Planting and Growing
Urban Churches

Planting and Growing
Urban Churches

From Dream to Reality

Edited by Harvie M. Conn

Baker Books

A Division of Baker Book House Co
Grand Rapids, Michigan 49516

© 1997 by Harvie M. Conn

Published by Baker Books
a division of Baker Book House Company
P.O. Box 6287, Grand Rapids, MI 49516-6287

Fourth printing, April 2002

Printed in the United States of America

Library of Congress Cataloging-in-Publication Data

Planting and growing urban churches : from dream to reality / edited by Harvie M. Conn.
    p. cm.
    Collection of articles that have appeared in Urban mission.
    Includes bibliographical references and indexes.
    ISBN 0-8010-2109-X (pbk.)
    1. City churches. 2. Church development, New. I. Conn, Harvie M. II. Urban mission.
BV637.P53   1997
254′.1′091732—dc21
                                                  97-3223

For information about academic books, resources for Christian leaders, and all new releases available from Baker Book House, visit our web site:
http://www.bakerbooks.com

To Lee and Marion

Contents

Preface

Harvie M. Conn

In the first half of the nineteenth century William Wilberforce, the great British evangelical statesman, congratulated his son Samuel for turning down a call to become pastor in Lancashire. By rejecting a ministry in this rapidly industrializing city and remaining in a semi-rural area, argued Wilberforce, Samuel could be more devoted to the gospel. In 1854, another Englishman, J. Hudson Taylor, had a different gospel vision of the city. He arrived in Shanghai, a city with a ten-year history of industry, foreign trade, and international contacts. Four of the ten largest cities in the world were then in China—Beijing, Canton, Hangchow, and Soochow.

Taylor did not desert the cities with his vision of reaching "inland" China. They were, in fact, a key part of his strategy from the moment that the first missionary team of China Inland Mission arrived in 1866. "His aim was to occupy the strategic centres, first the provincial capitals, then the chief prefectures, and then the smaller towns and villages."[1]

The pattern began. Hangchow, the sixth largest city in the world (700,000 people by 1850), became the first base for the new team. Other city bases sprang up—Nanking, Yangchow, Tientsin, Anking. By 1901, CIM missionaries had begun work in Kaifeng, the capital of Honan Province. Taylor's plan to occupy all the provincial capitals was fulfilled.

The modern history of the mission of the church since those days in the nineteenth century has continued to reflect the same choices—Wilberforce and the country, Taylor and the city. In fact, the challenge of the city has grown in the years that have followed, as urbanization has swept across the world. But the church has not always kept up. In recent decades that picture may be changing. There are growing signs of a new evangelical interest in reaching the cities of the world for Christ, and new sensitivities about how deeply that concern must go.

---

1. Marshall Broomhall, *By Love Compelled* (London: China Inland Mission, 1947), 25–26.

The Global Consultation on World Evangelization, sponsored by the AD 2000 and Beyond Movement in Seoul, Korea, in 1995, may indicate movement in this new direction. One of the key tracks in the initiative developed in Seoul was the "Cities Network." Viv Grigg, the co-chairperson of the Network, supported that emphasis when he wrote, "Today we are moving into . . . the fourth era of the modern missions—reaching the cities. . . . The future of missions is urban."[2]

Seoul 1995 concentrated a special focus on the 1700 least evangelized cities and called for special prayer for, and evangelistic attention to, the "100 gateway cities" of the world's 10/40 window.[3] No urban concern of similar strength developed twenty-one years before at the 1974 Lausanne Congress on World Evangelization (though subsequent Lausanne-sponsored gatherings began to give the cities the attention they deserved).

Out of Seoul have come strategic pleas for the mobilization of urban mission—intensification of prayer focus, research consortiums, the formation of regional city networks, indigenous city leadership teams, adopt-a-city programs.

Seoul, we suggest, symbolizes the growing concern of the world church for the city. Cities are no longer simply the concern of Western missionaries. Three-quarters of Seoul's financial underwriting and two-thirds of the delegates were from Africa, Asia, and Latin America; it was "the only large global Christian mission conference that has ever had *more than half* of its participants from the former mission fields of the world."[4]

Does Seoul also signal that more holistic focus on the city that the Lausanne movement has championed? Only the future will tell. But certainly the spiritual dimensions of reaching cities were there, with a heavy emphasis on prayer and evangelism, underlined by a strong Pentecostal and charismatic presence. And there were those such as Viv Grigg, who sought to connect this spiritual power with strategy planning, church planting, and "the transformation of major sectors of society and culture as they are impacted by the kingdom of God."[5]

Strong consideration of these emphases is in the collection of essays in your hands. Drawn from twelve years of the publication *Urban Mission*, they reflect more than the commitments of its institutional origins in Westminster Theological Seminary, though the Seminary has generously subsidized it through the years. They reflect a growing global dedication, shared by the

    2. Viv Grigg, ed., *Transforming Cities: An Urban Leadership Guide* (Auckland: Urban Leadership Foundation, 1995), 3.
    3. The 10/40 window is a rectangle of world geography lying from West Africa across Asia and from 10 degrees north latitude to 40 degrees north latitude. Many of the world's unreached peoples are said to live in this "window."
    4. Ralph Winter, "Editorial Comment," *Mission Frontiers* 17, nos. 7–8 (1995): 4.
    5. Grigg, *Transforming Cities*, 15.

Seminary and journal, "to the advancement of Christ's church and kingdom in cities throughout the world."

The essays in this volume circle around the issue of church growth and planting. They take up themes that are becoming more familiar to the world church—networking, unreached peoples, strategic research, ministry to the urban poor. Each author has been given the opportunity to make minor revisions and update his or her contribution; two have done so. It is our hope that an enthusiastic reader response to this volume will encourage publication of similar books. There is ample material in past issues of *Urban Mission* from which to develop other emphases also.

The gifts of three people have enriched this collection. Susan Lutz, a busy pastor's wife, has served as assistant editor during all of *Urban Mission*'s history. Her remarkable gifts of judgment and editing skills have often transformed an essay from a good one to a much better one. Her touch is clearly present in this volume.

Thanks also must go to Carol Ajamian, whose Christian enthusiasm for this project and for the goals of *Urban Mission* has been translated into long hours of typing and retyping, checking and double-checking copy. This book would not be before you without her sacrifices.

And Roger Greenway, the founding editor of *Urban Mission*, kindly provided the introduction to this volume. His vision and skills saw the journal through its first six years. Six of these seventeen essays appeared under his tenure. His undiminished excitement for reaching the world's cities for Christ is part of the Christian heritage on which we continue to build.

We and the contributors join in inviting you now to think and pray and do. Expect great things from God for the city; attempt great things for God in the city.

Contributors

Ray Bakke is executive director of International Urban Associates, a network of church and mission leaders seeking to empower God's people in the largest cities of the world. Since 1979 he has been associated with Northern Baptist Theological Seminary and served as senior associate for large cities with the Lausanne Committee for World Evangelization. He wrote *The Urban Christian* (InterVarsity, 1987).

David Britt, Ph.D., has been director of planning and research with Metro United Way in Louisville, Kentucky, since 1990. Prior to this appointment, he was a youth minister in two congregations and served for seven years as director of admissions and student records at Southern Baptist Theological Seminary, Louisville.

Kriengsak Chareonwongsak, Ph.D., is the president of Hope of God International and founding pastor of the Hope of Bangkok Church, the largest and fastest growing congregation in Thai history. Active in the media and in social, political, and economic affairs, he is also director of the Institute of Future Studies for Development.

Harvie Conn, Litt.D., is professor of missions on the staff of Westminster Theological Seminary, Philadelphia, where he has served since 1972. He was a missionary in Korea from 1960 to 1972, working under the combined supervision of the Orthodox Presbyterian Church and the Reformed Church in the United States. His latest book is *The American City and the Evangelical Church* (Baker, 1994). He continues to edit the quarterly journal, *Urban Mission*.

Craig Ellison, Ph.D., is professor of counseling and urban studies at Alliance Theological Seminary, Nyack, New York. Under his leadership and direction, the Seminary was involved for a number of years in an innovative program of summer urban extension studies in New York City. He is the author, co-author, or editor of six books, including the first volume to deal with counseling in an urban setting, *Healing for the City* (Zondervan, 1992).

James Engel, Ph.D., is distinguished professor of marketing, research, and strategy at Eastern College, St. Davids, Pennsylvania. Prior to taking this post in 1990, he served for eighteen years on the faculty of Wheaton College (Illinois). He has written more than twenty-five books and monographs and is known as a pioneer in the application of audience-oriented strategic planning for Christian missions. His 1975 title, *What's Gone Wrong with the Harvest?*, co-authored with H. Wilbert Norton, is still in wide use.

Mark Gornik, M.Div., is the founding pastor of Baltimore's New Song Community Church, a congregation associated with the Presbyterian Church in America. He plans to establish a New York City church with the same commitments to Christian community development. He is a graduate of Covenant College, Chattanooga, Tennessee, and Westminster Theological Seminary, Philadelphia.

Roger Greenway, Th.D., is professor of world missiology at Calvin Theological Seminary, Grand Rapids, Michigan. After twelve years as a missionary in Sri Lanka and Mexico, he served for six years as the Latin America secretary for Christian Reformed World Missions and several years as executive director of that board. He was professor of missions at Westminster Seminary from 1982 to 1987. He has published a dozen books on missions, including *Discipling the City* (Baker, 1992).

Viv Grigg, M.A.Miss., is the international director of the Urban Leadership Foundation and coordinator of the Cities Resource Network of the AD 2000 and Beyond Movement. A New Zealand engineer, he has catalyzed global missions interest in the slums of the world, pioneering teams in Manila and Calcutta. A graduate of the School of World Mission at Fuller Theological Seminary, he is the author of *Cry of the Urban Poor* (MARC, 1992).

C. Kirk Hadaway, Ph.D., is minister for research and evaluation at the United Church Board for Homeland Ministries, an agency of the United Church of Christ. He came to this post after lengthy service as a church growth specialist for the Southern Baptist Convention and directorship of the Center for Urban Church Studies. His latest book, co-authored with David Roozen, is *Rerouting the Protestant Mainstream* (Abingdon, 1995).

John Holzmann, M.Div., with his wife, Sarita, is the founder and director of Sonlight Curriculum, Ltd., a home school curriculum supply house dedicated to meeting the needs of American expatriates. After graduation from Westminster Seminary, he served as a staff member of the U.S. Center for World Missions, Pasadena (1984–1989) and of the Caleb Project (1990–1992).

Robert Linthicum, Ph.D., is the executive director of Partners in Urban Transformation, an international Christian association strengthening urban ministry networks and providing resources for organizations committed to empowering the urban poor. Prior to accepting this post in 1995, he served as director of Urban Advance, a ministry of World Vision International. He is the author of several books, including *City of God, City of Satan: A Biblical Theology of the Urban Church* (Zondervan, 1991).

Rebecca Long has served with Wycliffe Bible Translators since 1974. She has worked particularly among the Zapotecs in Oaxaca (Mexico) and Los Angeles and is currently involved in a second translation project in another dialect of Zapotec. Other labors have also included responsibility as literacy coordinator for Wycliffe's Mexico branch.

Ralph Neighbour Jr., D.Min., S.T.D., is president of Touch Outreach Ministries, an organization committed to training pastors and church leaders in cell group evangelism and church formation. His advocacy of cell group churches has taken him around the world in research, lecturing, and consultations. Since 1990 he has served as associate senior pastor of the Faith Community Baptist Church in Singapore. Using the cell group strategy exclusively, the congregation has grown from 350 to 6,000 members in just over four years.

Benjamin Pierce, M.Div., is associate pastor of evangelism and mission at First Presbyterian Church, San Mateo, California. Before graduating from Fuller Theological Seminary in 1991, he served as a missionary in Zaire from 1984 to 1987.

Dick Scoggins has been a church planter for nineteen years. During the past seven years he has shifted from planting traditional churches to house churches in network. The Fellowship of Church Planters, of which he is a member, now oversees four teams in New England which have planted close to thirty house churches. In 1995 he relocated to England to start a similar team there and to facilitate such work in Europe. He also serves as a consultant to Frontiers.

Fred Smith, Ph.D., is regional director of Latin America North for the Christian and Missionary Alliance, a post he has filled since 1991. Prior to that, he served fifteen years in Peru and Ecuador with the Alliance. A graduate of Fuller Seminary's intercultural doctoral program, he also directs the Alliance program for unreached peoples, Within Our Reach.

William Travis, Ph.D., has served as professor of church history at Bethel Theological Seminary, St. Paul, Minnesota, since 1978. He is co-author with Norris Magnuson of *American Evangelicalism: An Annotated Bibliography* (Locust Hill, 1990) and of *Religious Traditions of the World* (Zondervan, 1991), written with James F. Lewis.

James Westgate, D.Min., is executive director of the Fresno Leadership Foundation. The organization has targeted six of the poorest and highest crime rates in Fresno for spiritual revitalization and economic development. He also teaches urban ministry at the Mennonite Brethren Biblical Seminary in Fresno. He brings to these ministries twenty-five years of pastoral experience in urban and inner-city settings.

Introduction

Roger S. Greenway

The first issue of *Urban Mission* appeared in September 1983. From an economic standpoint, it was a poor time to begin a new publication, because many established periodicals were having financial difficulties. But from a strategic standpoint, Harvie Conn and I believed the time was ripe for a journal that focused on mission to the city. The world was urbanizing fast, but mission agencies and training schools were dragging their feet. The missionary world needed a sharp nudge to move from "pith helmet" thinking to vigorous engagement with urban realities.

We knew that urban realities were not popular topics for discussion among evangelicals, including a majority of mission leaders. In fact, urban challenges were so unpopular that a friend of mine, editor of a leading Christian magazine, advised me against using the word *Urban* in the title. But we did it anyway, convinced that we had to convey our message loud and clear.

From the beginning *Urban Mission* aimed to accomplish at least three things. First, it aimed to develop a biblical theology of the city that would address a wide range of issues affecting urban life. The sponsorship of the journal by Westminster Theological Seminary in Philadelphia was more than merely a convenient organizational arrangement. It signified the commitment of the journal and the Seminary to address urban issues in ways that would be holistic in the best sense, theologically valid, sociologically informed, and missiologically strategic.

The second goal was to publish material that would have practical value for Christian workers in the city. In the first "Editor's Viewpoint," I observed that the fiercest battles for minds and hearts are waged on city streets. Satan launched his urban strategy years ago, and he has taken many captives. The church needs to challenge Satan's control of urban life. By God's power, captives can be set free. But for this to happen, theories must be translated into practical ministries on the streets where traffic flows and masses live.

Third, *Urban Mission* set out to deal with the global missionary task as it took on different forms and shapes around the world. The focus would be upon the growth and development of vital Christian congregations in the cities of Africa, Asia, and Latin America, as well as North America and Europe. This was a broad mandate; some said it was too broad. But the journal stayed the course, publishing articles and case studies dealing with urban issues and ministries from around the globe.

How wonderful are the ways of God, and how his purposes exceed our dreams. When *Urban Mission* began back in 1983, we could not imagine that within a decade we would be discussing church planting in countries that were then part of the Soviet Union and entirely out of reach of Christian missions. Yet a change occurred, and we now discuss church planting in cities of the former USSR.

Similarly at the beginning, *Urban Mission* faced an uphill battle just to capture the attention of evangelical leaders. But that changed too. Every mission leader now recognizes that evangelizing the world means seizing the "gateways," which invariably are towns and cities. This is illustrated in the current worldwide effort to focus intercessory prayer on one hundred gateway cities of the "10/40 window," the least evangelized part of the world. Until Satan's hold on the urban gateways is broken, world evangelization will hobble along. That is what *Urban Mission* said from the beginning, and we rejoice that its voice has been joined by a chorus.

The focus of this collection of articles from *Urban Mission* is on the planting and development of city churches. My initial vision for urban church multiplication and growth came from the late Donald A. McGavran, founder of the Church Growth Movement. My wife and I were missionaries living in Mexico City in the mid–1960s when McGavran came to the city to lecture. After his meetings were over, McGavran asked me to take him to one of the densely populated squatter areas on the edge of the city. Standing in the center of a dirty, smelly street, surrounded by children, McGavran said to me: "Roger, it's great what you are doing out there in the mountain villages, and God has blessed your work. But I challenge you to rethink your strategy and turn your attention to the city. This is where the greatest challenge of the future lies."

I took McGavran's advice. Planting urban churches became my passion. Along with seminary and Bible school students, and anyone else I could convince to come along, I started house churches in various parts of Mexico City. Our basic method was to go door to door selling Bibles, praying for anyone that was sick or in special need, and starting Bible studies in the homes. By his numerous letters, McGavran encouraged us to push ahead. At the end of one letter he wrote: "Plant churches passionately!" McGavran's vision of great cities filled with vital churches proved to be contagious.

Four Basic Principles

Four basic principles, I believe, should govern all plans and strategies for urban church planting. I hammered out these principles years ago and have tested them over and over against the teaching of Scripture and the data of missionary experience. Their validity is borne out in every successful church growth work I have encountered.

1. In Christ Alone Is There Salvation.

The task of missions is to proclaim salvation through the one Lord Jesus Christ with conviction and passion, calling all people to believe in Christ alone, renounce their false allegiances, and spend their lives as Christ's disciples (Acts 4:12; 1 Cor. 9:19–23; 2 Cor. 5:11–21).

This is so basic, so plainly biblical, that some people may wonder why it needs to be spelled out. I offer two reasons. First, in the history of urban missions many workers have become so immersed in ministering to people's physical and social needs that they lost sight of spiritual needs. Human hurts are many in cities, and urban workers cannot avoid ministering to the needs of abused and suffering people. But in the course of their many important ministries, urban pastors, missionaries, and other Christian workers must present the news of how Jesus meets the greatest human need of all, that of reconciliation with God. Otherwise they are robbing city dwellers of the highest good and neglecting their calling to be Christ's emissaries.

The second reason why this principle needs to be underscored has to do with the pervasive ideology of pluralism, and the resulting anti-missionary, anti-evangelism mood. Pluralism, by its nature, plays down the place of Christ among the world's religions. Today the traditional Christian position regarding the uniqueness of Christ is under attack as never before, and the center of the storm is the city.

The ideology of pluralism seems to fit the city. In cities, Christians, Buddhists, Hindus, Muslims, atheists, and others rub shoulders every day. Pluralism has an alluring appeal in this context because it appears to offer the best possibility for persons of different religions and cultures to live peacefully together. Consequently, in wide areas of urban society it has become unacceptable to support or engage in overt acts of evangelism. In public conversation it is considered indiscreet to take the position that conversion to Christ is important and necessary, or that following an untrue religion may have dire consequences for one's soul. In the conduct of many urban ministries, the overall impact of ideological pluralism is that interreligious dialogue replaces evangelism and community workers avoid speaking the gospel out of deference to other people's feelings.

However, if God wants the world to hear the gospel and sinners won to him, which the Scriptures plainly teach, we have to base our urban ministries on the principle that, along with whatever else we do in addressing human needs, the gospel must be communicated with a view to personal conversion to Christ. With this urban mission begins.

2. Believers in Christ Should Join Communities of Faith.

In churches they gather to worship God, teach his Word, baptize, celebrate the Lord's Supper, enjoy fellowship as members of Christ's body, pray, serve, witness, challenge, and equip one another for consistent living. This means that planting and developing churches is an important and necessary part of missions in all times and places.

Even a casual reading of the New Testament leads to the conclusion that in apostolic times mission work and church planting were virtually inseparable. The apostle Paul consistently planted churches in the cities he visited. His strategy was to preach the gospel to groups, individuals, and households and to gather those that believed into congregations under local spiritual leaders called "elders." That churches be organized wherever there were believers became a governing principle of Christian missions.

The Church Growth School of missiology reminded us that the numerical growth of the church through conversions from the world is important. McGavran taught that wise strategy calls for focusing on those groups that God in his providence has made receptive to the gospel. Every group has its *kairos,* McGavran said, that moment of divine grace when gospel opportunity and receptivity come together, making great Christward movements possible, and we must seize those moments for Christ.

Effective mission work does not consist of transferring Christians from one church or denomination to another and calling it "church growth." There is a great deal of transfer growth among churches, and the only good it does in my opinion is to make a handful of churches big, rich, and famous. But the kind of church growth that the Bible describes and praises focuses on winning the unsaved, the unchurched, and the uncared-for. It consists in proclaiming the gospel passionately, indiscriminately, by every legitimate means, hither and yon, and gathering those who heed Christ's call into vital Christian churches whose focus is on equipping members for ministry.

From the standpoint of the New Testament, vital churches are those whose teachers and pastors take as their primary goal equipping members for righteous living and fruitful ministry. Whether paid or unpaid, seminary trained or not, their leaders diligently teach God's Word so that the members grow in spiritual knowledge and understanding, faithful discipleship, and the active pursuit of truth and righteousness among themselves and in society. They have a global vision and follow with prayerful interest the expansion of Christ's kingdom throughout the world.

Vital churches are organized according to biblical patterns and contextualized to meet local circumstances. Pastors, elders, deacons, teachers, and evangelists carry out their duties joyfully and faithfully, and equip members to participate fruitfully in God's service in the world. Vital churches demonstrate concern for the poor and suffering, nearby and far away. Vital churches consist of "missionary people" who define themselves in Christ's terms as light, salt, and leaven in a sinful, divided, and hurting world.

3. Churches Are God's Missionary Instruments.

As such they transform the communities around them. Vital churches challenge the assumptions that govern the politics, economics, academics, and cultures of people committed to other gods and masters. Besides this, every day, and in a multitude of ways, they offer cups of cold water in Christ's name to thirsty lips.

By the example of Christ, the church is instructed as to its responsibilities to the community. In his preaching and teaching ministry, Jesus called men and women to personal and costly discipleship. He taught them about a kingdom in which covenantal obedience to God is expected. At the same time, by his words and actions, Jesus challenged the centers of power, both Jewish and Roman, religious and political. He challenged them on the basis of an authority that came from a higher source than either Rome or Jerusalem represented.

In the worldview that Jesus embraced, and in which the church operates, the base assumption is that the one true God has revealed himself and his will. God is sovereign over all of life, and humans are accountable to him for everything they do, think, and say. On the basis of this worldview, Jesus taught, responded to authorities, rebuked Satan, cast out demons, and by words and actions pictured for his followers the nature of his kingdom and his will for the church.

The church's actual performance has always fallen far short of the ideal. Yet the church can still claim to be history's most beneficent institution. In his book, *The Gospel in a Pluralist Society,* Lesslie Newbigin offers this moving tribute to the church's role in society:

> The Church is an entity which has outlasted many states, nations and empires, and it will outlast those that exist today. The Church is nothing other than that movement launched into the public life of the world by its sovereign Lord to continue that which he came to do until it is finished in his return in glory. It has his promise that the gates of hell shall not prevail against it. In spite of the crimes, blunders, compromises, and errors by which its story has been stained and is stained to this day, the Church is the great reality in comparison with which nations and empires and civilizations are passing phenomena. The Church can never settle down to being a voluntary society concerned merely with private and domestic affairs. It is bound to challenge in the name of the one Lord all the powers, ideologies, myths, assumptions, and world views which do not acknowledge him as Lord. If that involves conflict, trouble, and

rejection, then we have the example of Jesus before us and his reminder that a servant is not greater than his master.[1]

What does this mean for urban church planting? It means that when we plant a church that throbs with biblical vitality we introduce into urban life a force for good, for justice and reconciliation. It happens when churches pursue the agenda of the kingdom of God, as Jesus did.

Churches bless individuals, families, and neighborhoods when they consistently perform three roles. *First, they teach the biblical worldview regarding:*

- who God is, his nature, and how he reveals himself;
- who human beings are, men and women equally made in God's image and morally accountable to God;
- the nature of the human problem, sin, and how sinners can be reconciled to God;
- biblical values concerning the family, how husbands and wives ought to treat one another and raise their children;
- the value and importance of work, time, and stewardship of all God-given resources;
- the proper role of human authorities and their ultimate accountability to God;
- moral values, and the consequences of vice, waste, and self-destructive habits and entertainments.

Find any city or neighborhood on earth where vital churches are vigorously teaching large numbers of people Christian beliefs, values, attitudes, and lifestyle, and where church members demonstrate by their lives the impact of God's Word. Here you will see a community where people are being empowered for good, where unemployment is declining, where the quality of life is improving and poverty is diminishing.

Second, the church in the urban community serves, with diaconal ministries, those who cannot escape poverty, or have been devastated by a calamity like an earthquake or war, or are afflicted by long-term handicaps. To such people, the church's deacons come as representatives of Christ the Healer, Christ the Merciful One, Christ the Servant of God who cares about his creatures, weeps when they suffer, and meets their needs.

Church-based community development programs offer the best hope for depressed neighborhoods. They provide the skills, resources, and training that can turn a neighborhood around. Oftentimes the line between destitution and a decent standard of living is narrow. All it takes is some training in management, organization, and technical skills to achieve a major improve-

---

1. Lesslie Newbigin, *The Gospel in a Pluralist Society* (Grand Rapids: Eerdmans, 1989), 221.

ment in a family's living standard. But usually the benefits are short-lived if the persons receiving help are not changed inwardly and outwardly by the teaching of God's all-encompassing Word. For that reason, community development programs should be based in or closely linked to churches.

Third, vital churches cry for justice and plead for freedom to create, initiate, and enjoy the benefits of labor. All these are prerequisites of social transformation. When churches raise such cries, they must expect trouble, conflict, and rejection. As Newbigin reminded us, the powers of this world do not take kindly to reproof and calls for reform. In such instances, the church's modeling role may be the most crucial factor in its service to the community. Regardless of oppressive conditions in society, the community of believers must strive to model moral integrity, biblical values, prudent stewardship, and the freedom to be all that God intended humans to be.

4. Care of the Environment Is a Christian Concern.

Strange as it may seem, that fact belongs in any discussion of church planting and urban mission.

How could the church ignore this for so long? For decades we have sung, *"This is my Father's world,"* while shrugging off the God-insulting misuse of air, water, soil, and space. Largely due to pressure from secular forces there is now more concern for protecting the environment. How sad that Christians were not in the forefront of the movement from the beginning! And shame on those church planters who even now ignore environmental questions when they choose new sites, design buildings, and pave parking lots. We ought not to abuse our Father's world, even when pursuing the holy calling of planting churches.

These principles have echoed through the pages of *Urban Mission,* and they are reflected in the chapters of this book. They bear repeating, because from Madras to Geneva, São Paulo to Moscow, we see a virtual explosion of church planting institutes and training programs. It is safe to say that never before have there been so many church planters and would-be church planters. I hope they take these principles seriously and that this book will inspire them as, in their particular contexts, they plant churches through which multitudes find entry to the city with solid foundations, whose architect and builder is God.

Part 1
Research:
Searching for the Right Questions

Introduction

Harvie M. Conn

"Research," says James Engel, "is the gathering of information for use in decision making."[1] More particularly, the research introduced in this volume is applied research, applied specifically to those questions revolving around church growth and planting in the cities of the world.

How will a study of the history of the Protestant churches in Acapulco help us in developing a strategy for church planting? Why does an increase in housing construction in specific zip code areas and the replacement of old housing with new housing seem to promote growth among otherwise declining American mainline churches?

Our purpose in this introduction is to review the progress of that urban church research over the past several decades.

Urban Church Research: New Beginnings

Urban studies in the behavioral sciences have become prominent since the 1960s.[2] But similar research on the urban church has accelerated more slowly. Literature in the 1960s came largely from the United States and was oriented toward churches dealing with neighborhood transitions; the coun-

---

1. James Engel, *How Can I Get Them to Listen?* (Grand Rapids: Zondervan, 1977), 13.
2. Harvie M. Conn, *Notes on Urban Studies and Christian Missions: A History and Case Studies* (Philadelphia: Westminster Theological Seminary, 1995), 1–21.

try had begun to wrestle with "white church flight" and the growing movement of African Americans and Hispanics to the cities.

Some in the mainline white churches found a model for interpreting these and other shifts in the positive motifs of the theology of secularization, emerging during this time.[3] Predicting the end of human religiosity as we knew it, the movement called for a new social activism by the church, oriented to and for the world.

The theology of secularization left a strong accent on social context for the church's agenda but faded fast as a permanent foundation for urban mission. It had misjudged the persistence of human religiosity and minimized the dark side of secularization. And, as Harvey Cox said of himself, its perception of the city was that of "a relatively privileged urbanite. The city, secular or otherwise, feels quite differently to those for whom its promise turns out to be a cruel deception."[4]

White evangelical churches remained largely aloof from the movement and the urban social context, self-insulated from dealing with such issues as racism by their continued division of personal from public life, of evangelism from social transformation. Fearful also of programs and theologies that sounded too much like a revived social gospel, they moved deeper into "the suburban captivity of the church," drawn to the growth potential of the suburbs. Urban mission for many was a synonym for evangelism in the city.

Impetus from the Church Growth School

The 1970s brought a research wake-up call for evangelicals. It came from Donald McGavran (1897–1990), the father of the Church Growth Movement. His early focus on the global picture touched the heartstrings of the evangelicals' long concern with "foreign missions" but had the unintentional effect of bypassing their massive, growing escape from the U.S. city.

He drew attention, not to the needs of American cities, but to the overseas field and to its growing urban populations as "perhaps the most urgent task confronting the Church."[5] From McGavran's command headquarters at Fuller Seminary, there began a slow trickle of materials by faculty,[6] students,

3. Harvey Cox, *The Secular City: Urbanization and Secularization in Theological Perspective* (New York: Macmillan, 1965); Colin Williams, *Where in the World?* (New York: National Council of Churches, 1963); Gibson Winter, *The New Creation as Metropolis* (New York: Macmillan, 1963).

4. Harvey Cox, "*The Secular City* 25 Years Later," *The Christian Century* 107, no. 32 (1990): 1028.

5. Donald McGavran, *Understanding Church Growth* (Grand Rapids: Eerdmans, 1970), 295.

6. Donald McGavran, ed., *Crucial Issues in Missions Tomorrow* (Chicago: Moody, 1972), 227–65; C. Peter Wagner, *Frontiers in Missionary Strategy* (Chicago: Moody, 1971), 179–97.

and those he influenced,[7] calling for empirical mission surveys of church growth.

McGavran's optimism, anchored in a call for the traditional values of evangelism and church planting, spoke to the heart and dispelled earlier fears. His emphasis on careful research to remove the fog of pietistic clichés and missionary newsletter jargon, to really see what was going on, was well received. It was a message exemplified by the work of McGavran's Fuller colleague, Alan Tippett (1911–1988),[8] and picked up and amplified by research specialists such as Edward Dayton and James Engel.[9] His call to reach "winnable people groups" turned the direction of missionary interest from picking up individuals one-by-one "against the stream" to a deeper focus on ethnic and socio-cultural influences in evangelism and church planting.

It was McGavran's attention to "winnable people groups" that gradually moved to the center of research interest. The concept was refined by ongoing discussions that moved the focus from the winnable to definitions of the "unreached,"[10] And World Vision's Missions Advanced Research and Communication Center (MARC), in collaboration with the newly formed (1974) Lausanne Committee for World Evangelization (LCWE), pioneered in the development of a growing computer database on unreached peoples. At this stage its database remained demographically oriented to larger geographical and social units, rather than to cities. More recently, some efforts are beginning to appear with a more urban focus. The Foreign Missions Board of the Southern Baptist Convention, for example, has undertaken a database survey of cities with populations over 100,000.

Research Encouragements along the Way

At the same time, within evangelical research circles in the 1980s, attention to the urban focus has developed on other fronts. A mini-track of the LCWE-sponsored Global Consultation on World Evangelization, held in Pattaya, Thailand, in 1980, was structured around "Reaching Large Cities." Out of it came a follow-up program oriented to world-class cities. Its coordinator, Ray Bakke, with the support of MARC and the LCWE, has traveled extensively since then, promoting the urban cause around the world through consultations. Lausanne II, in Manila in 1989, pushed the urban dimension

7. Roger S. Greenway, *An Urban Strategy for Latin America* (Grand Rapids: Baker, 1973); Timothy Monsma, *An Urban Strategy for Africa* (Pasadena: William Carey Library, 1979).

8. Alan R. Tippett, *Solomon Islands Christianity* (New York: Friendship, 1967); *People Movements in Southern Polynesia* (Chicago: Moody, 1971).

9. Edward Dayton, *Planning Strategies for Evangelism: A Workbook*, 6th ed. (Monrovia: MARC, 1978); James Engel and Wilbert Norton, *What's Gone Wrong with the Harvest?* (Grand Rapids: Zondervan, 1975); James Engel, *How Can I Get Them to Listen?*

10. Ralph D. Winter, "Unreached Peoples: The Development of the Concept," *Reaching the Unreached*, Harvie M. Conn, ed. (Phillipsburg, N.J.: Presbyterian and Reformed, 1984), 17–43.

even more strongly, serving as a platform for dialogue and consultation "oriented specifically toward urban mission."[11]

During this time there appeared a growing body of literature, focusing on the macro-level and on the institutional church. World-class cities of a million people or more have received dominant attention.[12] City-wide surveys, centered on the church and produced by large-scale, team collaborations, have appeared on Brisbane [13] and Auckland,[14] and on Nairobi[15] and Mexico City.[16] An ongoing, in-depth study of Miami is nearing completion under the direction of Latin America Mission;[17] nine other cities of Central and South America are also being surveyed under their Christ for the Cities program. The Caleb Project, whose methodology is described in chapter three, is an excellent sample of how this city-wide research can also be undertaken by smaller teams oriented specifically to unreached peoples.

Modifications, Directions, and Shifts

New agenda concerns, a growing global interest in the urban church, and a call for increased sophistication in methodology have affected urban church research in the 1980s and 1990s.

The world church recognizes the need for urban mission and research as preparation for that mission.

Urban church thinking in England has been greatly stimulated by the extensive study initiated in 1983 by the Archbishop of Canterbury's Commission on Urban Priority Areas. Published in 1985, the commission report is a rich study, especially strong in its exposition of the national and institutional context.[18] It has stimulated many organizations in the United Kingdom that have moved through often-turbulent transitions in urban mis-

11. Samuel Escobar, "From Lausanne 1974 to Manila 1989: The Pilgrimage of Urban Mission," *Urban Mission* 7, no. 4 (1990): 22, 24.

12. David B. Barrett, *World-Class Cities and World Evangelization* (Birmingham: New Hope, 1986).

13. Ralph Neighbour Jr., ed., *No Room in the Inn . . . Brisbane . . . Resistant or Neglected?* (Queensland: Torch Ministries International, 1987).

14. Ralph Neighbour Jr., ed., *A City that Neglects Its Religious Institutions . . . Auckland . . . Resistant and Neglected* (Houston: Torch Ministries International, 1989).

15. Larry Niemeyer, *Summary of the Nairobi Church Survey* (Nairobi: Daystar University College, 1989).

16. *México Hoy y Mañana. Documento No. 1: Directorio Evangelico de las Gran Ciudad de Mexico* (Mexico City: *Vision Evangelizadora Latinoamericana* and *Instituto Misionologica de las Americas,* 1987).

17. Scott Nyborg, "Christ for the City—Miami: A Global Outreach," *Urban Mission* 12, no. 3 (1995): 16–21.

18. *Faith in the City: A Call for Action by Church and Nation* (London: Church House, 1985). A follow-up study appeared five years later, *Living Faith in the City: A Progress Report by the Archbishop of Canterbury's Advisory Group on Urban Priority Areas* (London: General Synod of the Church of England, 1990).

sion.[19] The Evangelical Coalition for Urban Mission (ECUM), founded in 1980, is one such networking focal point. It is among many worthy of attention for their promotion of mission and research.

The Australian continent was the setting for a massive church survey in 1991. With the cooperation of more than 6,000 congregations from 19 denominations, a nationwide National Church Life Survey was conducted. Though the survey was not explicitly limited to urban areas, Australia's deeply urban population base of 85 percent makes it an exemplary model for such full-scale studies, one of the first to tackle an entire nation. The database remains one of the most comprehensive of its kind in the world. Results of the study are beginning to appear. [20]

Monitoring such research since the 1970s has been Scaffolding, an interdenominational support and resource network. Not primarily oriented to urban church research, it nevertheless plays a significant role in encouragement, information dissemination, and exchange and collection of resources.[21]

The picture in Africa, Asia, and Latin America is less developed. The need for urban church ministry and research flows out of rapid urbanization and its related problems.[22] Scattered individual research results circulated outside the regions have been published, some substantial,[23] others more oriented to expectations.[24] But financial problems must be overcome before more surveys like those of Daystar University College on Nairobi or the research project on Mexico City and those of Latin America Mission are repeated and implemented.

Encouraging further networking and mission explorations in these regions is the work of International Urban Associates (IUA), founded in 1989

19. For a history of the United Kingdom's struggles in urban mission, consult: Colin Marchant, "Witnesses and Dreamers," *Urban Mission* 13, no. 1 (1995): 13–20.

20. Peter Kaldor with John Bellamy, Merilyn Correy, and Ruth Powell, *First Look in the Mirror: Initial Findings of the 1991 National Church Life Survey* (Homebush West, Australia: Lancer, 1992); Peter Kaldor with John Bellamy, Ruth Powell, Merilyn Correy, and Keith Castle, *Winds of Change: The Experience of Church in a Changing Australia* (Homebush West: Lancer, 1994); Peter Kaldor, John Bellamy, and Sandra Moore with Ruth Powell, Keith Castle, and Merilyn Correy, *Mission Under the Microscope: Keys to Effective and Sustainable Mission* (Adelaide: Open Book, 1995).

21. Vaughn Bowie, "Scaffolding: Urban Mission in Australia," *Urban Mission* 2, no. 5 (1985): 46–51; Rowena Curtis, "Crossing Boundaries," *Urban Mission* 11, no. 4 (1994): 25–31.

22. "Seeking the Peace of the City: The Valle de Bravo Affirmation," *Urban Mission* 7, no. 1 (1989): 18–24; Bong-rin Ro, "Urban Cities and the Gospel in Asia," *Urban Mission* 6, no. 5 (1989): 20–30.

23. Aylward Shorter, *The Church in the African City* (Maryknoll, N.Y.: Orbis, 1991); Keith Hinton, *Growing Churches Singapore Style: Ministry in an Urban Context* (Singapore: OMF Books, 1985).

24. Bong-rin Ro, ed., *Urban Ministry in Asia* (Taichung, Taiwan: Asia Theological Association, 1989).

by Bakke. IUA aims at the empowering of regional partnerships and resource networks through leadership consultations and strategic planning.

*An interest in the American context has resurfaced with new vitality in the
American churches.*

Some of this has come from the growing attention of C. Peter Wagner and
Church Growth School-related institutions to applying church growth principles to the United States setting. [25] But, until recently, these studies have
been more generic than urban-focused.[26] American mainline denominations, whose research interests in the past have been more structured around
wider social and pastoral issues,[27] are also turning their attention to issues of
growth.[28]

More directly influential and more urban in focus has been the concern
of America's ethnic churches, which were energized by the civil rights movement of the 1960s into vibrant African American and Hispanic communities. Against the background of the country's increasingly multi-ethnic cities,[29] they have wrestled with issues of church growth as they are touched by
problems of racism, poverty, and powerlessness.[30] Some of the richest of
these studies have drawn their strength from pastoral experience in, or case
studies oriented to, congregational life.[31]

Issues of theological education for the city are now being addressed out
of this new sensitivity. Can traditional institutions, their curricula oriented
to a white and (increasingly) suburban agenda, meet the needs of the city?[32]
Is research ever "urban-neutral"?

25. Donald McGavran, *Effective Evangelism: A Theological Mandate* (Phillipsburg, N.J.:
Presbyterian and Reformed, 1988), 92–94.

26. One striking exception is Charles Van Engen and Jude Tiersma, eds., *God So Loves the
City* (Monrovia, Calif.: MARC, 1994).

27. For an excellent survey of those concerns, consult Loyde Hartley, "Recent Directions
in Urban Church Literature," *Word and World* 14, no. 4 (1994): 433–41.

28. David A. Roozen and C. Kirk Hadaway, eds., *Church and Denominational Growth*
(Nashville: Abingdon, 1993); C. Kirk Hadaway and David A. Roozen, *Rerouting the Protestant
Mainstream* (Nashville: Abingdon, 1995).

29. Harvie Conn, *The American City and the Evangelical Church: A Historical Overview*
(Grand Rapids: Baker, 1994), 161–80.

30. Orlando Costas, *The Integrity of Mission: The Inner Life and Outreach of the Church* (San
Francisco: Harper and Row, 1979); Orlando Costas, *Liberating News: A Theology of Contextual
Evangelization* (Grand Rapids: Eerdmans, 1989); Manuel Ortiz, *The Hispanic Challenge: Oppor-
tunities Confronting the Church* (Downers Grove, Ill.: InterVarsity, 1993); C. Eric Lincoln and
Lawrence Mamiya, *The Black Church in the African-American Experience* (Durham, S.C.: Duke
University Press, 1990); Oscar Romo, *American Mosaic: Church Planting in Ethnic America*
(Nashville: Broadman and Holman, 1993).

31. G. Willis Bennett, *Guidelines for Effective Urban Church Ministry* (Nashville: Broadman,
1983); Samuel G. Freedman, *Upon This Rock: The Miracles of a Black Church* (New York: HarperCollins, 1993); Joe Ratliff and Michael Cox, *Church Planting in an African-American Community* (Nashville: Broadman and Holman, 1993).

32. Eldin Villafañe, *Seek the Peace of the City: Reflections on Urban Ministry* (Grand Rapids:
Eerdmans, 1995), 77–96.

New training centers are appearing, as answers to these questions are sought. Some, such as Chicago's Seminary Consortium for Urban Pastoral Education (SCUPE) and Boston's Center for Urban Ministerial Education (CUME), build on more relational, historical ties to established theological schools and their models; others, such as Boston's Emmanuel Gospel Center (EGC), are modeling more informal, more directly church-related training methods. Substantive research results have already appeared from the EGC, focused on Boston and its churches.[33] SCUPE's biennial Urban Congress has become a focal point for global networking.

A more holistic concern, long a feature of cultural anthropology, has begun to augment urban church research.

Earlier compartmentalization of evangelism and social transformation in the white evangelical camp has begun to erode under pressure from several directions. Third World churches saw early on the social and cultural dimensions of evangelism. And the explosion of urbanization in their countries only reinforced that perception. Cities were more than merely large numbers of people; they were interacting networks shaped by social, political, and cultural movements.

At the 1974 Lausanne Congress, those socio-cultural perceptions were articulated by leaders like Orlando Costas, Samuel Escobar, and René Padilla.[34] For evangelism to be effective, those networks must be understood. For church growth to be full dimensioned, those organic connections must be tapped.

Minority churches in the United States sent similar signals. Long feeling the pressure of life on "the underside" of urban systemic structures, they could speak with more ease of the evil side of those structures, of poverty, racism, and oppression. The continuing role of African American and Hispanic churches as voices not only of their fellowships but also of their communities has kept them, for the most part, from building a high wall between the church and the world or the public and the private.

Reinforcement has also come from a third, perhaps surprising, source. America's mainline denominations, pushed by serious membership declines in recent years, have undertaken extensive studies of their own growth patterns. Deeply oriented to sociological research methods and to theological pluralism, they have questioned what they perceive as the simplistic theological [35] and unbalanced institutional[36] emphases of church growth ideas in the past.

---

33. Rudy Mitchell, ed., *The Boston Church Directory (1989–1990)* (Boston: Emmanuel Gospel Center, 1989); Douglas Hall, Rudy Mitchell, and Jeffrey Bass, eds., *Christianity in Boston* (Boston: Emmanuel Gospel Center, 1993).

34. J. D. Douglas, ed., *Let the Earth Hear His Voice: International Congress on World Evangelization, Lausanne, Switzerland* (Minneapolis: World Wide, 1975), 116–46, 303–26.

35. Dean R. Hoge and David A. Roozen, eds., *Understanding Church Growth and Decline: 1950–1978* (New York: Pilgrim, 1979). The volume was intended as a reaction to the 1972 book

In doing so, they appear to be moving toward a clearer recognition of the significance of evangelism for church growth. And their own emphasis on the social context in shaping institutional growth may be supplementing and balancing what they see as a weakness of past church growth research. Through the sophistication of research methodology, they are underlining by another route the socio-cultural dimension crucial to church growth. And with their emerging acknowledgment of the place of evangelism as a major factor in church growth, [37] the studies may be coming closer to a holism from the opposite direction. Their own minimizing of biblical and theological direction in their reflecting, however, leaves an imbalance in that support.

In the meantime, old patterns of a more restricted view of evangelism and church growth have continued. And debates go on.[38] But even within the Church Growth School, such 1994 titles as *God So Loves the City* appear to move toward a wider understanding. And more now hope that the global city will provide the contextual and social instrument for seeing that larger picture.

Adding their distinctives into discussions of urban church research are the Pentecostal and charismatic communities.

These churches have long been a dominant force of church growth both in the minority churches of America's inner cities and of the urban churches of Africa, Asia, and Latin America. But only recently has their strong emphasis on healing, exorcisms, prayer, and spiritual warfare found growing support in the larger Christian community. The 1989 Lausanne II Congress at Manila helped to open that door.[39] And the 1995 Global Congress on World Evangelization held in Seoul opened it farther.

Wagner has played a significant part in legitimizing that merger with church growth thinking.[40] And others, many closer to these communities, have articulated for a larger church the connections between church growth and the city,[41] between urban mass evangelism and gifts of healing and prayer.[42]

---

by Dean M. Kelley, *Why Conservative Churches Are Growing* (San Francisco: Harper and Row). Kelley's thesis was that mainline church decline was a result of their institutional inability to advance a belief system that would foster ardent membership commitment.

36. Kenneth Inskeep, "A Short History of Church Growth Research," in Roozen and Hadaway, eds., *Church and Denominational Growth*, 136.

37. Ibid., 45, 351.

38. John R. W. Stott, "Twenty Years After Lausanne: Some Personal Reflections," *International Bulletin of Missionary Research* 19, no. 2 (1995): 51–52.

39. Roger Greenway, "Reflections on Lausanne II," *Urban Mission* 7, no. 3 (1990): 4.

40. C. Peter Wagner, *The Third Wave of the Holy Spirit: Encountering the Power of Signs and Wonders* (Ventura, Calif.: Regal, 1988); C. Peter Wagner, *How to Have a Healing Ministry Without Making Your Church Sick!* (Ventura, Calif.: Regal Books, 1988).

41. John Dawson, *Taking Our Cities for God: How to Break Spiritual Strongholds* (Lake Mary, Fla.: Creation House, 1989); Floyd McClung, *Seeing the City with the Eyes of God* (Tarrytown, N.Y.: Chosen, 1991).

42. Ed Silvoso, *That None Should Perish: How to Reach Entire Cities for Christ Through Prayer Evangelism* (Ventura, Calif.: Regal, 1994).

In the process, research has been linked to strategy in what is called "spiritual mapping," an instrument for identifying the spiritual principalities and powers over the different cities and regions. Coined by George Otis Jr. in 1990, the term involves "the researching of a city to discover any inroads Satan has made which prevent the spread of the gospel and the evangelization of a city for Christ."[43]

Linked to traditional study agenda issues, the process involves research into the history of a region or city—its demographics, its cultural self-understanding, its politics, its worldview loyalties. But all these elements are also oriented around an effort to see the city "spiritually."

Crucial in the process is spiritual discernment, unmasking the Satanic deceptions that are hindering the work of God and developing a combat strategy to break these demonic strongholds. Often this discernment is to be exercised through what are described as special gifts of prophetic insight and revelational confirmation from the Lord.

Wagner, not himself a member of the Pentecostal or charismatic movements, sees this new spiritual focus on research and strategy as a needed addendum to past Church Growth emphases on methodology. And surely the character of research as a spiritual discipline needs underlining. Time will tell whether all of its focus will be acceptable in those parts of the Christian church where charismatic emphases are seen as in conflict with a finished view of revelation.[44] Undoubtedly modifications will appear.

And Now Tomorrow

Where should research go in the future? The past we have sketched has enough loose threads to keep us busy for a long time to come. But some demand attention more loudly than do others.

1. *Research methodologies will need refinement.* The warnings of Roozen and Hadaway demand more careful attention; stronger and more sophisticated connections between the urban context and the urban institution on both the national and local levels will have to be made. Past studies of the urban church, we must admit, have sometimes shown more attention to the institutional (congregation and denomination) in relative isolation from the larger socio-cultural context.

2. *A more balanced urban hermeneutic is needed.* What is the proper mix between the urban horizon of the biblical text and the contemporary urban horizons of Minneapolis and Mexico City? How can the academic disciplines

---

43. Cindy Jacobs, "Dealing with Strongholds," in C. Peter Wagner, ed., *Breaking Strongholds in Your City* (Ventura, Calif.: Regal, 1993), 77.

44. An interesting and supportive perspective, written out of this traditional community, will be found in: Don Dunkerley, *Healing Evangelism* (Grand Rapids: Chosen, 1995), 123–30.

of urban sociology and urban anthropology aid our search of Scripture, and vice-versa, as we develop a functional theology for urban mission?

3. Recent mission studies have followed earlier academic interests in focusing on urbanization, on the process of urban demographic populations. *Christian scholarship must now turn as well to the issue of urbanism, to the city as a way of life,* and to the proper connection between "religion" and urbanism.[45]

4. *Research on a macro-level and micro-level scale must be encouraged in those areas of Africa, Asia, and Latin America where it has often been minimal.* Here, after all, is where the great urban explosion shows few signs of let-up. And here is where the majority of unreached peoples reside. Increased networking on both the formal and informal levels will encourage that attention.

5. *For that research to be effective in winning the cities for Christ, it will need to be user-friendly on three levels—that of the theoretician, the strategist, and the practitioner.* Particularly the practitioner will be key, as he or she digs up the raw data and shares it with the other two sifting members of the missiological team. As yet, published research, with few exceptions, aims toward the theoretician and the strategist.

---

45. Harvie Conn, "A Contextual Theology of Mission for the City," in Charles Van Engen, Dean S. Gilliland, and Paul Pierson, eds., *The Good News of the Kingdom: Mission Theology for the Third Millennium* (Maryknoll, N.Y.: Orbis, 1993), 96–104.

Learning from Urban Church Research

C. Kirk Hadaway

The primary goal of all research is to further the understanding of some phenomenon or event. Whether the question is "How do urban churches grow?" or "What is the structure of the atom?" the goal is essentially the same: to add to our knowledge by answering a question.

In a university or seminary setting it is often enough that the questions posed by research be of value to a particular discipline. The study may not necessarily be practical, at least in any immediate sense. For this reason those working in "applied" settings, like denominational agencies, often see little value in such research. In fact, I recently heard the comment that researchers are "answering questions that no one is asking."

Stinging references to research of this sort are easy to understand, because those who need research the most are frustrated by expensive efforts to answer questions that they view as either trivial or irrelevant. Often, however, it is not the subject of research that is the problem, but the translation of research into useful forms. Not everyone who needs research has time to glean some gems that he or she can use in an area of ministry from a technical paper or computer printout. Yet there may well be such a gem buried in the report or printout.

The purpose of this chapter is to show how research, especially research dealing with the urban church, can benefit churches and denominations and help them be more effective. It is my view that some very good research has been conducted, but much of it has not been publicized or translated in such

This chapter first appeared in *Review and Expositor* 80, no. 4 (1983): 543–52 and was reprinted in *Urban Mission* 2, no. 3 (1985): 33–44. Used by permission.

a way that it can be used. I also feel that a great deal more research must be conducted if we ever hope to deal with misconceptions that may cause a denomination to guide entire programs by faulty assumptions. Without good research to test our assumptions, activity proceeds without the knowledge that what we are doing works or that there might be a better way.

How Can Research Help?

Good research can help our churches and agencies in a variety of ways. One of these is simply to provide facts that are essential for decision making. Applied research questions of this type are often phrased in terms of "what": What is the number of black members in the Southern Baptist Convention? What is the number of churches added to the Convention last year? What percent of SBC members are located in metropolitan areas? Much of the analysis which the Research Services Department at the Sunday School Board conducts on the Uniform Church Letter fits this style, especially that published in the handbook edition of *The Quarterly Review.*

Research facts are needed in order for intelligent decisions to be made. Agency planners need to know if the Convention grew in Sunday school enrollment over the past year in order to determine if efforts are effective. Similarly, knowledge that Southern Baptists are under-represented in large metropolitan areas was part of the motivation for the Home Mission Board's "Mega Focus City" emphasis, and also a reason why other agencies have begun to join in this commitment to our largest cities.

In addition to providing facts, research can also provide tests of ideas, programs, and strategies. Strategies are often developed and even carried out with little expended effort to find out if they will work, or after the "campaign" is over, to find out if they did work. The recent mass evangelism campaigns conducted by Campus Crusade for Christ ("Here's Life America" or "I Found It") and the Baptist General Convention of Texas ("Good News Texas") are classic examples of good intentions but little evaluation. In each case test cities should have been studied and the results carefully analyzed. Instead, the campaigns proceeded without anyone knowing if they were effective. "Here's Life America" is perhaps the worst example because there was plenty of opportunity for continued evaluation as it moved across the United States. In retrospect, from the little independent evaluation that has been done, it appears that these campaigns were not very effective in attracting new converts to the churches. In fact, they may have been somewhat counter-productive, as they drew resources and energy away from local churches. Research could have helped the planners either revise their strategies or decide that the entire process was a waste of time.

In a similar manner, research could be used to evaluate the effectiveness of many ongoing SBC programs and strategies. Unfortunately, not much is currently being done in this area. This lack of evaluation is likely due to fears that the results might show that strategies are not working in the way they were intended (and, no doubt, because such research is also quite difficult).

A final way research can help is through the development of new ideas, models, and strategies, that is, through basic research. Research of this type involves a great many styles, from case studies of particularly interesting urban churches to large-scale surveys. The purpose of each effort is to find out something new that could possibly be used by the denomination. For instance, a research project might investigate the style and techniques of effective urban pastors and the experiences that helped them succeed in this difficult setting. The goal of such a project could be the development of a list of training needs for present or prospective urban pastors. Seminaries and agencies could then use this information in the development of curriculum and urban training events.

Another possibility, which could determine the strongest correlates of church growth and decline, is a denomination-wide sample survey of urban churches and pastors. This type of project has already been conducted by the United Presbyterian Church and proved very helpful in determining what factors stimulated growth in their churches. The results of such a survey could be used to show churches how to grow. The findings also could be used by our seminaries to teach prospective pastors what they need to do once they receive a call to an urban church.

Providing needed facts, testing ideas and strategies, and developing new ideas and models—these are the primary ways in which urban research can help our churches and agencies. All three applications should be pursued by those engaged in research, though not in every project, of course. Too much emphasis on providing facts can lead to a reduction in the importance of a research organization, as it becomes simply a responder to immediate needs and relegates evaluation and basic research to the back burner. On the other hand, a research organization that focuses too heavily on evaluation, at the expense of data collection, might lose the trust of those it is seeking to serve, and one that only conducts basic research is in danger of losing touch with the practical needs of churches and agencies. A balance must be maintained if a research organization is to effectively make some lasting contribution to the kingdom.

Examples of Urban Research

Nearly any question can be answered through some research procedure, although in some cases the appropriate technique would be so involved and expensive that funding would be impractical. This is especially true in religious research, where the problem is not so much, "How can I answer this question?" but "How can I answer this question without spending much money?" This typically becomes an extremely difficult and artful process, since cutting corners too much can result in invalid findings.

In this section I want to consider several examples of urban-related research which range in objectives from information providing to good basic research. My goal is to show why such research is needed, how the projects were designed with an eye on both cost and effectiveness, and how the research either was or could be used.

Measuring Metropolitan Concentration

As indicated earlier, it is often the case that a manager wants (or needs) to know the answer to a seemingly simple "what" question (an applied research question involving data collection). In this case the question which came from both the Home Mission Board and the Southern Baptist Theological Seminary was "What percentage of Southern Baptists live in metropolitan areas?" This question was deemed important for several reasons. First, these agencies believed that an urban emphasis was necessary in the SBC, but little documentation could show that American cities were underevangelized. Second, the research was needed in order to establish a baseline for evaluating subsequent Baptist efforts in major cities. Finally, the research was needed to inform two major program emphases that were being developed by the Metropolitan Missions Department at the Home Mission Board: "Mega Focus Cities" and "Metro Thrust."

The methodology for this project was simple but rather laborious. The U.S. Census Bureau defines metropolitan areas in terms of counties. Thus, a given Standard Metropolitan Statistical Area (SMSA) may be defined as one county, as in the case of Los Angeles (Los Angeles county), or as cluster of several counties, as in the case of Atlanta (fifteen counties). Also important was the fact that the Uniform Church Letter asks each church in the SBC to indicate the county in which it is located, and Research Services at the Sunday School Board produces a computer printout each year which gives county totals for membership SMSAs and their constituent counties by entering the number of SBC churches and resident members from the Uniform Church Letter.

This information has proven quite useful. In 1980 Southern Baptists had 41 percent of their churches and 57 percent of their resident members in metropolitan areas. What does this say regarding our penetration of metropolitan areas? Nothing by itself, until we compare the figures to the percent of the national population, showing clearly that Southern Baptists are underrepresented in metropolitan areas. Further analysis into these data shows that Southern Baptists are over-represented in non-metropolitan areas and severely under-represented in the fifty largest SMSAs. SBC concentration in smaller SMSAs is often very weak.

Research for Associational Planning

Another example of urban church research which primarily involves data collection and interpretation but relatively little analysis is the planning studies which the Center for Urban Church Studies conducts for selected metropolitan Baptist Associations at the request of the Home Mission Board. The purpose of these studies is to help a metropolitan Association better understand its churches and city and thereby enable it to set meaningful long-range objectives as part of the strategy planning process.

In 1983 the Center worked with the six Southern Baptist Associations in the greater Los Angeles metropolitan area. Each of these Associations convened a two-day strategy-planning retreat, during which a representative from the Center for Urban Church Studies presented a data report that helped pastors and laypersons develop a list of needs for their Association. Broad objectives and more specific goals followed from these needs, and the result was a locally owned strategy to guide the Association over the next five to seven years.

The research that goes into the development of a data report for an Association involves the collection of information from a variety of sources. Census data is needed to give an overview of what is happening to the population in an Association's territory. We look at population growth or decline in the Association as a whole and also try to identify areas of the Association that are growing (or declining) most rapidly. Of similar importance are race and ethnicity. We show the racial composition of the area and how it may have changed over the past decade. In doing so, we try to point out various racial and ethnic populations that may merit greater attention by the Association. Additional data on age, income, housing values, marital status, mobility, and other factors are discussed, in each case drawing implications for ministry and evangelism. The census data employed in most cases are received from Census Access for Planning in the Church (CAPC), an interdenominational organization which purchases summary census tapes and allows member denominations access. In certain cities it is also necessary to consult with the local planning commission for census breakdowns that would ordinarily be too expensive or time-consuming. This was the case in Los Angeles, because rather arbitrary boundaries which cut across Los Angeles city limits led to difficulties in computing Associational totals.

Church data are also important to an Association's awareness of its situation. Pastors may be familiar with the health of only their own and a few other nearby congregations, and even the director of missions may not have taken time to analyze thoroughly the overall direction of his or her churches. Thanks to the Sunday School Board, Uniform Church Letter data for the past ten years are available on computer tape. We conduct a five-year trend analysis on all the churches in an Association of membership, baptisms, Sunday school, additions, total receipts, WMU, church training, Brotherhood, and church music. A special computer program developed for "Mega Focus Cities" allows this trend analysis to be printed out in tabular form for each Association.

Finally, our report to the strategy planning group includes an analysis of the growth and decline of other denominations in the area. These data are available for 1971 and 1980 from the Glenmary Research Center in Atlanta. Graphics produced for several census and church items heighten impact, and the entire report is distributed to all persons attending the planning retreat.

The data that go into this report come from a variety of sources, and most are obtained at a very low cost. Through selective memberships in strategic data-collecting organizations and the knowledge of where to obtain the right information, research materials can be compiled that are effective and inexpensive.

Urban Church Growth

My first example of basic research involves a statistical analysis of church growth and decline factors. Our initial step was to divide the sources of church growth and decline into institutional and contextual factors. Institutional influences are those internal to the church—its pastor, worship, programs, outreach, ministries, and the like—while contextual factors are external to the church—population change, racial transition, even broader social events like wars, revolutions, and value shifts.

We decided early on to try to measure the influence of each major contributor to church growth and decline, the final result of which would be a rating of the relative impact of each. It seemed appropriate to look first at the influence of the local context on church growth and decline. First, we reasoned that the setting of a church is causally prior to whatever the church decides to do in reaction to that setting; and second, the context was much easier to research objectively. So we proceeded to show how much impact the context has on church growth and to isolate the major reasons for the expected influence before moving on to research the church as an institution.

Our research procedures involved collecting data on church membership from all the churches that belonged to the five largest denominations in five geographically and religiously distinct American cities: Memphis, Tennessee; Omaha, Nebraska; Springfield, Massachusetts; Columbus, Ohio; and Sacramento, California. We plotted all these churches on census maps to obtain tract locations and thereby were able to isolate population characteristics of the neighborhoods surrounding each church. All the church membership data and census data were coded into our computer, and we determined what census characteristics were associated with the growth and decline of churches in each of the five cities. Using various statistical procedures we were also able to measure the overall impact of the context in each city and the relative importance of different aspects of the environment as well.

Our findings indicated that a major part of the growth or decline of urban churches results from changes in and characteristics of the context. Population growth or decline is the most important factor, followed by racial transition, neighborhood social class, and the proportion of young children in the area. This means that without knowing anything else about a church, information about its setting can give a fairly accurate prediction of whether it will grow or decline.

Additional research has looked into why the context has such a large impact in the city. This research has shown that, by and large, churches tend to resist change while their communities are drastically changing. They become so out of step with their communities that before long they essentially lose the ability to attract nearby residents. Often the problems stem from the early years of growth, when new houses were being built, population was increasing, and a homogeneous group of new residents was flooding to the church. Easy growth like this tends to spoil a church; it thinks its growth is due to its own minimal efforts. When population growth finally stops, church growth becomes much more difficult, and the church is unlikely to figure out the reason for a plateaued or declining membership.

We now know enough about the context to state without equivocation that it must be considered when analyzing the growth of any church. The context, however, does not determine the growth or decline, but rather makes it somewhat easier for some churches to grow and somewhat more difficult for others. Clearly, some churches are able to grow in spite of what we might describe as poor contextual situations. This does not invalidate our findings, but instead underscores one of our main points: It is not the context that makes a church decline, but how a church adjusts to that context.

Unfortunately, most churches are growing because of their contexts, not in spite of them. The overwhelming majority of growing mainline churches are located in suburbs where the white population is increasing. Despite this situation, much of the additional research conducted at the Center for Urban Church Studies will focus on the exceptions—churches that do grow "in spite of their contexts." We know a great deal about the context; now it is time to investigate institutional sources of growth and decline.

Racial Transition

A second example of basic research is a project which analyzes both institutional and contextual factors and represents an initial effort to investigate "the exceptions." The study is one of churches in communities experiencing racial or ethnic (Hispanic) transition during the 1970s.

The origin of this project was a request from the administration of Church Program Services at the Sunday School Board. Because of related interest and funding needs, however, sponsorship also came to include the Metropolitan Missions Department and Research Division at the Home Mission Board. These units wanted to discover what institutional characteristics helped growing churches in areas experiencing racial or ethnic transition.

We began this project by selecting twenty metropolitan areas out of the 100 largest SMSAs. Selection was based on the percentage of blacks and Hispanics in the area and the number of SBC churches. We wanted to ensure that the city had enough transitional neighborhoods and that each SBC church initially had an equal chance of being selected for this study.

For the final selection procedure census information was obtained for the tracts with SBC churches in the twenty cities. Tracts were defined as transitional on the basis of substantial increases in the black and Hispanic populations rather than by the perceptions of local church leaders. Churches located in these transitional tracts were classified as growing, plateaued, or declining through an analysis of records from the Uniform Church Letter. We then sampled from the growing and declining lists in each city and conducted personal interviews with the pastor of each church. The number of interviews varied from city to city according to the number of SBC churches present. A total of 150 interviews were conducted in five other metropolitan areas.

Our first finding was that decline is far more typical than growth among churches in transitional communities. This was not unexpected, of course, given our previous research into the influence of the context on the church. In a few cities, however, such as Birmingham, the effect was devastating. In Birmingham thirty churches were defined as in transition; only one was growing. An interview with the pastor of this growing church revealed no special ministries and little openness to blacks, but a visit to the community provided the explanation for its growth. The tract was split by major geographical barriers (a large hill and a railroad), effectively segregating whites from blacks. A regional church, this congregation is located on a major thoroughfare leading to several large, growing neighborhoods.

In other cities the situation was not as extreme as in Birmingham, but it has still been difficult to find transitional churches that are clearly growing in both membership and Sunday school attendance. Those that are growing fit a definite pattern, and we have begun to develop a typology of these growing transitional churches.

Type 1: Ethnic Churches

By far the most typical growing situation is the church where over 85 percent of the membership is composed of the racial or ethnic minority that is producing the transition. This is not surprising, since we can expect black churches to grow in areas where blacks are increasing in numbers, in the same way white churches tend to grow in areas where white population is increasing. Some of these churches were once white or Anglo and changed as the community changed, while others were started as black, Hispanic, or Asian congregations.

Type 2: Multiple Mission Churches

In this type, the mother church (usually Anglo) shares its facilities with one or more ethnic missions. The mother church counts the membership of these missions along with its own, so growth often results even if the Anglo congregation is losing members. It is legitimate to say these churches are growing, especially if their missions share facilities with their mother church. Even if the original congregation eventually dies, it leaves behind one or more viable ethnic churches to carry on the work in that community.

Type 3: Multi-Ethnic Churches

These churches are made up of a relatively stable mix of groups which worship together, rather than separately. For this to work, the racial or ethnic populations must be largely assimilated, so that members share common expectations for worship. Few good examples of this type can be found, although a number exist in California. Most are made up of Anglos, Hispanics, and Asians. In the south, a very few examples of white/black congregations can be found, and most that do exist are in the process of becoming all black.

Type 4: Regional Churches

Regional churches tend to be less affected by changes in the immediate context because they draw their members from a wider area than most churches. There are, however, relatively few regional churches in most cities, and some have not escaped declines caused by racial transition. The growing regional churches are usually located near the edge of the city proper, near freeways, and draw their members from suburbs and exurban territory. Several of the pastors from these churches who were interviewed had not even noticed that blacks had become the majority in nearby housing.

Type 5: Satellite Churches

These are churches that have started a satellite congregation in the suburbs and add the membership of this outlying congregation to that of the transitional congregation. Typically, the satellite is growing, and its growth cancels out the decline of the church in transition.

Thus far, these are the only types of growing churches in transition that we have found. Another possible type is an inner city "super-church." However many types are found, the church in transition has only one legitimate and viable option: radical change within itself to reach the group(s) producing the transition. As we proceed in this study, a special effort is being made to find out how those churches that made the shift toward reaching blacks or ethnics were able to do so. How was prejudice overcome? How were the first ethnic families attracted? What changes in church structure, worship, and staffing were made? These and other questions are being asked in order that these successful churches in transition can help others in similar situations.

New Directions for Research

Research is often seen as a luxury for a denomination. Yet if we want to design programs that work, if our programs are to be guided by accurate information, if our programs are to be objectively evaluated, and if we want to do effective planning, research should be seen as a necessity.

This is not to say that new research organizations should be created in the Southern Baptist Convention, or that all existing programs should be expanded (although they probably should be). Research takes place in many areas of any denomination. Seminary faculty and students, college faculty and students, state convention personnel, associational personnel, even pastors and church staff may contribute to the production of research. All too often, however, either the research that results is not practical for the church, the issue is trivial, the design is poorly developed, or the results are not shared. This is also true of denomination-wide research.

There is nothing wrong with knowledge for the sake of knowledge. It is certainly legitimate for a student to choose a dissertation topic that has little practical value, and it is legitimate for a pastor to choose a Doctor of Ministry project that will not be read by anyone except his or her committee. Still, it would seem that students, faculty, and anyone else interested in both research and in helping churches ought to consider an important and practical project.

Basic research is what is needed. Simplistic programs based on simple solutions are not getting the job done in this complex urban world. We need to understand the complexity of the issues facing urban churches; to do this, carefully designed research is essential. I have stressed church growth research because it is a current research interest of mine and because much more research is needed in this area. Despite the assurances of church growth professionals, most of the growth strategies have not been tested in any sort of objective and systematic fashion. Instead, we are being taught "what has worked for me."

Research is needed in many areas: how new churches are developed; effective ministry techniques; alternative structures for the urban church; model development; how to reach apartment dwellers; how to retain members. In the area of church growth we need to know if the homogeneous unit principle actually works as a programmed growth technique; we need to know the role of the pastor in church growth; we need to know why churches in so-called good contexts manage to decline; and we need to test all the growth strategies being promoted by various agencies of the Southern Baptist Convention. These are just a few of the practical research topics relating to the urban church. Obviously, there are other areas of equal or greater significance.

My final suggestion to those beginning the research process is to note that a narrow gap separates good research from poor research. Sampling techniques, control groups, proper questionnaire construction, and appropriate statistics should be used. When in doubt, or just to be safe, one should consult a research professional. Usually it is easy to make a few modifications and turn a flawed project into one that is potentially very useful.

Using Research Strategically in Urban Ministry

James R. Engel

The greatest challenge to world evangelization is urban ministry. Urban centers are complex mosaics, increasingly resistant to traditional evangelistic methods. The challenge can be met only by strategies that are adapted to the context, through planning based on accurate understanding of those to be reached.

Strategic planning has three foundational pillars, all of which are undergirded by openness to the leadership of the Holy Spirit: (1) intuition, (2) experience, and (3) research. The planning process logically begins with intuitive hunches, which are clarified and enriched by experience. Only recently, however, have Christian leaders come to see that these two bases are not complete by themselves.

There is growing recognition that research is needed to narrow the risk of error by providing further clarification and greater certainty. In fact, the pendulum has swung so far that we are increasingly inundated with numbers. Those who attended Lausanne II in Manila, for example, were given a laundry list of information on the numbers of unreached people in various areas of the world. Again and again I heard the lament, "How can we ever make sense of such abstract stuff?" "What does it mean right where I live?"

It is necessary to differentiate between macro and micro research. Most of the data on unreached peoples is macro, meaning that figures are provided for large population groups, such as an entire province or metropolitan area. While this has its role in area-wide strategy, it means far less to a church planter working in a twenty-block area.

This chapter first appeared in *Urban Mission* 8, no. 4 (1991): 6–12. Used by permission.

Left unanswered are such crucial strategic questions as religious beliefs and attitudes among the diverse people who live there, their motivations and needs, and their receptivity. These questions can only be answered by micro research on a geographically defined target area.

The purpose of this chapter is to demonstrate the practical significance of micro research in cross-cultural urban strategy. The world in which I have lived all my life is marketing, the arena in which micro research perhaps reaches its zenith. Hence, I can only write about what I know—information that is practical, actionable, and understandable to those who live and work on the strategic firing line.

The Nature of Strategic Research

In its essence, ethnography refers to the process of describing a culture from the perspective of those who live within it.[1] The central tool is participant observation,[2] with help from surveys and published data sources. Only recently have ethnographers begun to acknowledge the contributions from quite a different field—consumer research.

Consumer surveys are a mainstay in the secular marketing world, and a sophisticated literature and body of methodology have evolved around use of survey methods.[3] The focus is distinctly practical, because the goal of marketing is to influence thinking and behavior through insights gained into the ways in which consumer decisions are made.

Marketers also use research to provide vitally needed feedback on response to various strategies. This is done before the strategy is undertaken (pre-testing) and after it has been executed (post-testing). How many listened? How many understood what was said? What impact was made on thinking and behavior?

Market analysis has studied consumers with these measures in the secular world since the turn of this century, and methodology is well developed. Only recently, however, has it found its way into Christian ministry. This change is long overdue, because without consumer research it is exceedingly difficult to assess the effectiveness of evangelistic efforts.

A Focus on the Decision Process

Consumer research has pioneered in the study of how decisions are made, and it is here that a significant common ground has been established with

1. James P. Spradley, *The Ethnographic Interview* (New York: Holt, Rinehart and Winston, 1979).
2. James P. Spradley, *Participant Observation* (New York: Holt, Rinehart and Winston, 1980).
3. See James F. Engel, Roger D. Blackwell, and Paul W. Miniard, *Consumer Behavior*, 6th ed. (Hinsdale, Ill.: Dryden, 1990).

ethnography. Through the understanding that is gained, it is possible to develop strategies that begin where people are emotionally and move them step-by-step to a point of commitment through changing awareness and understanding attitudes, intentions, and behavior.

Research in spiritual decision processes, of course, is undertaken in full acknowledgment that the Holy Spirit plays a crucial role that transcends the scope of research instruments. A model of spiritual decision processes (the so-called Engel scale) has served as the guiding paradigm for a number of studies worldwide.[4] The latest version appears in Figure 1.

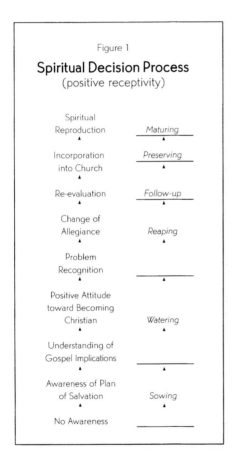

Figure 1

Spiritual Decision Process
(positive receptivity)

Spiritual Reproduction	Maturing
Incorporation into Church	Preserving
Re-evaluation	Follow-up
Change of Allegiance	Reaping
Problem Recognition	
Positive Attitude toward Becoming Christian	Watering
Understanding of Gospel Implications	
Awareness of Plan of Salvation	Sowing
No Awareness	

Purity versus Practicality

There are two schools of thought among micro researchers. Both share a central concern over whether the research accurately measures what it says it measures. But there can be differences in what is considered to be methodologically valid.

One group, especially those undertaking basic research in environments where experimental control is possible, rightly insist on research purity. This leads to probability sampling, measures of instrument reliability and validity, and rigorous statistical analysis. The other group is made up of applied researchers, especially those working in the urban context in the Two-Thirds world. Realities of their setting often force them to relax research rigor.

Here is one example where tension arises. There is general agreement in research texts that sample designs should be developed in which everyone in the target population has an equal chance of being selected—the randomly chosen sample. This presents no great challenge when there are defined dwelling units, each consisting of one nuclear family,

4. An initial exposition appeared in James F. Engel and H. Wilbert Norton, *What's Gone Wrong With the Harvest?* (Grand Rapids: Zondervan, 1975). For a review of decision process research and resulting changes in this scale, see James F. Engel, "The Road to Conversion: The Latest Research Insights," *Evangelical Missions Quarterly* 26, no. 2 (1990): 184–93.

and sufficient budget to contact all who are selected. It is quite different in the large slums of Nairobi, however, in which a half million or more people live.

In these teeming neighborhoods, there is no neat grid of streets with single-family homes. No one knows how many live in the shacks that literally are built on top of one another. It is impossible to define who is the head of the family. How, then, can a sample be designed which guarantees that everyone has an equal chance of being selected?

The only option is to resort to non-random samples, a method largely ignored in some research textbooks. There are ways in which non-random samples can be designed that are representative of the larger population. Representativeness, after all, is the goal of all sampling, and to resort to non-probability methods does not compromise validity, even though some purists may consider it unacceptable.

Qualified researchers who make such tradeoffs are fully aware of what they are doing. Their focus is on the central determining criterion in applied research studies: Does the information provided prove to be accurate and helpful in strategic planning? Fortunately, the evidence over many decades is decidedly affirmative.

Researching Unreached People

The focus of the remainder of this chapter is on micro analysis of a defined target group among those who are unreached. Here are the categories of data that are most helpful in planning evangelistic strategy:

Receptivity

The goal is to discover those who, for one reason or another, are seeking change (which may or may not be religious in nature). All things being equal, they are most open and hence serve as a primary target audience. Receptivity is measured, first of all, by questions focusing on satisfaction with life as it is and willingness to change. If people are satisfied (a very common response once basic survival needs are met), spiritual truth tends to fall on non-fertile soil. The opposite response often is an indicator of a readiness to consider a new direction in life. A second dimension of receptivity is commitment to an alien religious belief. Receptivity varies inversely with strength of this commitment.

Understanding of Biblical Truth

What do those in a target audience believe to be true about God, the nature of humanity, the person of Christ, and the means of salvation? Most have little correct understanding, so seed must be sown. A call for commitment is appropriate when responses indicate a positive attitude toward the act of receiving Christ.

Motivations and Felt Needs

Biblical truth takes on power once it is perceived in the context of motivations and needs. Otherwise it is little more than an abstraction. Therefore, this connection between teaching and life becomes an important research goal if we are to follow the example of Jesus. He demonstrated the relevance of the Christian message.

Attitudes toward the Christian Message

Based on an understanding of biblical truth in the context of motivations and needs, what is the attitude about the act of becoming a Christian? Positive responses among many in a target segment indicate a high likelihood of success using reaping strategies that call for commitment.

Decision-making Styles

Here are some illustrative questions: Is there a felt need for additional information? If so, are they readers, listeners, etc.? Are decisions made as individuals or in a family or larger group? Important clues can often be discovered in this way.

Surveys[5]

Survey research had its birth in the West, and most of the writing on methods takes little account of cultural nuances of surveying a non-Western population. Yet surveys are now being used worldwide by governmental agencies and businesses, in contexts ranging from primitive to highly sophisticated.[6]

My experience in all continents of the world has shown that survey research is no different from any other types of cross-cultural communication. The challenge is a familiar one—adaptation and contextualization. Here are a few examples of what has been learned at such research centers as Daystar University College in Kenya and elsewhere.

Research Design

Surveys are not uncommon now in most urban areas, and those under the age of thirty are familiar with questionnaires from school. Methods used run the gamut from in-home personal interviews to direct mail and telephone interviewing. While the telephone would seem to be totally off-limits (and it often is), there have been successful examples where a personal letter is sent

---

5. For an introduction to the use of survey research in Christian ministry, see James F. Engel, *How Can I Get Them to Listen?* This introductory research manual has been reprinted and may be purchased from the bookstores at Wheaton College and Eastern College. It was revised in 1991 by Robert Oehrig of Daystar University College (Kenya) and Engel under the title, *Using Research to Sharpen Ministry Effectiveness.*

6. For an excellent example, see Ane Haaland, *Pretesting Communication Materials* (Rangoon, Burma: UNICEF, 1984).

first, soliciting cooperation in research on a subject of personal importance and interest. Those who respond affirmatively (and this can be more than one might think) are interviewed at an agreed-upon time.

Sampling and Interviewing

I have already mentioned the difficulty of executing randomly chosen samples and the frequent need to use non-probability designs. But other challenges are faced.

An uninterrupted interview with a defined individual often is impossible. Many Muslim husbands insist on speaking for their wives. Large crowds gather around an interviewer, with everyone making a contribution. And on it goes. The best decision often is to undertake a group interview in the open air, taking full account of cultural protocols on who speaks first and so on. Incidentally, this method, known as focus group research, has become very popular in Western countries.

In other situations, potent barriers stand in the way of interviewing those who are chosen for a sample. Sometimes the key is to gain the approval of a gatekeeper (political official, bishop, or pastor) who authenticates the research process. The importance of the gatekeeper became clear to me in the 1970s. We lost access to all the churches of one denomination in a Brazilian city when the district superintendent proclaimed that the research was from the devil. Hopefully this was not the case, but nothing our local team members did could change his mind.

In another situation, in-home interviews were attempted in an upper-class neighborhood. It proved impossible to get past guards at the gate leading to the homes until certain key people within the neighborhoods intervened directly on our behalf.

Questioning

Questionnaires are nothing more than structured conversation. Therefore, all that we have learned about contextualization applies.

Survey research in the Western world, for example, makes extensive use of attitude scales, typically ranging from strongly agree to strongly disagree. But such scales do not always represent the way people think and their preferred form of response. We found this to be the case in Brazil, where it is common to reply using only the extremes. Therefore, scales were adapted and asked, first of all, whether respondents agree or disagree. Once this was decided, they were asked to mark a box showing how much they agreed or disagreed. Because of this two-step process, respondents made good use of all categories of agreement and disagreement.

Structured questions can be dangerous in that answers suggested by the categories are chosen by some respondents no matter what they believe. Therefore, effective use has been made of sentence completion questions such as "Jesus Christ is " and "Life would be better for me if _____." Such open-ended questions are useful. While the lack of structure makes tabulation more difficult, the quality of responses can be greatly improved.

Finally, measures of socio-economic status can be a challenge. There often is great hesitancy to reveal anything about income or wealth, but such external measures as a metal roof or a television set are good measures.

Reporting the Findings

Research will never be used if the analyst becomes enamored with his or her methodological lingo. Nothing can erect barriers more quickly than indiscriminate use of such terms as "correlation coefficient," "standard error," "chi square," and "95 percent confidence level." Matters are made even worse when a report is laden with numerical tables.

Perhaps the greatest contextualization challenge takes place at this stage. My experience has shown that Christian leaders around the world, regardless of their educational level, are fully capable of excellent strategic thinking if they are approached correctly. Here are some imperatives if the research is to be used:

1. Make maximum use of charts and graphs.
2. Do not use technical terms.
3. Present only the data which have major implications for strategy. Explain what these implications are. Suggest the strategic options that should be considered, stressing the most relevant considerations.
4. Trust the users to make good decisions as they interact and seek the leadership of the Holy Spirit.

Phasing Research into Evangelistic Strategy

In my experience, getting the data is the easiest part. The greatest challenge lies in knowing what to do with it. It is here that God's people must not hesitate to be innovators. Innovators, in turn, are risk-takers.

Risk-takers, however, need not jump into the unknown in a foolhardy way. It can be a great mistake to launch a new project without testing and evaluation. Rather than pull out all the stops, try the strategy in a few test areas and see what God wants to teach us. Evaluate, adapt, and experiment until there are good signs that expected outcomes will be achieved.

Research, strategic planning, innovation, testing—these are tried-and-true components of the kind of stewardship God expects as his kingdom is proclaimed.

Caleb Project
Research Expeditions

John Holzmann

Caleb Project Research Expeditions (CPRE), commonly known as Joshua Project, engages in ethnographic surveys of urban centers of the largely unreached in the Two-Thirds world, usually in restricted access countries. We seek to determine the sociological realities of those cities in order that, based on this research, we can envision what culturally relevant churches might look like and how they might be planted among the various unreached peoples we find within those cities. At the same time, though our primary function is to engage in research and though we call ourselves "Research Expeditions," *research is not our primary purpose.* Rather, it is the means we use to achieve our purpose of mobilizing and training Christians to become strategically involved in church planting efforts among unreached people groups.

Missiological Presuppositions

There are a few presuppositions that underlie everything CPRE does.

1. God has commanded his people to make disciples among every ethnic group or "people" worldwide (Matt. 28:19; Acts 1:8).
2. Before "the end" comes, this mandate will be fulfilled (Gen. 12:3; Matt. 24:14; Rev. 5:9; 7:9).
3. It is by local congregations—churches—and not merely individuals that God intends to fulfill his purpose of discipling the nations. To es-

This chapter first appeared in *Urban Mission* 8, no. 4 (1991): 43–55. Used by permission.

tablish indigenous churches is a missiologically strategic goal (1 Cor. 12:14; Eph. 4:11–16).

4. God desires that every people have the opportunity to worship and serve him within a church that reflects their unique cultural and social structures, as sanctified by God. To establish indigenous churches is a biblically valid goal (Acts 10:9–11:18; 15:1–29).

5. A major barrier to the gospel's advance among many unreached peoples is the perception that Christianity and the church are "foreign," that one can't at the same time be both a member of his or her ethnic group and a Christian. Many are convinced that to become a Christian is to reject one's heritage.

6. Acquiring many individual converts does not naturally result in the establishment of churches.

The first four presuppositions are faith statements which arise from our understanding of Scripture. The fifth and sixth are the results of field observation. We have talked with many people who testify that they have studied the Bible and believe that Jesus died to save them from their sins, but they refuse to follow Christ. Further, there are hundreds of people groups around the world among whom, we are told, there are dozens, perhaps even hundreds, of indigenous Christians, yet no indigenous church. Why?

Observation 5 explains part of it. People who profess faith in Christ realize that if they openly acknowledge their faith by identifying with a church they will be perceived as traitors by their own people. Their neighbors will think they have joined a foreign culture. Missionaries make matters worse if they ignore ethnic realities and try to form churches by bringing together groups of converts who would never come together in any other context. In the Middle East, for example, Turk, Kurd, and Arab converts may live in the same city, but it would be more difficult for a missionary to successfully mix these groups when planting a church than to form a church comprised of people from both the lower and upper classes in the United States, which would be difficult in itself. Members of the two groups may seek very hard to get along. But no matter how hard they try, they will soon realize that their respective felt needs are irrelevant to, or ignored by, members of the other group. That is, the lower-class members' felt survival needs are not shared by the upper-class members' felt needs. The needs for a polished, professional quality music program are not shared by the lower-class members.

Missionaries go into church planting situations thinking that the ethnic barriers should be overcome in Christ. Therefore, they think, ethnic barriers can be overcome. And, indeed, we at CPRE pray that one day they will be overcome. But, realistically, we do not expect such changes to occur in one meeting . . . and certainly not in the foundational meeting of a new congregation!

Finally, especially in more restrictive cultures, converts don't naturally trust each other; indeed, they are often afraid someone in the group will turn them in to the governmental authorities. While new converts usually trust the missionary after the time they have spent together in fellowship and Bible study, they have no relationship with, and therefore no trust in, one another.

A Movement Mentality

Much missiological research has focused recently on the need for better, more effective gospel communication, how to help potential converts understand the gospel message. This emphasis has all been to the great good of mission work.

Growing out of our missiological presuppositions, however, CPRE has a different, complementary goal. We seek to discover how new believers in Christ can live out their faith as integral members of their society. What will the church look like if it is to be perceived as being "native" to that society?

Much mission research focuses on missionaries and missionaries' communication skills—helping them discover the specific words and forms of speech to use, the types of clothing to wear, the kinds of behavior to engage in. Caleb Project researchers focus instead on the society—on means for eliciting social change and on potential responses to such social change within the society. Among questions asked are: Who have the most influence within the society? What kinds of social deviations are acceptable? What happens to people who deviate? For instance, what would happen to a person who becomes a Communist?

Instead of asking, "How can we reduce the difficulties these people have in understanding the gospel?" Caleb Project Research Expeditions asks, "How can we help to reduce the perceived cost involved in accepting it?" Instead of concerning ourselves with how to narrow the cultural gap between missionaries and potential converts (the "E" Scale), we consider how to reduce the gap between potential convert(s) and the church (the "P" Scale).[1]

Instead of seeking to minimize distortion of the message, we seek to minimize social dislocation as members of the society become Christians and form a church movement.

Research Goals

Caleb Project research teams pursue information in four areas for every city in which they do research:

---

1. Ralph Winter and Steven Hawthorne, eds., *Perspectives on the World Christian Movement* (Pasadena: William Carey Library, 1981), 316–19.

1. Who are the peoples that require specific church planting efforts?
2. To what extent are the peoples reached (i.e., churched)?
3. What will healthy, fully functional churches look like among each of these peoples?
4. What evangelistic church planting strategies are likely to be most effective in order to produce healthy, functional churches?

CPRE in Bangkok: A Case Study

Preparation for the Bangkok Research Expedition began in mid–1987 as a result of conversations with missionaries from Thailand who said that most Christian work was being conducted among the ethnic Chinese rather than among the Thai people themselves.

We determined to discover whether this was true, and if so, whether this was a conscious or unconscious decision. We also wanted to discover what ethnic groups live in Bangkok and whether there were indications that some non-churched groups might be open to gospel work among them.

One of the key criteria Caleb Project Research Expeditions consider when choosing a city to study is whether there is an English-speaking population for team members to converse with, and whether researchers would be received well enough to carry out ethnographic work. We were assured that Bangkok met these criteria.

Prior to going, the team research coordinator gathered as much information as possible about Bangkok and its peoples. We ransacked local university research libraries, interviewed nationals who happened to come through our area, and telephoned people in mission agencies whom we knew had worked, or currently were working, in Bangkok.

Besides acquiring basic geopolitical, ethnographic, and demographic information, the coordinator sought to find out what was happening in the region, who was already working there, and the general felt need for the kinds of information our team(s) intended to gather.

Team Training

Pre-field training for most team members began in early October 1987. It consisted of thirteen weeks of low-intensity study at their homes, and five weeks of concentrated activity at Caleb Project's headquarters. By the time they arrived at Caleb Project headquarters, team members had read *The Ethnographic Interview* by James Spradley, the Caleb Project Research Expeditions training notebook, basic information about Bangkok and Thailand, and major portions of *Stepping Out*, the short-term missions manual. The research coordinator and team leader had also read *Siamese Gold: A History of Church Growth in Thailand* by Alex Smith, along with other more in-depth material about Thailand and modern sociology and anthropology. Nowadays, team members also read *Focus: The Power of People Group Thinking* by John Robb before they arrive at Caleb Project headquarters.

The Bangkok team spent five weeks at Caleb Project headquarters being built up as a team and receiving classroom and field training in six key areas:

1. *Missiology.* What are people groups? What do we mean when we speak of people group movements? What are our missiological assumptions?
2. *Research methods.* Interviewing techniques, note taking, and using a computer are among skills covered.
3. *Country briefing.* What is it like in Bangkok? During the country briefing, team members met some Thai nationals. The Bangkok team also had the opportunity to interview a Thai Christian convert.
4. *Mobilization.* Why are we doing this research? What will we do with our findings? How do we plan to achieve our overall objectives?
5. *Spiritual life.*
6. *Cross-cultural living and coping skills.*

Besides the classroom instruction, training included three ethnographic practice trips to Los Angeles' Chinatown and an extended, five-day field experience in Tijuana, Mexico.

On the Field

One of the unique aspects of CPRE is that we don't merely sponsor research; we sponsor research teams. The team dynamics enable team members to accomplish things that individual researchers could never do.

For instance, one could never hope to acquire credible research results—let alone have researchers survive—if one depended solely on individual researchers with the kinds of background CPRE expedition members have. About a third of all research team members have either never been overseas or had little overseas experience prior to their involvement with Caleb Project Research Expeditions. We believe it is only because of the team dynamics that these people are able to produce the kind of reports they do after only three months' field exposure—reports that, according to the testimony of at least one mission's field director, have saved years of groundwork and provided insights to use in strategy.

The coordinator of the Christian and Missionary Alliance's Bangkok church planting team said, "We on the scene are often so involved in the details of church planting that we sometimes overlook the big picture. What you [Caleb Project Research Expeditions] have done has really helped us do that."

Fourteen people—two married couples, four single men, and six single women—participated in the Bangkok research expedition. Among them, one single man served as team leader, providing pastoral care and facilitating team relationships. Another young man served as team research coordinator. His job was to provide oversight of most of the research activities and to ensure that data were recorded and stored properly. Other special roles included a team photographer, an accountant, and a computer specialist.

With fourteen people gathering data, all approaching the problem from their unique perspectives and continually interacting, the research progressed relatively rapidly. Further, while different individuals on the team may have become sidetracked or stuck in a research rut, the larger group dynamics were able quickly to help overcome these difficulties.

One final benefit of the CPRE approach is that the expeditions are set up as academic programs. That means team members are able to ask questions more directly and in a less intimidating fashion than if they were fulfilling another role. As team members approached people in Bangkok, they identified themselves as American students trying to learn about the peoples and culture of Bangkok. If they were ever asked about their religious convictions, they would freely identify themselves as Christians, but they did their best to avoid being viewed as or identified with missionaries.

Team Relationships

In Bangkok, the CPRE team stayed in the Christian and Missionary Alliance guest house. Especially in more restricted societies, we avoid any possible link with "missionary" endeavors. In Bangkok, however, being a Christian is not a great liability, and other Westerners, even non-Christians, stay at the C&MA guest house. So we felt the convenience and financial advantages were well worth whatever minuscule social costs would be involved in residing there.

Living together as they did meant that the team was able to eat breakfast, pray, and worship together at the beginning of each day and to enjoy mutual spiritual and emotional support at the end of the day as members prepared for bed. As one member commented, "Unless you happen to be an extrovert to the extreme, it takes a lot of physical and emotional energy to keep going out day after day to initiate conversations and relationships!" Thus, team members found that their times of fellowship with one another and with God were vital, not only for personal spiritual, mental, emotional, and physical health, but for encouragement, also, to press on in the task.

Research Stage 1: Exploration

During the day, the team split into seven "teamlets"—two people per teamlet—to do the ethnographic research. In Muslim societies, of course, we keep the sexes separate, but in Bangkok we had mixed-sex teamlets.

CPRE research usually proceeds in three stages: exploration, stratification, and envisioning. In Bangkok there was an additional item that needed to be studied. Unlike most cities where CPRE teams are sent, in Bangkok our researchers had to determine the relative reachedness ("churchedness") of the resident populations. In Stage 1, the team leaders took a map of the city and assigned the various teamlets specific neighborhoods to explore. Their purpose was to characterize their assigned area of the city, to discover what kind(s) of people lived there, to see if there were enough people in that section of the city who could speak English, and to begin establishing relationships. Since they were seeking the broadest possible exposure to the city and its peoples during this early exploration phase, team members went back to the same informants no more than once or twice.

During this same period, besides the initial field research, team members also participated in a three-week Thai language class to give them enough exposure to the language to get around the city comfortably.

The core of CPRE's ethnographic method comes from Spradley's *The Ethnographic Interview.*[2] There are two significant differences, however, between what Spradley espouses and what CPRE teams do. CPRE team members strive for much more informal conversations than Spradley suggests. For instance, they use no prewritten questionnaires; instead, they have a general subject that they will pursue with hypotheses to test and general lines of questioning. Further, if it seems that taking notes on the spot will cause their informants to feel uncomfortable or under pressure to give "correct" answers, CPRE researchers wait to record their notes until after the interview is concluded or, as one researcher suggested, "after having excused myself from the table so I could 'go to the bathroom.'"

The goal for Caleb Project researchers is to speak to their informants— and to have their informants speak to them—as one friend to another. Thus, researchers spend time with their informants and invest in their relationships with these people to establish a true friendship. In terms of the research itself, CPRE team members have found that it is in the context of such relationships that they will acquire some of their most important data. The higher the level of trust, the more one learns—or, at least, the more one is able to see society through the eyes of one's friend.

Bangkok team members aggressively initiated relationships—on the street, in restaurants, in stores—wherever they could locate English-speaking nationals. Further, they took time with their Thai friends to share themselves. If their friends were interested, they would show them pictures of "home," tell them about America, and participate in those things that were of interest to their Thai friends—whether that meant being an honored guest at a wedding, going to a museum, or visiting relatives in a nearby community. Of course, team members had to put certain limits on how much contact they had with any one informant, and they sought to redeem as much of

2. New York: Holt, Rinehart and Winston, 1979.

the non-research-oriented time as possible by carrying on conversations that would help to clarify their informants' personal views of the city and social relationships.

Besides the informality of Caleb Project research, the second difference from Spradley's methods is that, while he looks at the whole of anthropology, we focus mainly on sociology.

Whatever the quantity of handwritten notes they had collected at the end of the day, teamlets were required to enter field notes on computers. During their training they had been taught a standard format, so that they all used the same vocabulary, subject categories, and page setup. This process of typing notes at the end of each day forced team members to articulate what they had seen and heard—the specific behaviors or realities they had observed—and then to try to hypothesize as to the significance of their observations.

Teamlet partners would check each other's notes as they were typed into the computers, make corrections and suggestions for greater clarity, and then print a final hard copy of what they had written. They knew that these notes were important, not only as the database for their eventual final report, but also as a focal point for their weekly strategy meetings during the expedition.

The Weekly Strategy Meeting

One day a week, from 8:00 A.M. until 5:00 P.M., the CPRE team meets to discuss the information gathered during the three and one-half to four days of interviews in the previous week. There are several reasons for these strategy meetings. One is for team members to "come up to speed" on each other's findings to date. The idea is that everyone will go out the following week with, not only the information they have gathered the previous week, but everyone else's information as well.

During the strategy meetings, team members find that their data may confirm or conflict with others' findings. As one team leader has described it, "At the strategy meeting, we synthesize our data and compound our knowledge. It multiplies the effectiveness of our research." During these strategy meetings, team members remind themselves of their research goals during the previous week and consider their specific findings, and what their findings mean. Based on their answers to those questions, they decide what research goals they will aim for during the coming week.

The goal of these meetings is to reach group consensus—"We're convinced of this." "We need more information to know if this is true or not." From this consensus the group formulates hypotheses and lines of questioning for the different teamlets to pursue during the following week's research.

In Bangkok, with fourteen people collecting and recording field notes, by the end of each week there were between 100 and 150 pages of notes. The day before the strategy meeting, all team members read everyone else's notes. Before they read, the research coordinator assigned each team member a specific topic or angle to especially study. Everyone was to be familiar with all the data, yet prepared to interpret them from different perspectives.

Joshua Walks ("J"-Walks)

Beyond the living arrangements, the research teamlets and the weekly strategy meetings, the single most significant aid to Caleb Project research is the weekly Joshua Walk, or "J"-Walk as it is affectionately called. Team members go out, two by two, to walk through and pray over specific areas of the city. One of the CPRE team's goals when they set out on expeditions is that, by the time they have finished their studies, team members will have prayed through the entire city. Usually, team leaders keep a map on a wall of the team's living quarters and color in the areas where team members have J-Walked.

J-Walks have practical significance for the research in many ways. They provide a powerful impetus for team members to go out and meet friends. They remind team members of their ultimate purpose for doing the research. As one expedition member commented,

> "Suddenly, as you are praying Scripture for these people, you find your faith is built for what God can do. J-Walks give you a vision for what could happen. The significance of having a church established in that culture—what it will mean to those people—becomes a reality to you in a way that simply gathering more information will never make it. More information can lead you to despair if you don't have anything to hang it on—something to build faith and hope."

So J-Walks build faith and hope.

They also serve a more mystical function. "As you pray about the facts and information that you know, you find that God gives you impressions of what the church could or will look like. The facts and information become translated into something imaginable through prayer." Further, J-Walks "expose spiritual strongholds over peoples. . . . You pray for people with different eyes than those with which you research them."

Some things became more visible to the Bangkok team during their J-Walks: the materialism and materialistic aspirations of the city's Chinese population; the "god-shelves" in every Chinese business; the Thai spirit houses; the sense of spiritual oppression around Buddhist temples; the spirit of hedonism—especially the alcoholism and prostitution—that seems to dominate the city.

Research Stage 2: Stratification Studies

To *stratify* a population, CPRE studies any factors from race to religious affiliations, linguistics, class, political parties, locale, region of origin, stage of migration, education, or occupation. Our purpose is always to discover what criteria the people themselves use to distinguish themselves one from another (*emic* vs. *etic* perspective).

About the beginning of the third week on the field, the Bangkok team began its in-depth stratification studies. While teamlets continued to seek new informants throughout their visit, after the first couple of weeks they focused more energy on a few relationships.

As mentioned above, at each week's strategy meeting the teamlets were assigned specific topics to study during the following week. In Bangkok, with fourteen people and seven teamlets, the team as a whole was normally able to study three different stratification criteria each week. Each criterion was studied separately by two teamlets. Sometimes the teamlets required only a week to arrive at a strong consensus concerning a topic. At other times, they found they needed two or three weeks to complete their inquiries.

In Bangkok the team began its stratification studies by focusing on race, language, neighborhood, region of origin, and class—criteria they thought Bangkok residents would most likely view as their primary differentiating characteristics. When the stratification studies were complete, however, they had learned that region of origin, race/ethnicity, and education/occupation (or class) were the primary criteria by which residents distinguished themselves. Each of these criteria received different emphasis, depending on the segment of society.

After having identified the most important stratification criteria and having gathered extensive data on each one, the team set out to delineate Bangkok's peoples based on the Lausanne Committee Global Statistics Task Force's *operational definition* of a *mini-* or *uni-max people:* "the largest group movement without encountering barriers of acceptance or understanding."

The team hypothesized where church planting movements would encounter barriers of understanding or acceptance in various sub-segments of Bangkok society. The team based its hypotheses on the data it had acquired through the stratification studies.

About the seventh week on the field, the team came to a consensus that, though they could do more research—testing their hypotheses and further delineating the peoples—they had an accurate enough understanding of how Bangkok's society is stratified and where church planting movements would encounter barriers to acceptance and understanding. Their conclusion was that there are four major people groups in Bangkok: ethnic Chinese, Chinese-Thai, ethnic Tai, and Isaan (northeastern Thai; see Fig. 2). They were ready to press on into the next stages of research.

At this juncture, the team left Bangkok to spend a week surveying three of the areas from which many of the people in the city came: Northern and Central Thailand and Isaan. The team split up into three groups—one group to visit each of these areas. The entire team then gathered at the end of the

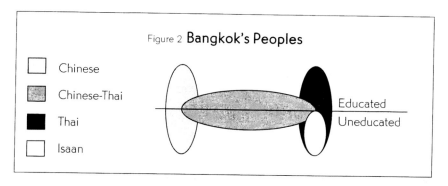

Figure 2 **Bangkok's Peoples**

Chinese

Chinese-Thai

Thai

Isaan

Educated

Uneducated

week to visit Jim Gustafson in Udon Thani to observe his "contextualized development" approach among the Isaan.

The purpose of these trips was to get a feel for the broader country—the context of which Bangkok is a part, to see the regions from which people were coming into the city, and to talk to Christian workers in those areas to find out what gospel work was being done.

Research Stage 3: Reachedness

In most cities where Caleb Project Research Expeditions work, there are no churches among the groups our teams study. In Bangkok, however, there is a sizable Christian presence. The team had to find out to what extent the peoples they were studying were churched. Did they all have equal representation in the churches?

In order to answer that question, team members visited churches—one teamlet per church, seven churches each Sunday morning. Following the service, team members talked with church leaders—the pastor, elders, whoever else they could find—to ask about the congregations' histories and to discover their ethnic composition. Besides local church leaders, team members interviewed some of the city's more prominent Christian leaders—both national and missionary. Who is turning to Christ? they asked. Where and why are they becoming Christians?

More than one church growth researcher has commented that the people who attend churches tend to be like their leaders. Whatever group their leader is from, that is the group from which church members themselves come. In Bangkok, most pastors said they had some ethnic Thai and/or Isaan members in their congregations. When a pastor made such a comment, team members asked him to identify these people so they could interview them directly. When team members asked these members themselves about their ethnic identity, almost every one identified with the Chinese or Chinese-Thai groups. In several instances, church leaders identified themselves and their churches as being Thai. However, it became clear that, while they spoke the Thai language, culturally they were all Chinese.

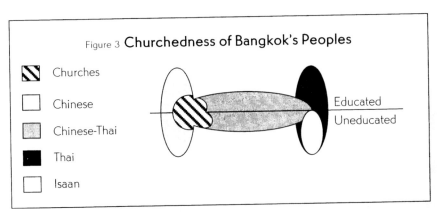

Figure 3 **Churchedness of Bangkok's Peoples**

By the time the expedition was over, team members had visited close to thirty of the most dynamic churches in Bangkok. It turned out that, as CPRE leaders have been told back in the United States, very few Isaan and even fewer pure Thai populate the churches of Bangkok. No matter what language they speak, almost all the pastors are Chinese or Chinese-Thai and the members of their churches are Chinese or Chinese-Thai as well (see Fig. 3).

Research Stage 4: Envisioning a Church

It seems that many missionaries never think strategically about how to start a congregation until they have acquired several converts. They figure that, once they have finished language training, they need to get to work with evangelism. After they have engaged in successful evangelism they will have converts. Once they have converts, they can start to establish a church.

They seem to assume that the big hurdle is conversion; once they have converts, all they have to do is "follow up" and churches will naturally spring into existence. As a result of this perspective, a lot of missionaries have defaulted to a strategy of random evangelism. They simply share the gospel with whomever they come into contact.

Caleb Project Research Expeditions seeks to approach church planting from the other end of the process. Our teams are taught to start at the goal—a culturally relevant church: What will a culturally relevant church look like in this population? What kind of people will be in it? What kind of leadership will it have?

Envisioning means imagining the future and then working backwards, asking the strategic questions concerning how to attain that goal. One CPRE leader has said, "When we have envisioned a church, we have formed a biblically based, research-informed, prayer-saturated hypothesis about what a contextualized church might look like within a people group." These elements tell us a lot about our role as planters:

Biblically based. What are the scriptural requirements of a church? We know it's not pews, choir robes, and steeples, but what is it?

Research-informed. A contextualized church is based on what the people themselves say about their feelings and cultural sensitivities.

Prayer-saturated. It is a spiritual work, not merely the result of an academic problem-solving approach. It is dependent on the Holy Spirit.

Hypothesis. We make a best-guess, not a rigid requirement or limitation on what God must do.

Our target is not merely to do better evangelism. It is to envision how to plant a church. The church that is finally planted may not look like the church the CPRE team envisioned, but it will look like a church and not merely a conglomeration of converts!

Having envisioned the final product, CPRE researchers seek to work back to the present day: What kind of evangelism is likely to bring the kinds of converts our envisioned church is going to need? Who is most likely to be successful at helping to lead these people to repentance?

In terms of research methodology, envisioning a church among target populations is no different from stratification; teamlets continue to interview their informants. The difference between envisionment and stratification resides in the topics researchers pursue.

In the envisioning stage, researchers no longer seek to identify group boundaries and bonds. Instead, they spend their time discussing leadership and relational patterns, institutional and associational forms, the social consequences of deviating from social norms, and potential entrance strategies. They try to determine where and how church planting work ought to begin. Should church planters work among the young? the old? men? women? married? unmarried? upper class? lower class? laborers? professionals? traditionalists? Westernized? Which of these distinguishing characteristics might make a positive (or negative) difference in terms of how the target population will view the envisioned church?

Every group Caleb Project researchers have studied has proven different in these matters. In Bangkok the team found that, even when ethnic Thais join a church, one of the primary reasons they subsequently leave has to do with the leadership patterns in the church. Among the Thai, a leader is self-effacing, who only steps forward to lead when the group insists upon it. To the Chinese, the Thai appear lazy and uninterested in leadership. To the Thai, the Chinese appear pushy and interested in power and prestige, rather than service.

Since most churches are Chinese, the Chinese are generally blind to the fact that leadership style is an issue to the Thais. Thais don't feel comfortable in churches run by people who lead in the manner of the Chinese and they are unlikely to become active members in Chinese churches.

So what will a Thai-oriented church look like? What leadership model should its leaders follow? The Bangkok team report made some suggestions. Besides leadership style, some of the other issues the Bangkok team dealt with included decision-making patterns, reversion patterns, appropriate locations, and schedules for meetings. In other cities, teams have made suggestions based on their research concerning such issues as entry strategies, class distinctions, and racial problems.

Besides envisioning churches, the Bangkok team members spent a lot of time during their third month on the field drafting a research report, trying to summarize what they had learned and confirming the things they weren't quite sure of. They also wrote a slide show script, took photographs, and put together a prayer guide and other materials that would become tools for mobilizing the church once they returned to the United States.

Return to the States

After twelve weeks on the field, the Caleb Project Bangkok research team returned to the United States where, besides unwinding from a high-intensity cross-cultural experience, they spent up to ten hours a day for three weeks producing the slide shows, prayer tools, and research reports they had been sent to Bangkok to produce.

Once they had made an initial public presentation of their materials and enjoyed a hearty thank-you/send-off party, they returned to their homes—some to raise support to go back to Bangkok to try to plant a church; others to become outspoken proponents of mission efforts to the people whose needs they had researched.

Resources for Doing Research

Blackwood, Vernon, Barbara Reichardt, and Sally Schreiner. *SCUPE Researchers and Resource Centers Directory*. Chicago: Seminary Consortium for Urban Pastoral Education, 1992 (30 W. Chicago Ave., Chicago, IL 60610). A listing of forty-nine centers in fourteen countries specializing in the collection, production, and dissemination of urban church studies. Each listing provides information on the center's purpose, research interests, and available reports and services. Not comprehensive but quite useful.

Conn, Harvie M., ed. *Urban Church Research: Methods and Models*. Collected Readings. Philadelphia: Westminster Theological Seminary, 1985 (Campus Bookstore, P.O. Box 27009, Philadelphia, PA 19118). Prepared for classroom use but useful on a wider scale. Extensive (now dated) bibliographies, including list of selected periodicals for study of missiology and world Christianity; ethnographic and demographic resources; fourteen samples of church growth survey questionnaires and instruments for research; copy of Engel's out-of-print title, *How Can I Get Them to Listen?*

Engel, James. *How Can I Get Them to Listen?* Grand Rapids: Zondervan, 1977. Out of print. Still the most user-friendly tool available for understanding basic techniques of sampling, questionnaire design, data collection, tabulation, and analysis. Oriented to practitioner needs.

Roozen, David A., and C. Kirk Hadaway, eds. *Church and Denominational Growth*. Nashville: Abingdon, 1993 (201 Eighth Ave., South, Nashville, TN 37203). Excellent samples of case study research focused on American mainline churches. Sophisticated use of data gathering and sociological analyses. Good blend of contextual and institutional factors in understanding church growth and decline. Not specifically oriented to urban needs.

Shipp, Harvey G. "Research as a Tool for Urban Evangelism in Developing Countries." Unpublished D.Miss. Dissertation, Fuller Theological Seminary, Pasadena, Calif., 1986 (available through University Microfilms, 300 N. Zeeb Road, Ann Arbor, MI 48106). General introduction to the urban context and to urban research methods and objects of study useful in evangelizing unreached peoples. The missionary author uses Belo Horizonte, Brazil, for his case study sample. Practitioner-level in orientation.

Stockwell, Clinton. *Urban Research Project: A Handbook for Urban Ministry*. Chicago: Midwest District, Baptist General Conference, 1985. Results of one-year study of the life and growth of twenty-one congregations in the Chicago area. Each church is profiled in terms of its mission and self-understanding. General observations and strategy recommendations are then drawn. Also includes extensive bibliography, in addition to resource tools for understanding church and community. Excellent examples of urban analysis.

Wiberg, Sally Johnson, and Clinton Stockwell. *Self-Helping Each Other: The Discovery Experience. Steps Toward Renewal and Outreach for Urban Churches.* Chicago: The Central Conference of the Evangelical Covenant Church, 1986 (3319 West Foster Ave., Chicago, IL 60625). A full description of the step-by-step process of self-study undertaken by the urban churches of one denomination. The survey reviews the planning process for the study, the seminar workshops held, and the role of the consultant. Seventy-four pages of appendixes provide extensive information on useful resources. Useful tool for planning a similar program.

Part 2
Strategy Planning:
Searching for the Right Answers

Introduction

Harvie M. Conn

"A strategy," defines Edward Dayton and David Fraser, "is an overall approach, plan, or way of describing how we will go about reaching our goal or solving our problem."[1] It takes the raw material of research and gives it purpose and direction.

Strategy planning looks at a shrinking church in a Philadelphia neighborhood that has shifted from African American middle class to African American lower class. It asks, "Does the church in its philosophy of ministry and its worship style still fit? What must stay? What must go?" Strategy planning looks at a slum neighborhood empty of churches in Bangkok and asks, "How do we begin?"

Non-Negotiables in Strategy Planning

Is it true that "if you fail to plan, you're planning to fail"? What about our Lord's injunction regarding the post-resurrection mission of the church to the Gentiles? In encouraging us not to worry about what to say, he assured us, "The Holy Spirit will teach you at that time what you should say" (Luke 12:12). Can we read that as an indictment against strategy planning, a call to sanctified non-planning?

---

1. Edward Dayton and David Fraser, *Planning Strategies for World Evangelization*, 2nd ed. (Grand Rapids: Eerdmans, 1990), 13.

Some in the history of the church moved in that direction. But worry is not the same as planning. The wisdom of the Spirit, in directing our Christian testimony at crucial moments of struggle, does not cancel Christ's mandate to be as "shrewd as snakes" (Matt. 10:16) in those encounters. Shrewdness is the dividing line between foolish virgins who don't plan and shrewd ones who do (Matt. 25:2).

Strategic planning is a human enterprise linked to who God is and who we are.

God plans. From all eternity, he has planned in electing grace to save a multitude of people through the sacrifice of his Son (Eph. 1:4–5, 11). In the freedom of his sovereign grace, and the omnipotent right of that freedom (Rom. 9:14–26), he exhibits his saving love "according to his eternal purpose which he accomplished in Christ Jesus our Lord" (Eph. 3:11). There is a priority of God's counsel and plan (Rom. 8:29–30; Eph. 2:10) that marks saints as also "the elect" (Col. 3:12; Titus 1:1).

That same divine strategy plans for the wilderness tabernacle (Exodus 25–40), for the proper exercise of cultic worship, for a legal system of justice and grace that sets apart Israelite society. God's plan distinguishes Israel from the idolatry and viciousness of neighboring city-states.

As images of God and not computers, we are called to mirror that divine strategy in our planning. The responsibility of being royal vice-regents and representatives of God (Gen. 1:27–28) is not negated by divine sovereignty but underlined by it. In a parallelism that no one can fathom, we "are created in Christ Jesus to do good works" but "good works which God prepared in advance for us to do" (Eph. 2:10). The same God who makes things grow expects also that one must plant the seed and another must water it (1 Cor. 3:6).

So, though their skills are given by God (Exod. 35:30–34), Bezalel and Oholiab are commended for offering them willingly in the building of the tabernacle. Even the unbounded generosity of the people of God must be restrained (Exod. 36:3–7). When plans of worship dictated by God are violated by the substitution of a golden calf (Exodus 32), God judges. When God's divine purposes for a just society are compromised by human plans that exhibit injustice toward the poor and helpless (Isa. 1:10–17), God rejects his own planned worship. God must still bless what humanity's urban vigilance can or cannot detect (Ps. 127:1).

The limitations of our creaturehood and the myopia of sin can misdirect strategy planning.

For God's fellow workers (1 Cor. 3:9), planning is a human enterprise. It's easier now because Israel's detailed civil and cultic law system no longer makes its elaborate tutorial demands on Gentiles who would enter the "glorious freedom of the children of God" (Rom. 8:21). Yet it is also more demanding because the Spirit gives us more elbow room to exercise our maturity in understanding how to do God's will in God's way.

Freedom in the Spirit is not easy to plan around, even for those who seek to imitate God's desires. Well-intentioned strategies for urban evangelism sometimes need rerouting by the Spirit (Acts 16:6–7). Planned urban visits need postponing (Rom. 15:23–28).

But, more frightening still, planning can head very much in the wrong direction, misshapen by greedy ambition (Joshua 7) or misplaced fear (Num. 13:31–33). Many Old Testament passages link this misdirected planning to the very building of cities.

Cain's planning and building of a city in honor of his son (Gen. 4:17) defied God's curse of wandering and sought a new self-created security in a substitute Eden. The city and tower of Babel were erected out of that same rebellious desire to settle down in resistance to the divine judgment of diffusion (Gen. 11:2). In contrast to God's promise to make Abram's name great (Gen. 12:2), the strategy of Babel's planners aimed to make their own name great (Gen. 11:4).

The tragic history of the monarchy testified to the power of urban planning that ignored God. Upon their entrance into the promised land, Israel did not, in contrast to the strategy of God, conquer all the city-states. And jealous over those urban patterns of rule, they called for a king "as all the other nations have" (1 Sam. 8:5).

But God's response to this plan became not a blessing but a curse. She would taste the fruits of a city-monarch strategy in the confiscation of her sons and daughters (1 Sam. 8:11,13), of her lands, her agricultural products, her servants, and her flocks (1 Sam. 8:14–17).

With the establishment of the monarchy came urban growth, preeminently in Jerusalem under David, but expanding beyond Jerusalem under Solomon. The writer of the Books of Kings often paints that picture with a judgmental eye. Created by a settled bureaucracy preoccupied with itself, the cities are built by Solomon with forced labor (1 Kings 4:6; 5:13; 9:15–22), disregarding the divinely planned boundaries of tribal groupings. Israel is reorganized into effective taxation districts (1 Kings 4:7–19). The people of God are reduced to living under an administrative package that closely resembles those of Pharaoh.[2]

In this context, Solomon's disobedience to God goes beyond the taking of many foreign wives or worshiping foreign gods. He builds cities with slave labor, not only non-Israelite (9:20–21) but Israelite as well (9:15), in disre-

---

2. On the significance of Solomonic tax districts, see Roland DeVaux, *Ancient Israel* (New York: McGraw-Hill, 1961), 133–38.

gard for the Mosaic legislation (Lev. 25:39–42). The names given to the cities, such as Baalath and Beth-Horon, were the names of foreign gods, cities devoted by their names to the false gods invading Israel. Says Jeremiah, "Your gods have become as numerous as your cities, O Israel" (Jer. 11:13). "The reference here is probably only to cities bearing the names of gods. But we must never forget the importance of a name: giving a name to a city is giving it the very being of the name it bears."[3]

This urban planning and building as a political demonstration of disobedience to God continues throughout the Books of Kings; the divided monarchies of Israel and Judah, following Rehoboam's example (2 Chron. 11:5–12), build fortified cities (2 Kings 17:9; 18:13), substituting military security for God's promised protection. And associated with this urban planning movement in the Kings narratives are the marks of apostasy—false worship on the city's high places (1 Kings 13:32; 2 Kings 17:9; 23:8), exuberant wealth and luxury (1 Kings 22:39), the perversion of justice (Isa. 10:1–4; Jer. 22:13–17), and oppression of the poor (Amos 2:6–7; 4:1–2; 5:12). And the end of that disobedience? The transformation of "fortified cities into piles of stone" (2 Kings 19:25).

Strategy planning must be God-centered in focus.

Against this dark side to urban planning in the Bible is another given: God's glory is displayed in the city. God's presence is the fulfillment of the city's original paradise purpose. The goal of strategic planning for the urban church flows out of this center—to proclaim, promote, and preview the salvation of God in Christ in the city as the kingdom sign of the new creation.

Uniquely, that goal flows around Jerusalem in the Old Testament. Out of the purification of judgment by God and exile among the nations, cry the prophets, "the glory of the Lord" will shine again on Mt. Zion (Isa. 60:1). Her walls will be Salvation and her gates Praise on that day when the Lord will be her everlasting light (Isa. 60:19–20). The Savior is coming to the city for royal enthronement. And when he does, Jerusalem will be called "Sought After, The City No Longer Deserted" (Isa. 62:11–12). Filtered through the imagery of creation (Isa. 65:17) and its pre-fall *shalom* (Isa. 65:20–25), God's presence on the Edenic holy mountain "will create Jerusalem to be a delight and its people a joy" (Isa. 65:18).

That eschatological joy in Jerusalem's urban redevelopment reaches far beyond the one city. The establishment of Jerusalem as the center of Israel's life under David's rule had brought together a divided people. And that unity, broken by the division of the tribes, a division sealed as Jeroboam erected competing shrines at Dan and Bethel (1 Kings 12:26–30), would

---

3. Jacques Ellul, *The Meaning of the City* (Grand Rapids: Eerdmans, 1970), 32.

one day be restored even more magnificently. With her salvation, God would also "rebuild the cities of Judah" (Ps. 69:35). And more as well.

She would become "the joy of the whole earth" (Ps. 48:2; cf. Pss. 68:31; 86:9; 137:1, 2, 5, 6). At the coronation ceremony of her divine King, Gentiles also would participate in her Messianic feast (Ps. 22:29). Jerusalem's pilgrims would include the cities of the world (Isa. 60:3). She would be set by God "in the center of the nations, with countries all around her" (Ezek. 5:5).[4]

In the same light, the writer of Chronicles, living in the post-exilic period and building on the history of the Books of Kings, sees the building of the temple and Judah's cities as a continued mark of God's covenant faithfulness to those promises fulfilled and yet to be. The Chronicler's treatment of David and Solomon reflects a "messianic historiography," their glorious rule and building plans in the past a typology of the Lord's urban hope for the future.[5]

Whereas in Kings, Solomon's wisdom is wisdom for ruling (1 Kings 3:7–15), in Chronicles it is wisdom for building (cf. 2 Chron. 2:12 with 1 Kings 5:7). Solomon and Hiram/Huram-abi, the craftsman of Tyre, are a second Bezalel and Oholiab.[6]

And, in keeping with this, one of the marks of blessing on the post-schism kingdom are the city building programs undertaken by Judah's kings—Rehoboam (2 Chron. 11:5), Asa (2 Chron. 14:6–7; 16:6), Jehoshaphat (2 Chron. 17:12), Uzziah (2 Chron. 26:2, 6, 9–10), Jotham (2 Chron. 27:4), Hezekiah (2 Chron. 32:3–5, 29–30), Manasseh (2 Chron. 33:14), and Josiah (2 Chron. 34:10–13). In Chronicles, wicked kings do not engage in urban building programs.[7]

Strategy planning must be Christ-centered in orientation.

One day Zion will lift up her voice as the bearer of good news and say "to the cities of Judah, Behold your God! Behold the Lord God comes with might and his arm rules for him" (Isa. 40:9–10 KJV). The message of the New Testament is the good news that in Jesus that call to the cities to behold their God has been fulfilled.

In fulfillment of that prophetic urban dimension, Jesus' mission strategy turns to the cities. To "the other cities also" he must go, heralding the good news of the kingdom of God he has come to initiate (Luke 4:43 KJV). To those cities he sends his disciples in advance with word of his coming (Luke 10:1).

4. A rich analysis of these prophecies will be found in: Richard Mouw, *When the Kings Come Marching In: Isaiah and the New Jerusalem* (Grand Rapids: Eerdmans, 1983).

5. Raymond B. Dillard and Tremper Longman III, *An Introduction to the Old Testament* (Grand Rapids: Zondervan, 1994), 174–76.

6. Raymond B. Dillard, "The Chronicler's Solomon," *Westminster Theological Journal* 43 (1980): 289–300.

7. Contra Ellul, *The Meaning of the City*, 38–39.

The city is the audience that does not receive the message of the seventy-two (Luke 10:8, 10, 11, 12).

Luke gives prominence to the urban dimension through numerous stylistic twists. As in Acts, the Greek term *polis* (translated in older English versions as "city") is often added to the proper names of localities (Luke 1:26, 39; 4:31; 7:11; 9:10; 23:51), an addition not characteristic of other Gospels (compare Mark 1:21 with Luke 4:31). Even when he makes no mention of the city by name, the Gospel writer appears to think it worth noting that the city is the scene of Jesus' ministry or the background in his teaching (Luke 7:37; 8:4; 14:21; 18:2, 3; 19:17, 19).[8]

The centerpiece of Gospel attention, however, remains the mission of Christ, oriented specifically toward Jerusalem, the city of the great King (Luke 9:51; 22:10; 24:49), and toward his atoning death and resurrection. The Gospels, in fact, take on the appearance of an extended processional toward that city as the messianic goal.

In keeping with the prophetic literature, Jerusalem is the enthronement city of God's glory. And Jesus' redemptive work at Jerusalem is to be that divine exhibition of glory.

But the Gospels also suggest a transfer of that glory more clearly from the city per se to Jesus, the Royal Pilgrim. The One who is greater than Solomon (Matt. 12:42) comes to exhibit his wisdom in building, not a city but a church (Matt. 16:18).

Once again the city and its temple will be destroyed, predicts Jesus. But it will be restored and replaced by the resurrected Christ, the true temple of God (John 2:19–22). "One greater than the temple is here" (Matt. 12:6).

As fellow urban pilgrims, Jesus' newly formed Israel now shapes their planning around the cities. The Old Testament themes of the spontaneous, centripetal drawing of the Gentile city-kingdoms to God (Isa. 2:2–3) is reflected in the success and spontaneous expansion of the good news about Jesus in those cities (Acts 13:44, 48–49; 14:21–22; 17:4, 12; 19:10, 17–19; 28:30–31). A Pauline strategy, as described by Acts, shapes itself around the cities as places of socio-political importance and geographical influence, places where Jews gathered and diverse ethnic groups traveled and intermingled.[9]

Slowly in this gospel expansion, Jerusalem's place recedes into the background, as the preaching and teaching centered in Christ move into the foreground. Her predicted fate as the bearer of the wrath of God for her denial of the Messiah-Builder (Luke 21:20–24) begins its manifestation.

---

8. A fuller discussion of these urban features to Luke–Acts will be found in: Harvie Conn, "Lucan Perspectives and the City," *Missiology* 13 (October 1985): 409–28.

9. Dean Gilliland, *Pauline Theology and Mission Practice* (Grand Rapids: Baker, 1983), 287–88; Roland Allen, *Missionary Methods: St. Paul's or Ours?* (Grand Rapids: Eerdmans, 1962), 10–17. Strangely, Allen also argues for a distinction between deliberate planning by Paul (an idea Allen rejects) and strategy (which he affirms).

Her place as the center of activity shifts to Antioch, the home base for the mission to the Gentiles (Acts 13:1–3; 14:26–28). Her last appearance in the narrative is the scene of the temple riot where Paul is accused of profaning the holy place (Acts 21:27–29) and saved by Gentile intervention (Acts 21:30–40). When the narrative concludes, Jerusalem as the embarkation point for the gospel into the cities of the world (Acts 1:4) has faded against the prominence of Rome, "the ends of the earth" (Acts 1:8). Preaching about the kingdom of God has become synonymous with teaching about the Lord Jesus Christ (Acts 28:31).

Implications for Urban Strategy Planning

If planning is to empower the church and its strategies, its agenda will be shaped by certain biblical dispositions. Without those perspectives, the pitfalls of strategy can overpower. What are some of those?[10]

Strategy planning must be a call to exercise discrimination.

Unlike the Old Testament people of God, we do not possess the Urim and Thummim with which to clearly discern the will of God and plan our urban strategy (Num. 27:21; Deut. 33:8). How will we discern those felt need keys to change that Craig W. Ellison so richly treats in chapter five? How will we discern those needs that lead us most assuredly to church growth?

Even the path of "spiritual mapping," discussed in the introduction to Part 1, can lead astray. What appears to be the direction of the Spirit sometimes is personal inclinations and the cloaking of human intuitions with the Spirit's imprimatur. In the search for a strategy, more than one church leader has misread history that was too dated already to give clues for present understanding.

"Why don't you judge for yourselves what is right?" asked Jesus in Luke 12:57. In asking that, our Lord issues a call to discern what is fitting to do in a given set of circumstances. The Christian planner is not called to credulity. Our suspicions must be open to the leadership of the Spirit. And that Spiritual leadership is shaped by prudence and discrimination. Wisdom in strategy planning must give "prudence to the simple, knowledge and discretion to the young" (Prov. 1:4).

Those two words, *prudence* and *discretion*, appear together only three times in the Scriptures (Prov. 1:4; 8:12; Dan. 2:14). In their deepest theological sense, they are intimately related to the knowledge of God. But they also carry the meaning of tact, discrimination, shrewdness, and good sense. In fact, discretion's most basic sense, argues C. H. Toy, is "the power of

---

10. With significant modifications, the bulk of the following material is drawn from sections of my essay, "Micro Reminders for Macro Researchers," in Vernon Blackwood, Barbara Reichardt, and Sally Schreiner, eds., *SCUPE Urban Researchers and Resource Centers Directory* (Chicago: Seminary Consortium for Urban Pastoral Education, 1992), 5–12.

forming plans or perceiving the best line of procedure for gaining an end, then the plan itself, good or bad."[11] "A prudent man sees danger and takes refuge, but the simple keep going and suffer for it" (Prov. 22:3).

Our calling to strategy planning is a calling to "preserve sound judgment and discernment" (Prov. 3:21), to listen to sound words "that you may attain discretion" (Prov. 5:2). To alter slightly Proverbs 11:22, "Like a gold ring in a pig's snout is a strategy planner who shows no discretion."

Strategy planning must be oriented to hope, not shame over past failures or guilt over missed opportunities.

Hope does not make one ashamed; it does not disappoint (Rom. 5:5). It transforms the strategist into a pilgrim (Heb. 11:13–16), longing for what is better because he or she has seen Christ, who is past and future. Like Abraham, we look in hope at the city now, remembering that a better urban future is to come (Heb. 11:10). Poverty and injustice are realities for the urban strategy planner. But they are not overpowering realities. Not ideology, but eschatology, expects *new* things to happen. Not utopia, but hope in the coming "God of hope" (Rom. 15:13), gives our planning a socio-political preview of change to come.

Strategy planning itself can be overwhelming. Our initial reaction to a well-intended 1988 book, *Seven Hundred Plans to Evangelize the World,* was exhaustion more than inspiration. At the 1989 Singapore Global Consultation on AD 2000 and Beyond, delegates pondered a 50-page, 104-point "kaleidoscopic global plan" for evangelization. Some there, we were told, saw the plan as too detailed to be effectively communicated to their constituency.[12]

Behind these frustrations is there a demonic pessimism that needs to be cast out? As we send out our little bands of Joshua and Caleb strategists to spy out the land, are they too overwhelmed by the size of the cities, the macro dimensions of the task (Num. 13:28)? Hope cast out fear then; it still does.

Strategy planning must be an exercise of faith.

Linked to hope by the writer of Hebrews, faith is not blind confusion of the role of the planner with that of a divine oracle. But, with the oracle, faith shares an enthusiasm for the future because the future is Christ's. This point is summed up in a sign long on the door of my daughter's room: "Do not be afraid of tomorrow: God is already there." Faith transforms the experience of research and strategy planning into a journey with fellow pilgrims, co-learners.[13]

11. C. H. Toy, *A Critical and Exegetical Commentary on the Book of Proverbs: The International Critical Commentary* (Edinburgh: T. & T. Clark, 1899), 7.

12. Art Toalston and Jay Gary, "Christian Leaders Pledge Cooperation Towards AD 2000," *World Evangelization* 16, no. 58 (1989): 37.

13. Harvie Conn and Samuel Rowen, eds., *Missions and Theological Education in World Perspective* (Farmington, Mich.: Associates of Urbanus, 1984), xi.

Second Samuel 24 records the history of a strategy project undertaken by David. He commanded that a census be taken from Dan to Beersheba by his military commanders. It brought God's judgment on David and a plague that swept away thousands of Israelites in days.

David's sin was not that of doing research or strategy planning. Census taking had been done at Mt. Sinai with the Lord's blessing (Numbers 1, esp. v. 54). And again at the end of the forty years of wandering (Num. 26), once more without the same dramatic judgment.

No, David's problem was not research or planning; it was planning without faith. David's intention was probably to raise a standing army.[14] His faith in Jehovah as the divine warrior was slipping. Self-sufficiency was eroding his confidence in the Lord of hosts.

Planning for church growth in the past twenty years has often seemed to some to have been reduced to a recipe list of do's and don'ts, with close attention to graphs and bar charts. The quest for better understanding sometimes seems almost to become a how-to search for better technology—strategy by computer. The spiritual side of research mapping needs underlining again. Five smooth stones in the hands of a person of faith can still bring down the Goliaths of the large cities.

Strategy planning must become the first step in evangelism.

One strong temptation in planning can be the elitism of abstraction. Cities offer an alluring fascination for the strategist. Research side streets always beckon—the nature of in-migration, assimilation patterns and demographic sheets, the differences between world-class cities and smaller cities, urban social and ethnic structures. But our research ultimately must always be applied research. And the objective of our application is to bring lost men and women to Jesus, our city of refuge. In strategy planning we are estimating costs before building towers, counting the strength of our army before going to battle (Luke 14:28–33).

And always before us in this process is our commitment to creating disciples (Luke 14:26, 33). Without this evangelistic dimension, planning produces manure, not salt.

In the essays of Part 2, that discipleship agenda controls the questions laid before us. How can a study of population shifts provide timely suggestions as to where and when hearts may be turned to Christ? How does the size and character of a city affect the decision-making process vital to making new disciples of the King? What part does our response to human felt needs play in building churches? These questions are not questions of pre-evangelism. They have evangelistic dimensions that should motivate our evangelistic intentions.

---

14. Joyce Baldwin, *I and II Samuel: Tyndale Old Testament Commentaries* (Downers Grove, Ill.: InterVarsity Press, 1988), 295.

Strategy planning must point to the obligations of urban service.

Like all gifts of the Spirit, the gift of strategy planning is a gift for ministry, for service (Rom. 12:6–8). Like the pastor and teacher, the strategist and planner prepares "God's people for works of service, so that the body of Christ may be built up" (Eph. 4:12). *Charisma*, says Paul, is best displayed, not in trophy cases, but in the *diakonia* strength God provides (1 Peter 4:11).

One of the rich tasks of urban church planning is to find the place where those *charisma*, those graces, may do their serving. And the study of the city's social structures is turning us again in a new direction. The Christian movement is becoming a movement toward the poor, the marginalized, the oppressed. By the year 2000, over 13 percent of our world will be squatters—a bloc nearly the size of Muslim or Hindu populations, doubling each decade. The mission of urban service among many is being redefined as a mission of "urban poor service." And the obligations of strategy planning must move in that direction also.[15]

Strategy planning must promote awe and reverence.

I sense, not awe, but alarm and distress as we look at our massive cities today. Mexico City overwhelms us; Tokyo boggles the mind; New York and Detroit tower over us.

But God promised, through Moses, to give the Israelites flourishing cities they did not build (Deut. 6:11). And Joshua's response to the report of the spies does not lose that perspective: "Do not be afraid of the people of the land, because we will swallow them up. Their protection is gone, but the LORD is with us" (Num. 14:9). Jesus' word to his servant Paul on an urban reclamation mission in Corinth retains that same confidence. Before him, behind him, the trail of an urban world, but with him a promise: "Do not be afraid . . . for I am with you. . . . I have many people in this city" (Acts 18:9–10).

The object of our fear, the city, is overcome by the subject of our faith, "the fear of the Lord" (Isa. 8:12–13). Timidity at the size of the urban church strategy task is to be replaced by wonder at the divine Task-giver. Reverence guards us from technological arrogance; awe moves us to humility. Strategy planning calls us to worship. Jerichos, no matter how strong they look to the strategists, fall like houses of cards when we are ready to shout, "The Lord has given you the city" (Josh. 6:16).

When the Israelites entered an urban promised land, God sent his fear before them (Exod. 23:27–28). In these last days he has sent his Son Jesus on a new Exodus (Luke 9:31). We watch a new departure, this time from a garbage dump called Calvary outside the city. And once again the cities are "filled with awe and say, 'We have seen remarkable things today'" (Luke 5:26). Jesus has come to give us the cities.

---

15. Viv Grigg, *Cry of the Urban Poor* (Monrovia, Calif.: MARC, 1992).

The Challenge
of World Evangelization
to Mission Strategy

Ray Bakke

As we examine the impact of world urbanization on our mission strategies, some assumptions should be stated at the outset to clarify the significance of the issues:[1]

Some Theological Assumptions

First, that our Lord God is urbanizing his world, and that he is not surprised or dismayed by the reality of a shifting center of power from the Atlantic to the Pacific perimeter.[2]

Second, that the gospel about an Asian-born Jesus Christ who became a political refugee in Africa must be proclaimed without apology in a world where half of the

---

1. This chapter was presented as a paper to the delegates at the Trinary Conference on Evangelizing World Class Cities, March 15, 1986, meeting at the Moody Bible Institute in Chicago, Illinois. It appeared in printed form in *Urban Mission* 4, no. 1 (1986): 6–17. Used by permission.

2. While the history of urbanization is not the focus of this paper, the author has in view classical interpretation studies such as Henri Pirenne's *Medieval Cities: Their Origins and Revival of Trade* (Princeton, N.J.: Princeton University Press, 1969) that show why Europe turned slowly from the Mediterranean to face the North Atlantic after the eighth century, and such current studies as that of Roy Hofheinz Jr. and Kent E. Calder, who in *Eastasia Edge* (New York: Basic, 1983), illustrate some of the dynamics in the macro shift to a Pacific perimeter world today.

newborn babies are Asian and fully half of the world's voluntary and involuntary refugees are Africans.[3]

Third, that the biblical resources are as vast as the exploding cities themselves. Indeed the more than 1200 references to cities are but a starting point for discovering God's urban agenda. We must be prepared to research the totality of the creative and redemptive themes of both Testaments. We must do the case studies, the ethnography of biblical passages, and reflect on a range of strategies and models that will hardly be obvious unless one reflects seriously on the contextualized experiences of biblical persons like Moses, Nehemiah, or Paul. Clearly, our Lord's agenda for the city is greater than the sum of our activity in it.[4]

Fourth, that the biblical pictures of God provide biblical people with the theological tools to address the whole systemic metroplex. The Creator grapples with the total environment. The resurrection redeems real bodies, Christ's and ours, from the grave. The heavenly Christology of the New Testament completes such passages as Isaiah 65:17–25 that describe God as an urban builder. We Christians are the only people on this earth who have the integrated worldview of matter and spirit that enables us to tackle sewer system development and the salvation of souls with equal gusto. In fact, the biblical picture of God who integrates the redemptive threads of the universe into a transformed eternal city should give us more than adequate permission to try and get our heads and hearts around the urbanization of the world.[5] When we reflect on nearly 4000 years of vast urban and cross-cultural mission experiences since Abraham, it should be self-evident that no one evangelism strategy could ever express God's total gift or planning design. Paul had a veritable tool kit of urban evangelism strategies, and others emerge from both Testaments.[6]

---

3. Jesus took sanctuary in Egypt for the same reason people come to Miami or Chicago today. Migration is a worthy biblical and historical study. The magnificent, two-volume work of Frederick A. Norwood, *Strangers and Exiles: A History of Religion's Refugees* (Nashville: Abingdon, 1969), is a good place to begin. Since Abraham, God's people have been pilgrims, and Israel is not the only nation to have its exodus, as prophets like Amos made clear. See Jeremiah's letter to the exiles (29:4f.) and note his counsel to them. In short, they are not victims but a nation sent on a mission; they are to invest families and put down roots; seek the just peace (*shalom*) of the city (Babylon, their enemy and that corporate Judas of the Old Testament), and trust God to rescue them when he pleases. See also the many sojourner passages of the Bible.

4. Classic passages such as Ezekiel 16 show how the ethnicity of the peoples merges into the geography and how cities are viewed by God as family, with suburbs and small towns as children of urban parents. How should such perspectives temper our understandings of the urban versus suburban dichotomy today?

5. Notice God's agenda for the New Jerusalem that he is building in Isaiah 65:17–25, where his blueprint for public health and happiness, infant welfare, secure housing, unexploited markets, the sanctity of labor and families plus the absence of violence are spelled out. If God's Spirit is in us, should we be happy with less in our communities?

6. There are dozens of urban ministries in both Testaments from Nehemiah's radical urban development model to Paul's diverse strategies for reaching the cities of the Roman Empire.

Our starting point, then, is theological rather than sociological. The author has studied Chicago seriously for twenty years and world urbanization for nearly as long. What follows grows from the conviction that the God who prepared the early church for urban evangelism by exile and by diaspora in the cities of the Middle East is the God who can be seen in the exodus of whole people groups and cultures to the cities today. Our first task, before we rush into evangelism analysis and program design, must be to reflect upon God's mission in the world and humbly inquire about his sovereign purposes in the radical, even awesome, urbanization of the world in our time.[7]

To accompany our theological assumptions, we may work from sociological assumptions:

Some Sociological Assumptions

First, urbanization refers not only to places called Chicago, but also to processes. The older classical urbanology did in fact define cities in morphological or structural categories, such as population density and geographical or spatial characteristics. In recent decades, however, cities tend to be seen in dynamic terms and defined by roles or functions. Thus we can speak of political, economic, or cultural functions of cities.[8]

The term *world class city* integrates both streams of urbanology if we understand the term to include two basic components: cities of 1 million or more persons, with international linkages or functions. That is how the term is used in this chapter.[9] This definition allows us to broaden our perspective

7. Beyond the many patterns of involvement are the numerous theological principles. William Temple was correct in his *Christianity and the Social Order* (New York: Seabury, 1977), when he pointed out that the God of the Bible works with dirt at the beginning, and at the ending of the Bible resurrects real material bodies of Christ and us. Christianity is the only religion in the world that can integrate spirit and matter or the salvation of souls with the development of sewer systems for the city. If we are consistently biblical we will struggle to hold together the transcendent Christology of Ephesians and Colossians in tension with the immanent Christology of Philippians. The one legitimates our mission on public issues, the other on personal issues. New Testament Christology and ecclesiology and the whole creative and redemptive theme of both Testaments are required to give us a theology as large as the modern metroplex.

8. Compare, for example, the old studies of urban structures by Park, Burgess, and Wirth with the more recent studies of Mumford, Eames, and Goode, and especially the fine recent collection of essays edited by John Agnew, et al., *The City in Cultural Context* (Boston: Allen and Unwin, 1984), which seeks to move urbanological discussions away from the older structural and Marxian economic categories to a more balanced or interdisciplinary base. This book, together with John Palen, *The Urban World*, 4th ed. (New York: McGraw-Hill, 1992), are, in fact, balanced enough to be good basic textbooks for urban study courses. John Clammer models the best contemporary urbanology in his recent work, *Singapore: Ideology, Society and Culture* (Singapore: Chapman, 1985).

9. This definition combines both streams of urbanology into a simple definition: the morphological or structural matrix of a 1-million-plus "mega city," and a chief functional characteristic of internationality.

to see the larger picture of cities as the engines of cultural, economic, or political changes that reach into the hinterlands and threaten enemy space. The
ministry and evangelism significance of these realities will be developed later
in this chapter.

Second, urbanization is a primary reality on all six continents, though the actual number of residents in the cities of the developed world is declining. Put
simply, urbanization in the First World means cities are spreading out; elsewhere it means they are centralizing still.

*Third, urbanization today in the Two-Thirds world is different in at least three
ways from the nineteenth-century urbanization that produced the growth of Chicago or New York.* Chicago grew by immigration or transfer growth at a time
when urban life expectancy and birthrates were lower than those in rural areas. Today in most Latin American, African, or Asian cities, the immigration
adds to exploding urban birthrates.[10] This produces the paradox that centers
like Mexico City are growing younger and older at the same time. Another
reality today is that cities everywhere are shifting from labor to capital intensive economics. While they create jobs, they produce as much underemploy-
ment as employment. This, together with the inflated expectations of the
urban population, greatly increases the social threat levels. Cities also are
challenging the limits of the environment. Cities multiply pathologies and
toxins and, in many places, are threatened by loss of fuel, water, and even air
to breathe.

*Fourth, urban centers are more than large collections of people; cities structure
reality and package peoples.* In a rural area, most relationships are primary; in
the city, most are secondary. In the country, our senses tend to open outward
to the environment, but in the city, we close in to protect our space. To keep
from hemorrhaging emotionally, urban dwellers overcompensate to noise,

10. Some of the differences in contemporary urbanization can be studied in the urban An-
nual Reviews of Sage Publications, e.g., Brian Berry, ed., *Urbanization and Counter-Urbaniza-
tion* (Beverly Hills: Sage, 1976); George Tapinos and Phyllis T. Piotro, *Six Billion People* (New
York: McGraw-Hill, 1978); and older studies like Ronald Jones, *Essays on World Urbanization*
(London: George Philip, 1975), commissioned by International Geographical Union. The
World Watch Institute in Washington, D.C., has produced some excellent urban materials.
Alexander B. Callow Jr., ed., *American Urban History: An Interpretative Reader With Commentar-
ies,* 3rd ed. (New York: Oxford, 1982), is indispensable for the background to American cities.
Harlan Hahn and Charles Levine, eds., *Urban Politics: Past, Present and Future* (New York:
Longman, 1980), includes superb studies of urban power dynamics. Some of the best recent
international urban studies include the Cambridge series on urbanization in developing coun-
tries edited by Kenneth Little, the best known scholar of West African cities. As an example, see
Latin American Urbanization by D. Butterworth and J. Chance (New York: Cambridge, 1981)
in this series. See also A. Kelly and J. Williamson, *What Drives Third World City Growth: A General
Equilibrium Approach* (Princeton, N.J.: Princeton University Press, 1984). The relationship of
inner and outer city development is the subject of many studies. See also John Herington's *The
Outer City* (London: Harper, 1984), which looks at this phenomenon in Britain, as does Peter
Hall, ed., *The Inner City Context* (London: Heinemann, 1981).

crowds, and visual pollution by turning inward or turning off. The fact is that the more densely crowded we are, the less we communicate. Pluralistic interaction threatens those who lack identity or security, but to those who have confidence, life in a secondary relational matrix frees one up to specialize and create both personally and in ministry. What is urban bondage to some liberates others. Those dynamics are at work to some extent in any changing human environment.[11]

Fifth, we cannot escape world urbanization. Over 2 billion people live in cities and the number grows much faster than in rural areas worldwide. The people who sought to flee Chicago have bumped into the people who fled Los Angeles. There is no place to hide. It is absolutely critical that we consider the implications of such explosive urbanization for evangelism.

Some Demographics

The United Nations still struggles to decide how to count people and how to define cities. As a result, books appear with wildly differing numbers. By now there are some 2400 cities with at least 100,000 persons. About 286 cities had reached the mega, or million-plus, level by 1986. This is in a world of 4.9 billion. By 2000, more than half the world population will live in cities. Compare the lists below.[12]

In Table 1, even a casual observer can see remarkable trends between 1985 and 2000. Both the location of urban populations and growth rate change rapidly. Numbers are significant, but they do not help us differentiate

11. There are many Chicagos, of course, and according to Donald and Rachael Warren, *The Neighborhood Organizer's Handbook* (South Bend, Ind.: University of Notre Dame Press, 1977), there are at least six distinctive types of neighborhoods, each type with its own communication patterns and, therefore, its own church renewal or church planting development patterns. See also Howard Hallman, *Neighborhoods: Their Place in Urban Life* (Beverly Hills: Sage, 1984), a superb study.

12. Population figures vary widely because countries classify and count cities differently on all six continents. The United Nations is working to standardize these lists and you can see their progress by comparing *Estimates and Projections of Urban, Rural, and City Populations, 1950–2025: The 1980 Assessment* (New York: 1982) with its 1985 update. Compare these totals with those in recent studies such as John T. Marlin et al., *Book of World City Rankings* (New York: Free Press, 1986). Commissioned by the Council on Municipal Performance, this volume includes fascinating vignettes from more than 100 large cities on quality of life and work for international workers. Or see the urban data collection in *The New Book of World Rankings* (New York: Facts on File, 1984). Since these totals do not agree, stay with the U.N. data generally. David B. Barrett presents the most accurate updates in his book, *World-Class Cities and World Evangelization*, a study commissioned by the Foreign Mission Board of the Southern Baptist Convention (Birmingham: New Hope, 1986). This is one of several superb studies emerging in their AD 2000 series. Lots of interesting urban data analysis from population studies and conferences is available to subscribers to *POPLINE*, 110 Maryland Ave. NE, Washington, D.C., 20002, available free from the Population Institute. The most impressive published resource is Neil L. Shumsky and Timothy Crimmons, eds., *Urban America: A Historical Bibliography* (Santa Barbara, Calif.: Ohio, 1983), a massive encyclopedic work.

among cities in ways most helpful for designing evangelism strategies. For that we need to examine cities in other ways.

Table 1 **The World's Top 25 Urban Agglomerations**
Ranked by size in millions

1985		2000	
Tokyo/Yokohama	21.8	Mexico City	27.6
Mexico City	18.4	Shanghai	25.9
New York/NENJ	18.3	Tokyo/Yokohama	23.8
Shanghai	17.5	Beijing	22.8
São Paulo	15.0	São Paulo	21.5
Beijing	14.6	New York/NENJ	19.5
Los Angeles/LB	10.9	Greater Bombay	16.3
Greater Buenos Aires	10.8	Calcutta	15.9
Rio de Janeiro	10.4	Jakarta	14.3
Seoul	10.2	Rio de Janeiro	14.2
Calcutta	10.1	Seoul	13.7
Paris	10.1	Greater Cairo	12.8
Osaka/Kobe	10.1	Madras	12.3
Greater Bombay	10.0	Greater Buenos Aires	12.2
London	9.8	Greater Los Angeles	12.1
Rhein Ruhr	9.1	Karuchi	11.4
Moscow	8.7	Delhi	11.2
Jakarta	8.6	Teheran	11.0
Greater Cairo	8.5	Baghdad	11.0
Greater Chicago	7.4	Osaka/Kobe	10.9
Milan	7.1	Istanbul	10.9
Madras	7.0	Manila	10.5
Teheran	6.7	Paris	10.4
Delhi	6.6	Dacca	10.2
Istanbul	6.6	Bangkok	9.9

Some cities function as political capitals (i.e., Washington, D.C., New Delhi, Brazilia), and thus share a common ethos in their brokerage of power and decision-making. Other cities like New York or Hong Kong function commercially like giant markets, while Paris, Rio, or San Francisco invent ideas, fashions, and trends. Some cities combine many functions. London or Mexico City evokes many vivid images. When you see a list that includes Beirut, Belfast, Soweto, Berlin, or Nicosia, division and suffering come to mind.

Some Challenges

In the following ways, world urbanization constitutes a fundamental challenge to conventional mission theory and practice. Both personally and institutionally, the threats are real.[13]

The Structural Challenge

Because cities are interrelated sets of systems, a political decision in Washington to shift a Pentagon contract to Texas can mean good Christians will lose their jobs in Seattle.[14] Many rural farmers now share an experience with public aid mothers. They decide not to work because their labor does not generate enough money to cover the costs. Like the public aid mother, the farmer knows this ahead of time. The economy is international and unjust. Winners and losers live side by side. Cities have always competed with each other. Many Two-Thirds world cities are locked into extreme injustices. We can hardly be biblical and not care about that.[15]

In a meeting where leading evangelicals gathered to develop strategies for urban ministry and study, the tension this caring stimulates was demonstrated. After a robust discussion in which urban leaders shared concrete ways suburban people could be involved, one person said directly: "You know I really get thrilled when you talk about evangelism in the city, but I get very nervous when you talk about social involvement. It sounds like a social gospel to me." My question to this sincere brother was, "Where do you live?" He named the suburb, a very lovely community. When asked why he lived there he gave a litany of responses: "It is a nice community, safe, quiet, clean . . . with good schools and housing values." In fact, every reason this evangelical believer gave for living where he did was a social reason. He really believed in good, beneficial social structures. He had committed his life and family to the places where those values could be actualized.[16]

---

13. What follows emerges as primary data from visits to more than 100 large cities on six continents and from leading evangelism consultations in nearly seventy of them.

14. The author first realized that cities were not simply large collections of people when a political decision following the Kennedy–Johnson election of 1960 shifted Pentagon contracts from Boeing to General Dynamics and left many in his Seattle blue-collar congregation unemployed.

15. Farmers find themselves packaged or locked into futures markets in the grain exchange. The growth of the international economy means interdependencies that link us together on planet earth for better and for worse. These dynamics are described in the stimulating book by Jane Jacobs, *Cities and the Wealth of Nations: Principles of Economic Life* (New York: Random House, 1984), and reviewed beautifully by Fletcher L. Tink, "An Urban Missionary Encounters Jane Jacobs," *Urban Mission* 3, no. 3 (1986): 21–29. Tink is right. We may be distressed but we cannot ignore studies like this when we think strategically about large city evangelization.

16. In fact this conversation took place several years ago in the Graham Center at Wheaton College, but there have been many similar conversations, and some classic studies: James Dennis, *Christian Missions and Social Progress: A Sociological Study of Foreign Missions*, 3 vols. (New York: Revell, 1894); William Booth, *In Darkest England and the Way Out* (repr. ed., London:

Can anybody who deliberately located in a community with good schools and employment really criticize those who work to rehabilitate social systems in communities where they do not work? Those who say, "Let's just preach the simple gospel," usually live where good, working social systems are in place. Their plea for unadorned evangelism proclamation will have greater credibility when they live incarnationally alongside the people they wish to evangelize. And when these Christians do enter urban communities, they inevitably see that it is not a simple thing to evangelize.

Chicago has seventy-seven community areas that could be classified according to six paradigms: Integral, Parochial, Diffuse, Stepping-stone, Transitory, and Atomic. Each has its own communication and organizing dynamics.[17]

Why would missionaries and pastors who spend years studying Hebrew and Greek to develop exegetical skills, or personality theories to develop counseling skills, or who study linguistics and cultural anthropology in order to enter a single language tribal structure, think it unimportant to study the social structures and patterns that influence family or individual behaviors in the city? Cities are systems, like families or persons, and they will not usually yield to paternalistic, simplistic, *blitzkrieg* evangelistic strategies. These structures challenge mission agencies. The foreign boards would not think of putting missionaries on fields without special training. Our home boards do it all the time in cities, and the result is disaster.

The Pluralistic Challenge

Let us look at a familiar structural pattern of small midwestern towns (see Fig. 4).

Figure 5 illustrates the classic ex-rural town that is being urbanized by developers who package people on the fringe. Downtown is the church that ministered to people who think of themselves as "we"—a corporate ethos,

---

The Salvation Army, 1980); A. D. Gilbert, *Religion and Society in Industrial England: Church Chapel and Social Change, 1740–1914* (London: Longman, 1976); Ernest R. Sandeen, ed., *The Bible and Social Reform* (Philadelphia: Fortress, 1982); Ernest M. Howse, *Saints in Politics: The "Clapham Sect" and Growth of Freedom* (London: George Allen and Unwin, 1953); Gary R. Sattler, *God's Glory, Neighbor's Good: A Brief Introduction to the Life and Writings of August Hermann Franke* (Chicago: Covenant, 1982). A trilogy of studies on eighteenth- and nineteenth-century evangelical Anglicans includes H. C. G. Moule, *Charles Simeon* (repr. ed., Downers Grove, Ill.: InterVarsity, 1985; Robert Braithwait, ed., *The Life and Letters of Rev. William Pennefather* (London: Shaw, 1978); and Georgina Battiscombe, *Shaftsbury: The Great Reformer, 1801–1885* (Boston: Houghton Mifflin, 1975). Many volumes about evangelicals working in the slums and the massive studies of Latourette, Brauer, the Niebuhrs, Miller and Marzik, Rauschenbusch, Smith, Stead, Magnusson, and others argue forcefully for what Andrew Kirk calls the required "marriage of evangelism and social responsibility." See Kirk, *Good News of the Kingdom Coming* (Downers Grove, Ill.: InterVarsity, 1983).

17. The categories are from Warren and Warren, *The Neighborhood Organizer's Handbook.*

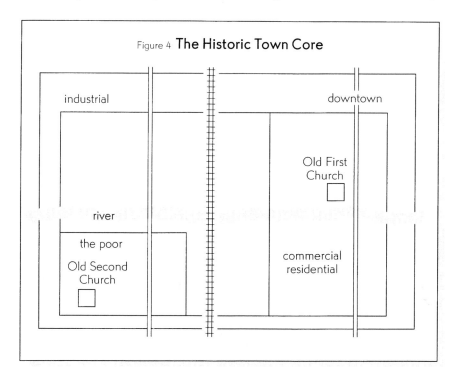

Figure 4 **The Historic Town Core**

known by family and who live out of functioning memories. These people "back" into the future. But now in the economically stabilized developments of the circle live the people who think of themselves as "I" and who are known by their vocations as they pursue their upscale futures.[18]

Obviously these are very different worldviews, and we have not even mentioned generation gaps and racial or language groups. How will the church respond to the twenty-four-hour urban clock without night and day staffs and similar strategies to those used by hospitals and police?

Ten years or so ago, if you walked into a Chicago supermarket, you saw a store with some 8000 products and a meat counter that closed at 6 P.M. while the store closed at 10 or 11 P.M. Today those remodeled stores stock some 22,000 products, stay open twenty-four hours a day, and have Asian aisles, Spanish aisles, salt-free, gourmet, and generic sections, multi-lingual checkers, and more convenient financial services than the local banks. Obviously such a store is in touch with local social realities, and it needs a profit to stay in business. The church nearby probably still uses English, and probably only at 11 A.M. on Sunday. Is it not obvious that to understand and respond

18. For a more complete discussion of these issues, see Raymond Bakke and Samuel Roberts, *The Expanded Mission of Old First Churches* (Valley Forge, Pa.: Judson, 1986).

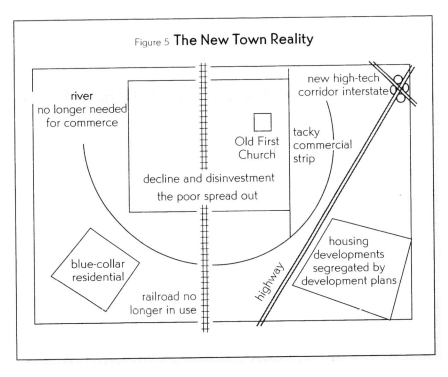

Figure 5 **The New Town Reality**

to the urban challenge, our ecclesiology theory and practice will be challenged at fundamental levels? Urban ministry is not so much a set of evangelistic techniques as it is a whole new way of envisioning the world about us.

This inevitable pluralism threatens pastors and peoples. Churches that grow will reach different personality types which constitute large urban audiences with hungers. Some we could call existential or event-centered peoples; others are relational and need church to function as a surrogate family. If they hunger for an absent father they may gravitate toward congregations with authoritarian pastors who can parent them. Others may move to body life or communal relationship churches. Other urban Christians are task or directional in orientation. Artists may be visual or verbal. Some folk live by sounds and cannot even jog without being wired up, while others crave their silent worship and a worship environment that compensates for the corruption of their external world.

The pluralism of the city goes beyond personality types. In most urban communities you will see the various profiles or clienteles:

Business management personnel
Commercial workers
Public Aid clients

Ethnic group members
Institutionalized persons
Deviants
Derelicts
Theater and visual artists
Students
Internationals
Politicians
Night people
Commuters
Middle-class people
Upper-class people
Lower-class people
Dropouts
Migrants
Elderly
Professionals

Subcultures and groups vary, and people overlap categories and move from place to place. In Chicago, as in most of the world's largest cities, whites are the ever-decreasing minority, and that brings its own kind of threats for them. The fact is, pluralism marginates us, and we may internalize that reality with negative consequences. Some respond by becoming authoritarian while others will develop programmatic approaches to compensate for their needs to control on the one hand, and to measure their significance on the other. The reality is that unless we have a strong sense of call, a personal sense of identity and security, a vision of God's kingdom as larger than our individual ministry, and a working support system, most of us will not survive in the city as God's evangelists.

The Leadership Challenge

Many of our most effective pastors and missionaries have had little formal higher education beyond Bible school training. Even at that, our small town pastors or missionaries may have been the best trained persons or most competent to minister to those in their regions.

Meanwhile, increasing numbers of those coming to the cities come for higher education and professional employment options which can propel them to successful careers. What happens when the village parsons and evangelists confront this urban challenge?

Immigrants and migrants come to the cities with cultural baggage from their sending environment. They will need a generation or more to sort through what is the gospel and what is culture, what is conviction and what is opinion. How will urban evangelists become sensitive to these processes?

Scholarship on migration social processes is vast and helpful. Must we fail to communicate because of inadequately prepared leaders?

Biblical examples show the importance of study and training. Consider Moses, who according to Stephen was learned in all the wisdom of the Egyptians, a student of Pharonic culture, economics, and government. After that he had forty years of sheep and desert cultural exposure, with some firsthand study of public health for primitive communities. Finally, in leadership he integrated his classical and developmental educational experiences and led a group of brick-making migrants from the slums of Egypt into one of the most hostile environments of the Middle East. There he built a culture for God's people and led them spiritually. Why can't Moses or the multi-cultural Paul become normative paradigms for our contemporary urban leadership roles?

In South America today the largest category of in-migrating peoples are young women fifteen to nineteen years of age.[19] In many of the most desperate slums and in the senior citizen cities of the United States, women are by far the largest group. The surprising reality is that God's Spirit is raising up marvelous women leaders. Nearly 70 percent of missionaries are women, and in the poorest urban communities the percentage may be higher. It seems some women are willing to serve God in places to which men refuse to go with their families. The Lord continues to work in spite of, if not because of, the church.

Not only has the Lord raised up leadership which may be radically and sexually different from our own; he may raise up denominations or large independent ministries that force us to question whether a church or mission really is needed. There will always be a need in urban outreach for every gifted and skilled evangelist, but the best stewardship of our resources may be in servant roles rather than in up-front leadership and decision making.

American evangelicals must remember that, for many, our banner symbolizes the "white fright and white flight" of the 1960s. But though many of our institutions and leaders left the cities, the Spirit of God did not. Rather the Spirit crossed boundaries of class, race, and language to produce the flower garden of urban churches we celebrate in our cities today.[20]

The Geographical Challenge

By definition, the world class city is international. Implicitly, that means the differences between the home and foreign mission fade in the urban context. The children of the foreign mission have come here. The Chinese Co-

---

19. See "Why People Move," chapter 2 in Douglas Butterworth and John K. Chance, *Latin American Urbanization* (New York: Cambridge University Press, 1981), 33–50.

20. The fastest growing churches in Chicago since 1970 are black. When the author last counted inner-city churches in Chicago in 1979, 1103 of 2167 were black. No doubt many were missed in the count.

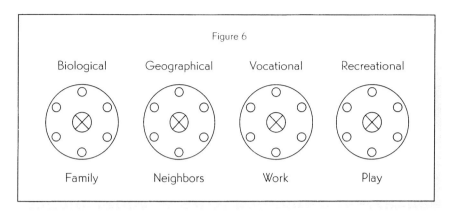

Figure 6

ordination Centre of World Evangelism, led by Thomas Wang in Hong Kong, has divided the whole world into forty-three Chinese regions. East London is becoming Asian where it is not Arab, or so it seems. Miami is a de facto capital of Latin America. Greater Los Angeles is the second largest Mexican city. The Turkish populations of West German cities, Japanese in São Paulo, Jews in New York, or Algerians in Paris add up to a new reality that forces us to acknowledge two distinct mission fields, the geographically distant (frontier) fields and the culturally distant fields which lie geographically within the shadows of our existing churches. The latter will not be reached unless we change our thinking about structures and adopt strategies of evangelistic partnerships that work at both ends of the migrant streams.[21]

Yet most denominations and mission executives guard their turfs tenaciously lest the urban mission on six continents threaten their traditional mission structures. In the words of Pogo, "We have met the enemy and he is us."

The Lay Challenge

The only way we will evangelize the city is to recruit, equip, and encourage laymen, -women, and -youth to identify and penetrate their respective worlds with the gospel. It will never happen by professional evangelism and "come-structured" strategies.

Urban laypeople usually stand at the center of four distinct worlds in their primary relationships—family, neighbors, work, and play (see Fig. 6).

Perhaps 90 percent of those who come to Jesus Christ in large cities were influenced by someone in one or more of their worlds. Massive door-to-door or media campaigns can never overcome the communication dynamics or

21. The work of MARC at World Vision International assists the Lausanne Strategy Working Group to facilitate consultations and stimulate research in these cities.

barriers to enable us to reach the masses. Urban people generally undergo identity shifts. Ask them who they are and they will tell you what they do. That should tell us evangelists that the most fruitful evangelistic urban world is the factory, school, or office.[22]

This means, of course, that while in the small towns and suburbs we visit people in their homes, we need to visit urban peoples in their places of employment and design strategies of witness for the marketplace. This requires a Copernican revolution in the minds of most church or mission leaders. To take the city seriously will require a fundamental shift in our thinking.[23]

Broadly speaking, evangelicals have been good at two historic urban ministries; we might call them the crusade and the franchise.

Crusades, from the era Gypsy Smith mobilized evangelicals in Chicago to eradicate slums in the 1890s until today, have been task- or event-centered, simple-issue strategies. They have power and have demonstrated effectiveness.

The franchise is a ministry like McDonald's or Wendy's. It simplifies the product, standardizes the service, and cranks up the delivery system so billions can be served. There is something very American and practical about designing strategies like these for mass production. The effectiveness is powerful and measurable.

The reader will recognize, of course, that such a description tends toward caricature, but the analogies do illustrate the strengths and limitations of much of our urban evangelism strategies. If our urban social analysis is correct, most of the city will not be reached without many gifted and empowered lay folks weaving the gospel into the fabric of their lives, delivering it personally to places and persons of greatest need.

Most of us went to Bible schools or seminaries where we learned to design ministry in our own image, that is, to sing the songs we appreciate and to preach sermons we would like to listen to. Unfortunately for us, the challenge now is to retool and design ministry strategies in the image of the unreached who may be very different from us culturally. These are not the only major challenges to conventional mission theory and practice, but they support the basic thesis. Cities will not yield to simplistic or reductionistic evangelistic strategies or to mission-as-usual thinking.

---

22. Since the city is a "secondary matrix," where generally we do not invest emotionally, these four primary networks of relationships are critical for evangelism, far more than are door-to-door "cold contact" in most urban multiplex housing communities. Urban pastors should visit people where they work in factories, offices, or schools to enable members to see their ministry potential in these worlds closed to pastors.

23. Remember that when you invite urbanites to your church you are asking them to give up their primary identity and enter the world of your sanctuary. Your world may intimidate or threaten them far more than you will ever know. There are many communication barriers in urban evangelism.

The Challenge of Internal Barriers

Since the Pattaya consultation of 1980, the Lausanne Strategy Working Group has sponsored urban evangelization consultations in more than seventy cities on six continents. Participants who are church or mission leaders are usually asked to identify the ten most significant barriers to be overcome if their city is to be evangelized.[24]

Responses fall generally into two categories:

1. Barriers in the city or environment
2. Barriers in the church

The results of these studies have stunned this observer. It does not seem to matter whether we are talking about Copenhagen (First World), Belgrade (Second World), or Cairo (Third World); the results are similar. Eight of the most often-named barriers are inside the church:

1. The politics of our denominations
2. The egos of leaders
3. The competition between pastors, congregations, or mission agencies
4. The acculturized, traditionalized ministry training of the seminary
5. The rural mentality of pastors, denominational executives, and lay leaders
6. The failure to take advantage of opportunities
7. The lack of organized prayer for the city
8. The lack of convincing ethics among Christians

Of course, Muslim or Marxist persecution or crushing poverty is a barrier in many cities. But more often than not, the real barriers indigenous urban leaders identify are those inside the church and missions structures.

Because of its size and shape, the fact of global urbanization will not be seen as good news by many of us. It fundamentally challenges the ways we have believed and behaved as evangelists. Obviously, we can and must meet the challenges. God help us do it.

24. For a more complete discussion of these issues see the author's essay on "Urban Evangelization: A Lausanne Strategy Since 1980" in *International Bulletin of Missionary Research* 8 (1984): 149–54.

Addressing Felt Needs
of Urban Dwellers

Craig W. Ellison

Why should we be concerned about addressing felt needs? How does a this-world focus of meeting felt needs fit with the eternal focus of evangelism? Doesn't such an approach distract us and dilute our ability to win people to Christ?

There are at least three reasons why evangelicals should address the felt needs of city-dwellers. To do so (1) provides a point of redemptive connection with those who are spiritually lost, (2) adds credibility to our communication of the gospel, and (3) is commanded by God and demonstrated by Christ. Let's examine each of these points.

First, addressing felt needs provides a point of redemptive connection with those who are spiritually lost. Urban life clamors for the attention of the city-dweller in a thousand different ways. In an urban world that is saturated with stimuli and crowded with choice, getting the attention of people is difficult. Only that which is novel and that which is personally relevant breaks through the din. Novelty gains only a temporary hearing. That which is seen to pertain to significant values, needs, and decisions is not only heard, but is sought.

Evangelization is essentially a communication process. It involves senders and receivers. In order for receivers to respond, they must hear and understand the message. Faith is the product of hearing God speak (Rom. 10:17).

Just speaking the Word of God isn't sufficient, however. Potential receivers must be aware that the message is being spoken and that it is worth listening to. We can say all the right things in the right way, but if we aren't in actual contact with the lost, or if they don't hear us as relevant to their lives, we are only talking to ourselves.

By addressing felt needs of city-dwellers, we connect with them so that they pay attention. Because we touch them at points of pertinence, our message gains a hearing. Often, in a natural way, their area of needs becomes an avenue for sharing the gospel. Because we have shown caring at the level of temporal need, we are given permission to express caring for their eternal need.

It should be noted that establishing a point of linkage via reaching out to felt needs presumes that a body of believers wants to reach out. There are times when it appears that some of the resistance to ministry through felt needs has more to do with a lack of heartfelt compassion for the lost than it does with aversion to the social gospel. Certainly the reluctance of the majority of evangelicals to get involved in more spiritually direct evangelistic outreach suggests such a possibility.

Second, addressing felt needs adds credibility to our communication of the salvation heart of the gospel. Evangelism is a special kind of communication process. Its intent is to persuade. It is meant to encourage people to move from spiritual death to spiritual life. It is intended to produce a fundamental change. The goal of evangelism is to promote deep personal commitment to Jesus Christ as one's Savior and Lord. Redemption requires a spark of faith sufficient for a person to entrust God with both temporal and eternal welfare.

When people are asked to change in a certain way, they do so if they feel the need to change and believe that making the change suggested will best meet their need. When we meet someone's felt needs, they can see that we are not hucksters. The urban world is full of exploiters—people who convincingly promise good and deliver bad. People see the good news as good when we have done good in their lives. Their past experience with us gives them confidence that what we say about something they haven't experienced can be trusted. As they come to see us as trustworthy they are helped to believe that the way we are pointing is trustworthy.

Conversion is predicated on the assumption that God can be trusted with future well-being. Such trust of the unknown is encouraged by reference to the known. If the lost have experienced caring for their current concerns from the representatives of Christ, it is easier to believe that Christ can be trusted with their eternal concerns. If we have met them with love and sensitivity, it is easier to believe that God will receive their toddling steps of faith in a similar way.

If we only go as far as the first two reasons for addressing felt needs, there is a serious danger. If we stop here, felt-need ministry may be seen as merely a means to an end. If that happens, we run a very high risk of manipulating people rather than ministering to them with integrity. The felt-need ministry of Jesus was motivated by compassion and not a compulsion for conversion. I am not suggesting that we downplay conversion. Rather, I am suggesting that integrity demands that compassion ministry must be accepted as its own biblically legitimate end and not just as a way to get something else.

Addressing felt needs is commanded by God and demonstrated by the incarnate Christ. We are saved by the grace of God through faith, not by works, but we are saved for good works, "which God prepared in advance for us to do" (Eph. 2:8–10).

The Bible says that "religion that God our Father accepts is pure and faultless in this: to look after orphans and widows in their distress," as well as "to keep oneself from being polluted by the world" (James 1:27). James continues his commentary on true and false faith in chapter two and finally concludes that "as the body without the spirit is dead, so faith without deeds is dead" (2:26). John picks up the theme by asking, "If anyone has material possessions and sees his brother in need and has no pity on him, how can the love of God be in him? Dear children, let us not love with words or tongue but with actions and in truth" (1 John 3:17–18). The difference between faith and philosophy is in the doing!

Paul urged Titus to teach the early believers to "devote themselves to doing what is good, in order that they may provide for daily necessities and not live unproductive lives" (Titus 3:14). In the same short book he exhorted the leaders to remind God's people "to be ready to do whatever is good" (3:1), and to speak confidently to them "so that those who have trusted in God may be careful to devote themselves to doing what is good" (3:8). In Galatians he instructed the believers not to lose heart in doing good but to "do good to all people, especially to those who belong to the family of believers" (6:9–10).

Evangelicals who try to distinguish between Pauline faith theology and a secondary Jamesian works theology not only fail to properly interpret these authors, but also are guilty of imposing a dual standard of scriptural inspiration. Furthermore, Matthew 25:31–46 records one of the most chilling passages in the Bible, the words of Jesus describing separation of the sheep from the goats on judgment day. The evidences of genuine saving faith recorded there are practical, caring actions addressing felt needs. The expression of righteousness is in an ethic and lifestyle of compassion. Those who will be invited to join the King will be those who have given food to the hungry, drink to the thirsty, clothes to the needy, health care to the sick, and comforting presence to the imprisoned. Jesus says there that as they ministered to the needs of the needy, they showed their love for the Son of Man.

On the other hand, those who will be consigned to eternal fire prepared for the devil and his angels will be those who ignored or somehow failed to address those needs.

The example of Jesus, summarized in Matthew 9:35–36, provides us with a clear model for urban ministry. He preached the good news of the kingdom (evangelism), he taught (discipleship), and he healed every kind of disease and sickness (compassion). He did not stop with the first two avenues of ministry and thereby give us a truncated theology. Rather, he was moved with compassion by the multi-dimensional needs of the crowds and touched them at their points of felt need.

Micah 6:8 answers the question, "With what shall I come before the LORD?" (6:6) with the clear response: "He has showed you, O man, what is good. And what does the LORD require of you? To act justly and to love mercy and to walk humbly with your God" (6:8).

Ezekiel 16:49–50 serves as a warning to those who close their hearts to those in need. The sin of Sodom which demanded God's judgment was their arrogance, which expressed itself in being overfed and unconcerned, not helping the poor and needy. Do we dare justify the same lack of responsiveness to felt needs in the name of evangelical faith? God severely chastised Israel as being worse than Sodom. Will he do any less with us if we evangelicals self-righteously reject acts of practical compassion toward those in need?

So, what's the problem? Why have (white) American evangelicals in this century been so consistently reluctant to include the addressing of felt needs as an integral part of theology and ministry?

Evangelical Reluctance

I believe there are five basic reasons for evangelical reluctance: (1) Greek-mindedness; (2) class captivity; (3) professional priesthood; (4) self-defense; and (5) misunderstood mandate. You will note that the most frequently expressed reason—avoidance of the social gospel—is not listed here. That is because, in my opinion, it is nothing more than an excuse for inaction. Indeed, it was never really the central issue in the liberal–fundamentalist struggle of the early twentieth century. Although fundamentalists ultimately focused upon it as a significant issue, it was secondary to the question of scriptural authenticity and interpretation. Seizing upon some of Rauschenbusch's theological distortion of the kingdom of God, fundamentalists found it convenient to throw the biblical baby of justice and compassion out with the bath water of liberalism. In the process they were as guilty of twisted theology and biblical reductionism as were the liberals; both reduced the gospel to less than what it was meant to be.

Greek-mindedness

This approach has been reinforced by the Greek-mindedness of Western society in general and the almost exclusive New Testament orientation of the evangelical community in particular.

Most of us in Western society have Greek minds; that is, our way of thinking focuses on analysis. Science and technology depend on this kind of thinking. We're educated to divide the whole into parts. The idea is that we will be better able to understand, predict, and control phenomena that way. We are taught to look at things and people from the viewpoint of a specialist.

We learn to see the parts of the whole as though they exist independently from each other and from their context. Because of our Greek-mindedness, we talk about spirit, mind, emotions, and body as though these intricately interrelated dimensions of the person can be separated and adequately addressed in isolation. We tend to have a segmented view of human beings. A brief glance at almost any introductory psychology text reveals this fragmentation. This is crucial to understand because our view of human nature significantly affects our practice of ministry. Ministry priorities and methods are established in relation to our concept of persons.

A major result of this orientation is our tendency to interpret the good news in one-dimensional terms. We have tended to treat the unsaved around us like disembodied spirits in our specialized emphasis on the spiritual. We have preferred to leave the rest of the person to other, usually secular, specialists.

Greek-mindedness is dramatically different from the Hebraic or Old Testament orientation, which sees people as a whole. Hebraic thinking focuses on fusion rather than fission, synthesis rather than analysis, intuition rather than empiricism, system rather than segment. It resists the kind of reductionism which makes people into less than what God created them to be, whether it is the reductionism of secularism or the reductionism of fundamentalism.

If urban ministry is to be effective, we must see people as complex, whole beings. That's the way God created us, and that's how he is redeeming us. (Even our bodies will be eternally redeemed in incorruptible form—1 Cor. 15:42.) Viewing people correctly, as integrated, multi-dimensional systems, will enable us to shape ministries that are powerful and persuasive.

Class Captivity

The resistance of American evangelicals to a felt needs approach can also be traced to the class captivity of evangelicalism. Several years ago Gibson Winter wrote a provocative book entitled *The Suburban Captivity of the Church*. Unfortunately, the term "suburban captivity" confuses geography with the real issue of class.

Most American-based evangelical theology has been generated by the theologians who come from the socio-economic context of the middle class. Our theology, approach to homiletics, and practice of ministry have all been born and nurtured in the cradle of the middle class. They have been transmitted by professors shaped by the socio-economic milieu of the middle class. This is not automatically bad, as long as we recognize and understand the influences that class has exerted on the white evangelical enterprise. Our ways of doing theology and ministry do not spring from some neutral void that is shaped directly by the Spirit of God without natural distortion, but from a specific socio-economic setting.

Failure to recognize the influence of class context leads to an unintended arrogance. What happens is that the contours of our class-based subculture begin to be structured into our Christianity. What is actually cultural begins to be absolutized as theological dogma, and a way of life becomes the way of faith.

A few examples will highlight this. Middle-class culture treasures predictability, privacy, possessions, and power. It teaches its members to dislike unpredictability, public display of feeling, poverty, weakness, and dependency. Because of economic and political positioning, the middle-class person is usually able to assume certain facts of life quality, such as relative safety and properly functioning public services. Individual members of the middle class have adequate resources to care for a variety of personal and family needs without overt dependency on others. In so doing, they live out the highest values of middle-class individualism. Anything less, anything which reflects weakness and dependency, is experienced as shame and guilt.

These values and ways of life have captured modern evangelicalism in some interesting ways. That the subcultural norms of the middle class have been translated into absolutes can be demonstrated by our very strong feelings about violations of the way we feel things should be said and done. For example, we conclude that sound theology should deal with matters of the Spirit, not matters material (except as necessary to avoid charges of gnosticism). Biblical references to the poor should be primarily interpreted as referring to the spiritually impoverished. Jesus' acts of healing must be viewed exclusively as signs of the coming kingdom, not as acts to be emulated by believers. Old and New Testament references to justice must be interpreted by reduction to the level of individual righteousness.

Homiletics are influenced, too. We adopt and absolutize one preaching style, which is primarily cognitive and dispassionate, linear and sequential. By so doing, we limit from the start the breadth of the audience that will truly hear our presentation of the gospel. Our preaching style and tightly structured order of service (expressions of class) help us to avoid eruptions of spontaneity, celebration, and passion lest we lose control and face moments of possible helplessness. We do it, of course, in the name of biblical order, but one wonders how Jesus would respond. For most people in cities, preaching speaks most clearly when it is in story form and when it arouses passion. The middle class looks down on this out of fear. For most city-dwellers, the best worship is celebration, not cerebralization; participation, not observation; releasing, not restricting. I don't think it's an accident that around the world, the most rapidly growing churches in large cities are Pentecostal. It has little to do with glossolalia, in my opinion. Rather, they've caught the heartbeat of urban dwellers and have shaped their ministry to the masses.

Our forms and focus of ministry are also shaped by the absolutizing of middle-class norms. We learn easily that bigger is better, so we freeze our church planting efforts into (usually suburban) settings which promise the largest number, given our middle-class forms of preaching and worship. Our ministry strategy is dominated by issues of property rather than by per-vasiveness of prayer. We are unable to move beyond spiritualization to the meeting of whole-person needs because people are supposed to take care of the earthly on their own. Our class context has subtly led us to formulate a theology of spiritual specialization appropriate for the middle class. When our sociology becomes absolutized into theology, however, and we argue against social compassion, we have become guilty of syncretism. This has doomed to failure most white evangelical efforts to minister to the poor and the working class in cities. Our sociology has shaped a one-dimensional, specialized theology that is neither sufficient for urban ministry nor fully biblical.

Professional Priesthood

The third reason for evangelical indifference to addressing felt needs has to do with the professional priesthood. Although the Reformation advanced the biblical concept of the priesthood of all believers, the Catholic priest-hood has simply changed form and garb in the practice of many evangelical churches. I should hasten to say that this has been changing slowly but surely in evangelicalism over the past fifteen years, but the professional priesthood has generally dominated. For all of its justifiable and good points, this has had a negative influence on whole-person ministry. Essentially we have insti-tutionalized the training of technicians who are highly skilled in the art of running a church. In fact, the job has been done so well that many pastors are expected to do it all, while the laity spectates, much like in Catholicism. Because of specialized training in spiritual ministry, the limits of time and energy, and the passive role of the laity, the minister is restricted to activities within the church. The church is confined as long as it is run in this way. It is self-focused, nonevangelizing, and usually rather boring unless the tech-nical skills of the preacher are so advanced that the people are drawn by the drama of superb rhetoric.

Until the laity are seen as an integral part of the priesthood and un-leashed, churches are evangelistically anemic and crippled in their expres-sion of compassion. Frank Tillapaugh, in his marvelous book on shifting the pastoral paradigm, *Unleashing the Church,*[1] has shown what can happen in an urban setting when laity are equipped, challenged, and released with the re-sponsibility to minister. The fastest growing churches in Third World urban centers seem to combine dynamic pulpit ministry and celebrative worship

1. Ventura, Calif.: Regal, 1982.

with laity who can carry their faith into the world and actively address both felt needs and spiritual needs.

Self-defense

The fourth reason modern white evangelicals have withdrawn from cities and avoided meeting felt needs is self-defense. Those who have it made don't like to lose it. As white evangelicals have captured material resources, they have in turn been captured by the comforts of the middle class. Addressing felt needs involves the possibility of releasing monetary resources to support such outreach, and it involves resetting priorities from self-aggrandizement to sacrifice. Instead of limiting one's concern to self and the nuclear family, the Christian must broaden the circle of love. This will mean time spent to help others, energy expended rather than guarded, an orientation of giving rather than getting. Comfort and recreation time may have to assume a secondary role to compassion and redemption time.

For many the cost is too high. They feel they have worked hard to get to the apex of middle/upper-class life and don't want to give up the rewards and risk their resources. As a result, most middle-class churches have been uninterested in ministry to those with significant needs who require more than an occasional guilt offering.

Misunderstood Mandate

Our basic mandate is to love the Lord with all our heart, soul, and mind, and to love our neighbor as ourselves (Mark 12:30–31). As we are filled with the love of God, we are moved to reach out to our neighbors in a variety of ways which will encourage their redemptive relationship with him. If we love, we care. Caring is not philosophical but practical. As we care in concrete, incarnational ways, we open a window to heaven for our neighbor. He or she begins to see God as God's love flows from us. He or she begins to experience children of God who are wholeheartedly committed to their God.

Just as parents who truly love are concerned about all dimensions of their children's well-being, so a Christian who truly loves is concerned with multidimensional needs. Anything less is a lie in the name of love.

John Wesley, one of the greatest evangelists of all time, reached out primarily to the working class. He neglected no opportunity for practical social expression. This man of God who preached more than 45,000 sermons and published 223 books and pamphlets, started the first free dispensary in England for medical aid to the poor, organized the Friends Society to aid needy strangers, supported efforts for elementary education, bitterly opposed the slave trade, and encouraged major prison reform efforts. Wesley's view of the biblical mandate was that "if good works do not follow our faith, even all inward and outward holiness, it is plain our faith is nothing worth. . . . The gospel of Christ knows no religion but social; no holiness but social holiness. . . . Holy solitaires no more express the Christian faith than do holy adulterers." The great evangelist George Whitefield preached that salvation makes an impact on society; he protested against cruel and inhuman treatment of slaves and raised money for orphan homes.

Felt Need Intervention

Felt needs may be addressed on individual and corporate levels. Traditional twentieth-century efforts at need-intervention by American middle-class evangelicals have primarily focused on the individual. Corporate or systemic intervention has been relatively rare among American evangelicals. When it has occurred, it has typically been reactive rather than proactive, and focused on a very narrow set of concerns (i.e., sexual and alcohol issues). Fortunately, a much more varied and vigorous positive model of systemic intervention was demonstrated by eighteenth- and nineteenth-century British believers.

There are three major types of intervention common to both the individual and corporate levels: informational, developmental, and mediational. In addition, addressing felt needs on the individual level may be diaconal in form. Table 2 displays specific expressions of these levels and types of intervention.

In communities where a substantial proportion of the people groups being reached are experiencing the same needs, it is wise to consider intervention at a systemic level which, if successful, may alter the root conditions causing the needs. This is much better stewardship than simply focusing on individual intervention in a diaconal form.

Based on a multidimensional view of human nature, five potential areas of felt needs emerge for ministry: the spiritual, cognitive, relational, emotional, and physical. Because humans are interactive systems, ministry intervention in any of the areas will make an impact upon other subsystems. The spiritual needs of people will be touched at least indirectly if we minister to other areas in the name and manner of Jesus.

Within each area or subsystem of the person, we can further specify several expressions of need. Table 3 illustrates this. The possibilities for ministry intervention are obviously overwhelming. Without adequate guidelines we can find ourselves paralyzed into inaction, or we may dilute our spiritual emphasis through over-extension. Neither extreme is desirable or necessary.

Principles of Felt-Need Outreach

Outreach balanced between the meeting of temporal and eternal needs is focused and selective. Ministry which effectively addresses felt needs will be guided by the following principles.

Table 2 **Types of Felt-Need Intervention**

	Individual	**Corporate (Systematic)**
Informational	Provide information to individuals on how and where to meet needs (job openings, health care, rentals).	Provide information to decision-makers on needs of a people group and a way to meet needs.
Developmental	Provide education to enable a person to productively and independently function within family and society (basic education, vocational or social skills training).	Provide economic/community development efforts to empower groups to develop their community and personal lives with a sense of dignity and worth.
Mediational	Intervene in problem areas to promote resolution, justice, and well-being (legal assistance, housing assistance, marriage and family counseling, employer/employee conflicts).	Apply influence and pressure upon various channels for either the enactment, change, or enforcement of laws and policies in a fair and just way (legal intervention).
Diaconal	Provide direct relief to meet immediate, personal crises (housing, food pantry, clothing, medical assistance).	

Inductive Foundation

The first principle is to ask, don't assume. By means of interviews with selected leaders, surveys of a large number of people, social science resources, and census data, assess your target community or primary people group. Talk with residents, attend community concern meetings, talk with school officials, listen to kids. Develop a catalogue of the most frequently and deeply felt needs. Determine what resources will be needed.

As you assess the community, also assess your church.

What are its current and potential resources in relation to the identified needs of the target community? Are there people who are sufficiently skilled to properly minister to an area of felt need? Is there sufficient motivation and commitment of resource people to do a particular ministry?

What kind of time will be required weekly to meet the identified needs? What amount of time do your people have available for each potential ministry? Over what period are commitments needed if the ministry is to be legitimate and fruitful? How will commitment to the felt-need ministry by the people in the church relate to their existing ministry involvements?

What kind of material resources necessary to meet the needs are either available within the congregation or reasonably accessible from other

Table 3 Intervention Possibilities for Urban Ministry

Spiritual/moral
1. Training of children: Sunday school; Christian school; parent workshops
2. Drawing closer to God: Neighborhood, workplace Bible studies; mentoring care
3. Finding forgiveness: Pastoral care; counseling
4. Purpose in life: Teaching; pastoral care

Social-emotional
1. Loneliness: Koinonia—interaction and caring opportunities
2. Internal and interpersonal conflict resolution: Teaching; counseling; small group exercises; mediation
3. Marital difficulties: Skills training; premarital and marital intervention and counseling
4. Parenting difficulties: Counseling; core circles; teaching
5. Depression: Pastoral care; comfort by koinonia; professional counseling
6. Substance abuse: Counseling; accountability within koinonia
7. Homosexuality: Counseling; accountability within koinonia
8. Other sexual problems: Counseling; accountability within koinonia
9. Threatened suicide: Pastoral care; professional counseling
10. Grief: Pastoral care and counsel; koinonia
11. Divorce recovery: Pastoral care; diaconal assistance; koinonia
12. Stress and anxiety: Teaching; accountability; counsel

Cognitive
1. Basic intellectual abilities: Parent-helpers in school; tutoring; nutrition; parental training; day care
2. Career guidance: Guidance counseling; Intercristo and other placement services
3. Second language acquisition: Language-learning programs and resources

Physical
1. Food and nutrition: Nutrition instruction; feeding programs; agricultural development; food co-ops; policy (Bread for the World)
2. Shelter: Temporary housing; project Nehemiah/Habitat; rental preservation; rent control
3. Clothing: Handouts; sewing skills development; materials co-op
4. Health care: Free clinics; improved sanitary conditions; pre- and post-natal care
5. Safety: Neighborhood watches; anti-drug programs
6. Quality of life: Economic self-development; self-determination; legal intervention

Table 4 Community Assessment

Potential target group:
Geographical location:

Degree of felt need					*Extensiveness*				
5	4	3	2	1	5	4	3	2	1
Intense				Moderate					Low
Pervasive									Isolated
80–100%		60–80%		40–60%		20–40%		0–20%	

Spiritual/moral
1. Training of children_____
2. Drawing closer to God_____
3. Finding forgiveness_____
4. Finding purpose in life_____
5. Other (   )_____

Cognitive
1. Basic education_____
2. Career guidance_____
3. 2nd language acquisition_____
4. Other (   )_____

Physical
1. Food/nutrition_____
2. Shelter_____
3. Clothing_____
4. Health care_____
5. Safety_____
6. Quality of life_____
7. Other (   )_____

Social/emotional
1. Loneliness_____
2. Conflict resolution_____
3. Marital difficulties_____
4. Parenting difficulties_____
5. Depression_____
6. Substance abuse_____
7. Homosexuality_____
8. Other sexual problems_____
9. Threatened suicides_____
10. Grief_____
11. Divorce recovery_____
12. Stress and anxiety_____
13. Other (   )_____

Primary Felt Needs (PFN)
in order of priority

Degree score × Extensiveness score
1.
2.
3.
4.

Table 5 **Church Resource Assessment**				
	Primary Felt Needs (PFN)			
People	**PFN 1**	**PFN 2**	**PFN 3**	**PFN 4**
1. Leadership				
2. Workers				
3. Necessary skills				
4. Motivation				
5. Long-term commitment				
6. Referrals				
Time				
1. Weekly time available				
2. Two-year time commitments				
Material Resources				
1. Start-up money and materials				
2. Ongoing resources to sustain the program for two years				
CR Score: 5 strong; 4 relatively strong; 3 adequate; 1–2 inadequate.				

sources? How will those resources be secured? By whom? What is necessary to start? To keep going?

As you assess available resources, be alert for referral and networking possibilities with people and material assets outside your own congregational pool. Be willing to link with those whose resources can be offered by referral without contradicting or compromising your theological commitments and spiritual ministry.

Systematic Planning

Once the community and the church have been assessed properly, priorities can be set. Prioritizing is crucial so that any compassion ministries undertaken can be done effectively and will appropriately interlock with the direct evangelism and discipleship ministries of the church. Priorities should be established in the context of frequent, intense, corporate prayer. Commitments to felt-need ministries should not be made until the church leadership and the laity have prayed together on at least three occasions and have a sense of the Spirit's leading. Once that occurs, begin training people. Also, start small, and plan for ongoing, regular evaluation and adjustments.

Planning should be done on both long-range and short-range bases, with appropriate goals and goal-paths visualized for a period of one month to five years.

Systematic planning also includes mobilization. Responsibility of the laity for evangelistic, discipleship, and compassion ministries should be regularly

---

Table 6 **Targeted Felt Needs**

Highest Combined Primary Felt Need Summary Score + Church Resource Summary Score =
Priority of Targeted Felt Needs
PFN + CR = TFN Priority

---

taught. Ministry possibilities and identified felt needs should be clearly and pervasively publicized through multiple channels of communication within the church. Ministry teams should be publicly commissioned with specific prayer for God's anointing. Periodic public reports should in turn be given to inform the church leaders and congregation of ministry endeavors, so that continuing, specific prayer is encouraged.

Lay Leadership

As has already been suggested, leadership for felt-needs ministry will be exhorted and reinforced by the pastor but supplied most naturally by the laity. They will evidence the supply of spiritual gifts and natural talents necessary to conduct various ministries. Guided by the pastoral staff with regard to their spiritual responsibilities, they generally have a variety of ability avenues which open up felt-need ministry more readily and broadly than if the professional ministry staff tried to do it all.

Self-development

Felt-need ministries must be carefully designed and executed so as to avoid creating or prolonging patterns of dependency. The goal is to help people acquire the skills and resources necessary for independence. Relief may be necessary on a temporary, crisis basis, but the teaching of responsibility is crucial to avoid a long-term welfare dependency. Felt-need ministries must empower people to care for themselves in dignified and effective ways. We must resist the temptation to empower ourselves by fostering dependency. That kind of paternalism eventually leads to manipulation and resentment of the provider by those locked into receiving assistance.

Reform as Well as Relief

Felt-needs ministry must be sensitive to the underlying legal, administrative, and policy conditions which create and perpetuate needs among certain groups of people. To ignore this is to choose poor management of ministry time, energy, and resources. If we ignore appropriate reform, we sentence ourselves to long-term and seemingly unending relief efforts toward a steady stream of needy persons. In many cases, especially those dealing with physical needs, a stroke of the governmental pen can instantly alleviate particular life needs of thousands. Stewardship demands reform as a part of meeting felt needs.

Structured Assistance

Aid should be channeled through screening bodies so that individuals are not seen as the source of assistance, thus opening themselves to manipulation, harassment, and charges of mismanagement. Whenever possible, assistance should be given in the form of goods and services, directly or through referral. Monetary requests should be cleared and provided in the framework of organizational ministry.

A Model of Balanced Ministry

In conclusion, I would like to highlight a ministry that is a sterling example of the blending of clear-cut evangelistic proclamation and programming with felt-needs ministry. While living in the Bay Area, I had the special privilege of developing a relationship with Dr. J. Alfred Smith, pastor of the Allen Temple Baptist Church in Oakland, California. Allen Temple reflects the outstanding servant leadership of this humble man of God. *Guidelines for Effective Urban Ministry* by G. Willis Bennett[2] provides a case study of Allen Temple and Dr. Smith. Because I will highlight only a few aspects of this ministry, I enthusiastically commend a thorough reading of the book.

The purpose of Allen Temple, as given in its constitution, is "the advancement of the Kingdom of Jesus Christ. It shall seek to attain the goal through the public worship of God, the preaching of the gospel, consistent Christian living by its members, personal evangelism, missionary endeavor and Christian education" (Article II). A corollary document, "The Local Church in God's Mission," written by Pastor Smith, pleads for a church which will be "the visible manifestation of the invisible Christ." He wants a church with a "harmonious balance between faith and works, theology and practice," one that is "committed to cultivating rich inner spirituality as well as courageous action outside of themselves for social justice." In another paper Dr. Smith asserts, "You see, Allen Temple the church assembled is concerned about regeneration and racism, hell and housing, justification and justice, evangelism and ecology, prayer and poverty."

In "The Bold Mission of the Church," Dr. Smith asserts that:

(1) The local church is an important Christian community for accomplishing God's mission in the world.
(2) Members of the local church need to be trained by the pastor to work harmoniously in order to accomplish God's mission in the world.

2. Nashville: Broadman, 1983.

(3) God's mission concerns itself with the personal acceptance of Jesus Christ as Lord and Savior, and this mission shares God's deepest concern for justice, human worth, and dignity.

(4) Commitment to God's mission requires a holy boldness on public issues of morality and ethics, and this boldness, when necessary, takes a strong stand against spiritual wickedness in the high places of power in our nation and world.

(5) Bold mission in the local church means the membership is prepared to accept the lifestyle and philosophy of Jesus Christ, while rejecting the lifestyle, false gods, and living standards of popular culture.

Out of this holistic theological foundation, Allen Temple grew from 1023 to 2498 between 1970 and 1980 and about doubled again by 1990. The church beautifully blends aggressive evangelism through revivals, special events, public invitations during worship services, evangelistic street ministries, visitation to rest homes, prison ministry, neighborhood Bible studies, and personal evangelism through felt-needs ministry.

Allen Temple is a seven-day-a-week church with outreach occurring both on its premises and where its people are. The church stresses education as expressed in its active support of public school education (Dr. Smith was given permission to run for the Oakland School Board, a position he handily won and retained for a second term), its tutorial program, scholarship program, adult education offered by the church, Spanish study to foster communication with Oakland's growing Hispanic population, released-time programs at the church in cooperation with a nearby elementary school, and courses for college credit at Allen Temple offered by a nearby community college.

With regard to health care, Allen Temple maintains bulletin boards, holds periodic programs and clinics, hosts its own blood bank, recruits volunteers to work in patient services at an Oakland hospital, provides space for dental clinics, maintains cancer screening and blood pressure testing programs, and honors members who are making contributions in the health field.

Allen Temple has built a seventy-five-unit housing site for the elderly, encourages the community by actively leading "sweep-up, clean-up" campaigns, organized a garden club to beautify the neighborhood in the area of the church, and assists with home repairs and improvements.

The church actively provides employment and economic information on bulletin boards and class, pulpit, and bulletin announcements. Referrals of unemployed persons are made available to business and service agencies. A Job Fair Committee, made up of resource people from industry, government, and educational institutions, provides assistance to high schoolers, college students, and recent graduates. People in emergencies are helped with direct assistance of cash, food, clothing, or shelter. There is also an annual flea market where people can buy a variety of items at low cost. A credit union at the church provides an avenue for investment and borrowing, protecting church members from the jaws of loan sharks.

Other felt-need ministries include recreational outlets, counseling programs, an anti-drug program (which brought threats on Dr. Smith's life), and citizenship development.

Bennett points out that "hardly a sermon is preached without a note of evangelism and social concern. These two are not to be divided but wedded. . . . The church has become known near and far for its involvement in society. The mayor of Oakland said, 'It is hard to think of any community action that hasn't been impacted upon by Allen Temple.'"[3] Allen Temple has found the redemptive balance.

As the evangelical church dignifies the daily, elevates the earthly, and ordains the ordinary in felt-need ministry to urban dwellers, Christ will be lifted up. People being touched by Christ's love will see our good works and glorify our Father who is in heaven (Matt. 5:16). As demonstration goes hand in hand with proclamation, the saving power of the gospel will be released in full measure.

3. G. Willis Bennett, *Guidelines for Effective Urban Ministry* (Nashville: Broadman, 1983), 102–3.

How to Create an Urban Strategy

Ralph W. Neighbour Jr.

Before launching or expanding a ministry, nothing is as crucial as the creation of an urban strategy. It is as important to the urban pastor or missionary as a business plan is to those who launch a new venture. An urban strategy is necessary if the entire metroplex is to be evangelized. While traditional church leaders tend to think in terms of parishes or "church fields," an urban strategist seeks to develop a pattern that will be effective in reaching all people groups present.

Finding the Tools

Each summer, I teach M.Div. and D.Min. students from Columbia Biblical Seminary and Graduate School of Missions a series of classes that take them to world-class cities. These students travel around the world, surveying churches in major cities. In each place, they are exposed to rapidly exploding cell group congregations. Finally, they remain in one major city for thirty days, learning the "tools of the trade" used by urban strategists.

In 1962, when Dr. Leonard Irwin of the Home Mission Board, Southern Baptist Convention, introduced these "tools" to me, I felt something like Alice when she stepped through the looking-glass. After planting more than a dozen churches without knowing what I was doing, a new way of praying and strategizing was opened to me.

I have found it possible to collect data in every part of the world I have visited—even when local missionaries said such information did not exist in their Third World nation. Reports have been created for Nairobi, Bangkok,

This chapter first appeared in *Where Do We Go From Here?* (Houston: Torch, 1990) and was reprinted in *Urban Mission* 8, no. 4 (1991): 21–31. Used by permission.

Singapore, Jakarta, Brussels, Auckland, Brisbane, and London.[1] In the United States, not only are data readily available, but special reports can be secured which will give one-, five-, and ten-mile detailed population reports from the intersections of any specific streets or highways.[2]

Developing an urban strategy includes the following steps:

1. Create a prayer base for your activity.

Nothing is more fraught with danger than seeking to do the work of the Master without "Listening Room" time. Taking daily findings to the prayer closet provides spiritual insights not provided by the crunching of numbers. It is recommended that the strategy team spend daily periods in prayer. There will be moments in the study when there is simply nothing to do but weep and pray over the lostness of the neighborhoods being studied.

Without question, spiritual eyes will discern "strongholds" of Satan within a city as the study develops. For example, in London's Southeast quadrant, Woolwich had been the site for manufacturing munitions for generations. All the soldiers who died on both sides of the Battle of Waterloo were killed with guns that came from this factory. After the Luftwaffe reduced the area to rubble in World War II, the British government developed it as a low-income housing area. Every attempt to plant a church in Woolwich failed for over forty years until Icthus Fellowship invaded it during Easter season of 1988, after concentrated weeks of prayer and fasting.

When one evaluates districts of sin and evil in a city, it is necessary to remember that the battle we fight is not against flesh and blood but against principalities and powers in the air. Let those who are spiritually blind to eternal warfare stay away from developing urban strategy.

2. Secure data.

Collect all available census data, sociological studies, and reports previously compiled about the city and the surrounding region. Sources for this will include United Nations studies, national census reports, and regional reports (including "Standard Metropolitan Statistical Area" data, city and county studies, and research materials completed through grants by local universities). Visits should be made to agencies developing highway systems for the area, and urban planning commissions sponsored by the national, state, or regional governments. Much information can be gleaned by interviewing the utility companies for the region; their forecasts of where telephones, electric-

---

1. The Brisbane and Auckland reports are available from Touch Outreach Ministries, Box 19888, Houston, TX 77079 for $25 each.

2. Contact Church Information and Development Services, 3001 Redhill Avenue, Suite 2-220, Costa Mesa, CA 92626.

ity, and gas will be needed can be valuable tools for studying exurbia and suburbia. Urban renewal commissions make recommendations about decaying inner city areas. Even the slums of Third World cities have been mapped, and the lifestyles of inhabitants described. In Bangkok, for example, a huge multicolored set of maps has been published, showing the location of hundreds of slums.

Basic questions to be answered about the city include:

1. How many children live here?
2. How many single-parent families are present?
3. How many retired and elderly live here, and where are they housed?
4. Where are the poor?
5. Where are the rich?
6. What ethnic groups are there, and where?
7. What are the educational levels and occupations?
8. What will the population be in five years? ten years?
9. What urban redevelopment will take place?

One must enjoy being a Sherlock Holmes during this investigative step, making friends at each location visited and asking endless questions. Many key documents not usually shown to the public will be "passed on" if you gain the respect of the official you are interviewing. In Singapore, I created the "Baptist Centre for Urban Studies" (of which I was the only staff), had calling cards printed, and left them behind with each government official. I was soon being invited to all sorts of functions held by sociologists, demographers, and urban planners. Most of the best "leads" come by asking who has information that might be of value to the study, and offering to share the results of your own research when completed.

Include visits to the religious headquarters of all religious centers in the region. Many denominational leaders have done studies which can be of great help. Secure listings of all known churches, synagogues, temples, and shrines from any available sources. In some areas this is a simple matter of getting a developed list; in other cities it will be the first time anyone has bothered to consider the matter. In doing an urban strategy for Brussels, interviews with the head of the state Protestant church and a Catholic cardinal provided significant data which influenced preparation of the strategy.

3. Create a strategy map.

From a government or private mapping source, purchase the largest, most detailed map available of the region. For Singapore, I purchased segments of a map from a government office and had them mounted on a cloth base. The map was eight feet high and thirteen feet wide, and showed every street

Figure 7 **Neighborhood Template, Pakuranga Central**

		Within the total population		Types of Dwellings	
Resident Population	2820				
Total Households	894	N.Z. Maori	45	Private dwellings	2823
Never Married,		Polynesian	15	Non-private dwellings	24
over 15 yrs.	684	Not Working	624	Separate houses	735
Married	1179	Born outside N.Z.	672	2 houses/flats, joined	99
Remarried	123	Among the overseas born are		3 or + joined together	60
Separated	60	U.K. and Ireland	393	Joined to business/shop	0
Widowed	108	Europe	102	Bach, crib, hut	0
Divorced	75	Australia	48	Temporary private dwelling	3
De Facto Relationship	57	Asia	39		

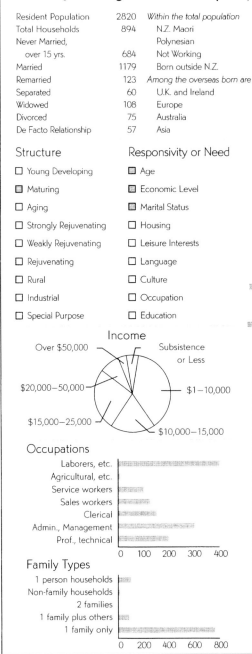

Structure

- ☐ Young Developing
- ☒ Maturing
- ☐ Aging
- ☐ Strongly Rejuvenating
- ☐ Weakly Rejuvenating
- ☐ Rejuvenating
- ☐ Rural
- ☐ Industrial
- ☐ Special Purpose

Responsivity or Need

- ☒ Age
- ☒ Economic Level
- ☒ Marital Status
- ☐ Housing
- ☐ Leisure Interests
- ☐ Language
- ☐ Culture
- ☐ Occupation
- ☐ Education

Male % Age Female %

| 65+ |
| 60–64 |
| 55–59 |
| 50–54 |
| 45–49 |
| 40–44 |
| 35–39 |
| 30–34 |
| 25–29 |
| 20–24 |
| 18–19 |
| 15–17 |
| 10–14 |
| 5–9 |
| 0–4 |

Income

Over $50,000 — Subsistence or Less

$20,000–50,000 — $1–10,000

$15,000–25,000 — $10,000–15,000

Occupations

Laborers, etc.
Agricultural, etc.
Service workers
Sales workers
Clerical
Admin., Management
Prof., technical

0 100 200 300 400

Family Types

1 person households
Non-family households
2 families
1 family plus others
1 family only

0 200 400 600 800

Generally, Pakuranga Central is made up of high-cost housing estates 10 to 20 years old. There is a high turnover of residents in the middle cost housing bracket as jobs transfer people in and out of Auckland. Families may stay two to three years, then move on. There is a large young population under 24 years old, which makes up about 30% of the population. Income is similar to that of greater Auckland, except for a slightly larger distribution of $25,000–50,000 incomes. It is also evident from the occupation chart that the laborer and clerical categories are relatively higher.

and track on the island. In Brisbane, we secured multicolored maps in sections about three feet by four feet in size, and developed each one as described below.

4. Delineate the neighborhoods.

This has often been done by urban planners. Much help can be gained by scrutinizing the Enumeration Districts (E.D.s) of the Census Tracts (C.T.s). While the C.T.s are shown on the census reports you purchase, the E.D.s are available only upon request from the Bureau of the Census. Expect to pay a special charge to have this material prepared for you.

The E.D. shows the area assigned to one person to survey when the census is taken. It will be a bite-sized area that can be covered on foot by the employee, who will not have to cross any highways or rivers to complete the task. This material is helpful in giving block-by-block reports of the number of residents, their incomes, education, religious preferences (in many countries), and even the number of toilets in their residences.

The boundaries of the city's neighborhoods should be carefully marked on the map, or maps, of the region. Use 1/16-inch bendable red chart tape for this purpose, carefully pressing it over the streets that mark the edges of each area. As you do so, put a 1/4-inch round sticker in each neighborhood, with a number written on it. Create a list of these numbers designating it with the commonly used name for that territory (e.g., "Woodlands, Section 1").

Also use round stickers to mark the exact location of all existing religious structures. In Philadelphia, doing so quickly revealed ethnic groups from Italy, Russia, and Greece and where they had clustered. In Singapore, Indian, Buddhist, and Sikh temples attract people who mingle in hawker stalls which prepare their ethnic foods; many live in housing estates miles away.

5. Create a template for your report.

To create a template for a report (see Fig. 7), I usually prepare a double-page spread for each neighborhood, showing a population pyramid, a small map showing boundaries of the neighborhood, housing information, immigration patterns, marital status patterns, income, employment, religious preferences, a brief description of the community, the neighborhood category (see part 7), and a recommended strategy for planting appropriate cell groups. A number of desktop publishing programs ease this task.

6. Make population pyramids.

Figures 8 and 9 show two examples of population pyramids which illustrate the facts revealed by research. In Figure 8 we see a slum area of Brisbane (Fortitude Valley). It includes prostitutes, night clubs, Chinatown, and a business district. Why should so many aged women live there? In our research, we discovered that the Catholics had established a retirement home for nuns in this neighborhood generations ago, and it remained as an oasis for them in the midst of a hellhole called Fortitude Valley.

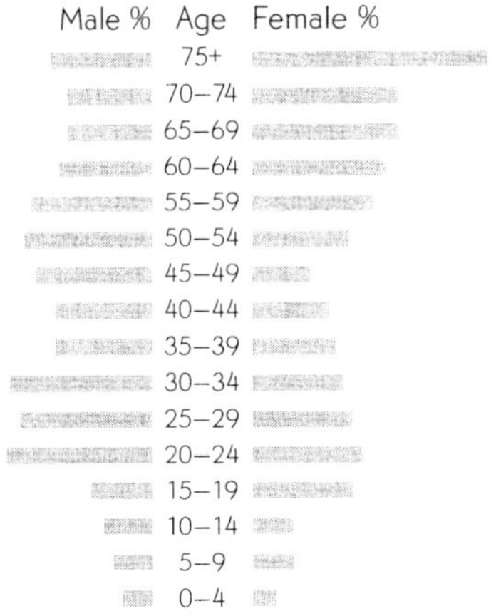

Figure 9 illustrates a typical pyramid of a community settled by young couples with lots of little children (Ferny Grove). This would be a prime area for the planting of a new work geared toward young adults.[3]

Figure 8 **Population Pyramid for Fortitude Valley, Brisbane**

Male %	Age	Female %
	75+	
	70–74	
	65–69	
	60–64	
	55–59	
	50–54	
	45–49	
	40–44	
	35–39	
	30–34	
	25–29	
	20–24	
	15–19	
	10–14	
	5–9	
	0–4	

7. Develop neighborhood analyses.

Using the template, fill in all the data for each category of the neighborhood. This requires simple compilations of statistics.

8. Cluster neighborhoods into categories.

The data collected should enable you to categorize a neighborhood as a young developing suburb, a maturing suburb, an aging suburb, a rejuvenating suburb, or a special-purpose suburb.

The Young Developing Suburb

These suburbs are still in the process of subdivision and construction. Their populations are increasing rapidly as young parents buy the homes and establish their families. Children through age nine comprise as much as 27 percent, and always more than 15 percent, of the population. The age groups sixty years and over usually comprise less than 5 percent of the total except in those young suburbs containing a large senior citizen's home. The social infrastructure needs of this type of suburb include kindergartens, child care facilities, primary schools, and playgrounds.

Target these areas by churches, for they contain some of the most responsive segments of the city.

The Maturing Suburb

This type of suburb has been in the process of development for at least twenty years. The population total tends to be fairly stable, although the composition of the population is undergoing change with a marked out-migration

---

3. From *The Brisbane Report.*

of young persons in the fifteen- to twenty-four-year-old age group as families mature and grown children leave the parental home. Such out-migration is partially balanced by new births (but at a much lower rate than in the young developing suburbs) and, in some suburbs, a small net immigration, as the remaining vacant lots are developed and filled.

The population structure is characterized by a concentration of older families. The age groups ten to twenty-four and forty-five to fifty-nine are usually predominant.

The social infrastructural needs of this type of suburb include a heavy demand for secondary schools, playing fields, and recreational opportunities for older children and younger adults.

An aggressive ministry to young people, with "Share Groups" led by people in this age group, can be a significant means of penetrating these areas. As adolescents and young adults seek to establish their own identity, they often search for a new set of values which contrast with those of their parents. If their peer group includes committed Christians, they will often choose to follow Christ. At this age, peers have more impact than older persons who seek to work with them.

Figure 9 **Population Pyramid for Ferny Grove**

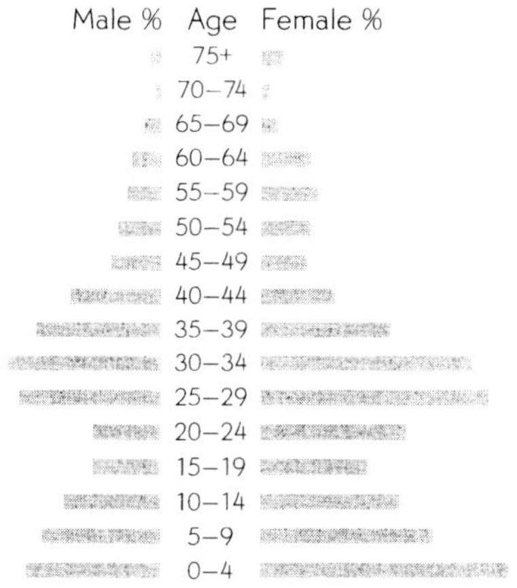

Male % Age Female %
75+
70–74
65–69
60–64
55–59
50–54
45–49
40–44
35–39
30–34
25–29
20–24
15–19
10–14
5–9
0–4

When the young people come to know Christ, they create a natural bridge, as they share their faith with other family members.

The Aging Suburb

The aging suburb typically consists of predominantly single-family homes more than forty years old. The population of suburbs in this category is invariably declining, some by more than 5 percent a year. Grown children are leaving the family home, persons in the older age groups (who form a major proportion of these communities) are moving to retirement homes or dying.

Persons over sixty years of age always comprise more than 12 percent of the aging suburb and in some cases as much as 26 percent. There is a marked lack of young children, the zero to nine age groups usually forming less than 12 percent, and always less than 14 percent of the total.

An important result of the population structure of this type of suburb is a low household size; many houses are occupied by widows or widowers living alone or by elderly couples whose children have left home.

The social infrastructure needs of these communities center around the provision of services to the elderly, such as meals for the home-bound, home nursing care, and social clubs. These suburbs often contain underutilized school facilities.

The gospel has particular relevance to these persons when shared in the context of relational small groups. Quite often they are neglected by their younger family members, who are intent on pursuing their own agendas. They want people who will care about them, listen to them, and encourage them. The leisure time of the elderly makes it easier to reach them during the daytime. The effective church in these areas will offer social and recreational life that is appropriate to senior citizens.

The Rejuvenating Suburb

A rejuvenating suburb differs from a young developing suburb in which the population of at least one young adult age group showed a net increase between censuses. A further distinction may be made between strongly rejuvenating suburbs, in which a decline in population has been reversed and weakly rejuvenating suburbs, in which the population decline has been slowed but not reversed.

Rejuvenating suburbs include most of the old inner suburbs where the housing stock has been through more than one cycle of ownership. Their age structure is similar to that of the aging suburbs, showing a heavy concentration in the older age groups and very few children. One marked difference, however, is a concentration of people in the twenty to twenty-nine age group, usually more than 20 percent of the total.

Household size in rejuvenating suburbs is small. As in the aging suburbs, there are many elderly people living alone, while the young in-migrants are most often singles or childless couples renting accommodations in old houses or in multiple dwellings.

The social infrastructure needs of this type of suburb will be those of the aging suburb, supplemented with the lifestyle requirements of the unattached adult: dining and dancing venues, sports centers, clubs, theatres, and other facilities for social intercourse.

Reaching this area must be done by two branches of Christ's body: one which focuses on the young adult and another which concentrates on the aging person. Many creative approaches can be used in these outreach strategies, including musical and drama groups, forum discussions, and sports.

The Rural, Industrial, or Special Purpose Suburb

These areas are rural or semirural. They have a small population whose structure often cannot be characterized under any of the foregoing types.

To these suburbs may be added those that are of a primarily industrial nature with virtually no resident population, and those in which dominant residential institutions distort the pattern of the population structure. These include such things as a prison farm or migrant hostel, a retirement village, nurse or student hostels, or military camps. They may also include seaside communities which contain many "second homes," often used seasonally or on weekends.

9. Take surveys of population awarenesses.

Once the neighborhoods have been systematically examined, a critical step must follow: Members of population categories must be interviewed to determine responsive segments. Local cultural factors may influence this significantly. For example, those working in Belgium a few years ago discovered that young couples with their first baby who spoke Dutch were unusually open to discussing salvation by grace through faith in Jesus Christ. French-speaking couples in the same circumstances were not as responsive.

On the other hand, some responsive segments exist in many differing cultures among the same groups. Youths and young marrieds are usually more responsive than middle- and older-aged persons. Better-educated people may be less steeped in the pressures of family religions than are the poor. Conversely, in some cultures the elite are resistant, and the poor are more responsive.

These matters must be discovered by surveys taken within the population. There are at least three ways to do this:

1. Discover which population segments are turning to Christ in existing churches and parachurch groups.
2. Discover which population segments are most vulnerable to the evangelism of the cults and what causes them to respond.
3. Interview people in different neighborhoods of the city. If it is discovered that there is responsiveness in a certain segment of people, then use the previous research to locate where pockets of such people are located.

10. Create your strategy document.

It is now possible to publish the results in whatever form seems most suitable. A document published jointly by Columbia Biblical Seminary and Touch International Ministries on Auckland, New Zealand, is an example of a comprehensive report. Over 450 pages long, it covers every neighborhood of the city, and includes an overview of the metropolis with population projections into the next century. It is useful to all churches and parachurch groups, and may be sold at a cost designed to recapture the cost of production.

As shown in the sample pages above, this strategy report should include a population pyramid, basic information about the geography of the neighborhood, income, marital status, immigration patterns, racial-ethnic mixes, types of employment, and religious preferences. Neighborhoods can be listed by zones, by census tracts, or alphabetically.

11. Select key areas for penetration.

With the strategy report available, it will now be possible to reach neighborhoods with similar characteristics. For example, couples with young children may be scattered throughout the metroplex, but would be reached by a common strategy. Another area may reveal a large number of middle-aged couples with teens; this would be of special interest to those seeking to reach youth. Through this selection, cell group churches seeking to penetrate an entire city will be able to plant cells appropriate to each area, targeting people with similar needs and interests.

In addition, much can be learned about specific population groups. A church seeking to build its membership around university students can pinpoint where they live.

When it is possible to include religious preferences in the strategy report, a further narrowing of the strategy can take place. When certain religious groups are open to the gospel, they can be located through the report, and a strategy developed to reach them. For example, if there is a responsive segment of immigrants in a city, they will be located for evangelism activity. The strategy may include radio broadcasting in their language as well as reaching them in the districts where they have clustered.

12. Use a checkerboard planting pattern.

The Ichthus Fellowship in Southeast London has a full-time staff worker who works on their strategy for penetrating the city. With more than 100 cells their strategy includes combining people from two or more cell groups to penetrate an unreached area between them.

For example, I participated in a prayer meeting and a street service in the district of Woolwich, sponsored by cells from either side of the area. We met for prayer and training in Greenwich, and then marched into the shopping district, singing praise songs. Before the day was over, a new cell group had been formed in the previously unreached area. Such "checkerboard" planting of cells can provide a powerful tool in evangelizing unreached areas.

Many years ago, I used this strategy to develop the ministry of "The People Who Care" in Houston, Texas. When we first began, the gap in our "checkerboard" was so large we would drive fifteen minutes or more between our homes for our cell meetings. Within a year, my wife and I were walking on foot to our cell group gathering.

The Full Gospel Central Church in Seoul has done the same thing with their "districts." When I first began to study them, they had only fourteen

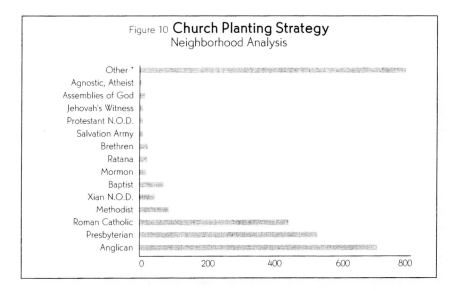

Figure 10 **Church Planting Strategy**
Neighborhood Analysis

districts, covering the entire city. As their cells grew, they gradually reduced the sizes of each district and added new ones. There are currently several dozen—and they continue to plan for further ones as they move past the 600,000 membership figure.

13. Create the actual strategy.

Questions for the church planter team to answer may include the following:

1. Who are the responsive segments we have discovered?
2. Should we seek to penetrate several groups as a test of receptivity before focusing on only one?
3. Which group, or groups, within the community should first be reached? How will this strategy lend itself to the expansion of the ministry into other segments of the community? Prepare both short- and long-range plans.
4. As we view the metropolis, where do these segments live or gather?
5. How should we seek to communicate with them? Should we use direct mail, word of mouth only, house-to-house survey, or other means?
6. What will be our reason for contacting them? Should we offer special small groups which focus on their problems or interests? (Examples: a "target group" for expectant mothers, or a group for lonely people).
7. Where will we meet with them? Can we use their own homes? If not, what facilities in the areas where they live might be available for us to use? Can we use our own homes for this purpose?

8. How many groups can we launch in the first six months, given our manpower and their available time?

In most cases, the original strategy is only theoretical (see Fig. 10). As the ministry is launched, the church planting team will require many adjustments to their preliminary plans. Above everything else, the initial penetration of the unreached in the community should be given much higher priority than the establishment of a worship service on Sunday mornings. The many hours spent in preparing and executing this service may better be invested in ministry to the target group.

Those who create an urban strategy will quickly realize that the kaleidoscope of a city requires church planting to be seen as a movement, not a helter-skelter task which can select certain portions of the community while ignoring other parts.

Resources for Doing Strategy Planning

Dayton, Edward R., and David A. Fraser. *Planning Strategies for World Evangelization.* Rev. ed., 1990. Grand Rapids: William B. Eerdmans Publishing Co., and Monrovia, CA: MARC (255 Jefferson Avenue SE, Grand Rapids, MI 49503). Walks through these key stages of strategy planning. Oriented around the concept of unreached peoples, it is useful both inside and outside the North American context. No specific attention to urban setting.

Faircloth, Samuel D. *Church Planting for Reproduction.* 1991. Grand Rapids: Baker Book House (P.O. Box 6287, Grand Rapids, MI 49516–6287). Generic overview of steps involved in church planting. Makes strong use of PERT management techniques in modeling the process.

Malphurs, Aubrey. *Planting Growing Churches for the Twenty-first Century.* 1992. Grand Rapids: Baker Book House (P.O. Box 6287, Grand Rapids, MI 49516–6287). Similar in focus to Faircloth but less rigidly defined by management process overlay. More time spent on discussion of personnel and principles. Of wider use than merely urban.

Marchak, Mark. *The Urban Church Planter's Book of Markers.* 1993. New York: Conservative Baptist Home Missions Society (166 W. 92nd St., New York, NY 10025). In-progress, loose-leaf binder collection of tools, methods, and "snapshot" case studies of urban church planting in New York. Good theological reflection on the nature of the city. Rambling in style but very comprehensive and extremely sensitive to the city context. Strong practitioner orientation.

Ratliff, Joe S., and Michael J. Cox. *Church Planting in the African-American Community.* 1993. Nashville: Broadman Press (127 Ninth Ave., North, Nashville, TN 37234). Strongly oriented to the practical in easy, readable style. Special attention to the relationship of organizing body to the sponsoring church and the role of the church planter. May need to be supplemented by references to Faircloth or Malphurs for insight on concrete steps in church planting.

Rusbuldt, Richard E., Richard K. Gladden, and Norman M. Green Jr. *Local Church Planning Manual.* 1977. Valley Forge: Judson Press (P.O. Box 851, Valley Forge, PA 19482–0851). Designed to help local churches do self-evaluation. Step-by-step instructions are given for developing a philosophy of ministry, building goals, objectives, and program plans. Over half the volume consists of tear-out sheets to be used in evaluation. Comprehensive in scope. Not specifically urban in focus.

Wagner, C. Peter. *Strategies for Church Growth.* 1987. Ventura, CA: Regal Books (2300 Knoll Drive, Ventura, CA 93003). Strongly oriented to the Church Growth School of thought, an introduction to the defense and practice of strategy, targeting, and goal setting in evangelism and church growth.

————. *Church Planting for a Greater Harvest.* 1990. Ventura, CA: Regal Books (2300 Knoll Drive, Ventura, CA 93003). Practical focus on ways and means to initiate church planting in the United States. Attention to essentials for planning, location decisions, and developing a nucleus. Twelve case studies for church planting are given, plus an excellent chapter on resources for church planters.

Part 3
Targeting: Linking Church to Urban Community

Introduction

Harvie M. Conn

Cities are not new. Nor is the church's checkered effort to target them for Christ. Have its perceptions of the city shifted through time? How have such shifts affected our understanding of strategy and planning? What insights remain as we plot new directions?[1]

Roman Colonialism, the City, and the Church

The Roman Empire in which the New Testament church was born was a commonwealth of self-governing cities, related to a single central power. Citizenship meant "city-zenship" (Acts 21:39). And the most envied urban affiliation was to be by birth a citizen of Rome (Acts 22:25–29).

The city in the Roman Empire was the seat of power and culture, and that power and culture was diffused outward toward Rome. In the urban centers of the Empire reigned the aristocratic minority. From those urban colonial centers the traders and merchants carried on their commerce and communication; for "all roads lead to Rome."[2]

---

1. This brief essay barely sketches this historical background. There is simply too much that we do not know. We present it more as an agenda for research, suggestions that need checking. A more extensive survey can be found in Harvie M. Conn, *The American City and the Evangelical Church: An Historical Overview* (Grand Rapids: Baker, 1994).

2. Stephen Neill, *Colonialism and Christian Missions* (New York: McGraw-Hill, 1966), 19–21.

In this context, it is relatively easy to see why the churches would turn to the cities of the Empire in their gospel work. Paul had "found Christianity a circle, centered on one city, Jerusalem, and left it an ellipse, with two foci, Jerusalem the mother city and Rome the seat of empire."[3] In the years following Paul, the ellipse shrank again to a circle, a circle where the center of Christian influence and urban imperial power coincided.

More and more that seal of the city was stamped on the church as its first three hundred years drew to a close. The Latin word *paganus* became the most used term to describe the unbeliever. The term originally meant rural dweller. Similarly, *heathen* originally pointed to "those whose homes were on the heath."

Can one also sense imbedded in this etymological history the beginnings of a neo-aristocratic, anti-folk sentiment, and with it a changing view of mission? The growing power of the church was finding new models for urban mission in the urbane arguments of Origen and Clement of Alexandria. So attached was the church to the city that people began to conceptually substitute the church for the city as the bearer of culture and the civilizing presence in society. In the course of time, argues David Bosch, that shift seduced Christian theologians to embrace "the typical Hellenistic feelings of superiority, particularly toward the *barbaroi*. . . . Mission became a movement from the superior to the inferior."[4] The city, whether Roman or barbarian, was the stage on which that drama unfolded.

Global Expansion, the City, and the Church

As the years rolled on, the city continued to play a strong role in the expansion of the Christian faith. The fourth-century imprimatur of Constantine not only gave approval to the church, it reinforced the church's growing self-perception as the transmitter of urban socio-political culture. Byzantium, the city poised between the Eastern and Western worlds, in 330 became Constantinople, the New Rome and, the Emperor hoped, the new model of that new urban world order. The earlier pattern of reaching the world by reaching the city was confirmed. Glances at African and Chinese church history illustrate what we mean.

Until the mid-nineteenth century reversed the direction, the progress of Christianity in Africa was outward from the cities to the rural areas.[5] With its anchor in Alexandria, one of the three great sees of the ancient world alongside Rome and Antioch, fourth-century Egyptian Christianity started "as a

3. Michael Green, *Evangelism in the Early Church* (London: Hodder and Stoughton, 1970), 262.

4. David Bosch, *Transforming Mission: Paradigm Shifts in Theology of Mission* (Maryknoll, N.Y.: Orbis, 1991), 193.

5. Jonathan Hildebrandt, "Church Expansion and Africa's Cities," *Urban Mission* 11, no. 1 (1993): 37.

religion of the urban imperial civilization with its Greek language drawn from outside Africa."[6] But it was able to cross the cultural and linguistic gap and appeal to the native Africans.

The churches of North Africa were not as successful. They were started in urban centers (Cyrene, Carthage, and Hippo). But, in contrast to Egypt, their position in the cities was weakened by heresies and splits, so that the gospel never really spread out to the nomadic population.

Thus, when Islam began its sweep through this area, Christianity could not hold on to the cities. By the eleventh century, the church had virtually disappeared from both city and countryside. Its extinction remains "one of the great mysteries of African history."[7]

The pattern of the city as a radiating center for the diffusion of the faith was repeated elsewhere. In Baghdad, a new Christian church grew up from the fifth century onwards. Out-of-favor but adventurous Nestorians spread eastward. Churches appeared in the caravan cities of Central Asia—centripetal points of cultural influence.

Eventually their path reached China. The Nestorian bishop Alopen was received at the Chinese Emperor T'ai Tsung's palace in Ch'ang-an in 635. Ch'ang-an was "possibly the largest city in the world of that day."[8] By the end of the seventh century, the capital had two churches, and at least nine others elsewhere, one in the eastern capital, Loyang. Political shifts, religious persecution, theological concerns, and missiological misjudgments brought an end to the Nestorian Chinese community in 980.[9] And with it came to a close the first encounter of China with Christianity.

The second encounter in the thirteenth and fourteenth centuries came during the Mongol empire of Kublai Khan. And again its entrance came through the city, this time Cambulac (Beijing), the Mongol capital and most splendid city in Asia. At the invitation of the Khan, a church was erected by Franciscans opposite the palace. By 1353 they had a cathedral and several churches and "lived at the Emperor's table." When Mongol power faded, so did the church.

A number of mission patterns emerge from these historical vignettes. Central to them is an understanding that the city is innovator and yeast for social, religious, and cultural change.[10] With a Christian presence in the broker cities, monasteries and monks were freer to become missionary agents

---

6. Adrian Hastings, *The Church in Africa, 1450–1950* (Oxford: Oxford University Press, 1995), 6–7.

7. Elizabeth Isichei, *A History of Christianity in Africa* (Grand Rapids: Eerdmans, 1995), 43.

8. Kenneth Scott Latourette, *A History of Christianity* (New York: Harper and Row, 1955), 324.

9. Samuel H. Moffett, *A History of Christianity in Asia. Volume One: Beginnings to 1500* (San Francisco: Harper San Francisco, 1992), 302–14.

10. S. N. Eisenstadt and A. Shachar, *Society, Culture, and Urbanization* (Newbury Park, Calif.: Sage, 1987), 134–35.

throughout the land, building and wandering with the message of the gospel. In the tenth century, to cite one more example, the Viking king Vladimir could send clergy from their base in Kiev over the countryside. Kiev was "the only city among the semi nomadic, primitive Slavs called the Russ."[11]

This open and even positive attitude toward the city by Christians frequently stirred urban "people movements" to Christ.[12] The Christward political and social trek that swept whole populations of Europe into the church in the early centuries, following their rulers, was also operating in Africa and China.

Nubia's surrender to Monophysite Christianity is such an example. Begun in the northern city of Aksum in the early fourth century, a people movement to Christ swept king and country into the church as the gospel followed other cities southward along the Nile. For centuries it was able to resist Muslim impact. Weakened by lack of teaching and finally overpowered by Muslim conquest, such movements like those in Nubia would finally fade. But their significance for the extending of the gospel, coupled with a prominent city's political favor, could not be denied.

"History in Africa indicates that the religion which controls the urban areas also controls the countryside. For the first eighteen centuries of evangelism and church planting in Africa, the strategy was to go to the urban areas first and then filter the message out to rural areas."[13] That filtering process moved along "people movement" lines.

Early Western Colonialism, City, and Church

From the fifteenth century on, the *Corpus Christianum* followed Portugal and Spain into an exploding world without boundaries. There were still those like the Jesuit Matteo Ricci (1552–1610) who saw access to the Chinese Emperor in Beijing as an indigenous urban door to China.

But more often, this role of the indigenous city as a power center was feared by the Western colonist. In Latin America, Iberian conquistadores ravaged and pillaged urban cultures of the Aztec, Incan, and Mayan peoples that predated their arrival by several thousand years. The cities they erected in turn—places like Cartagena (1533), Guayaquil (1535), Buenos Aires (1536), Santiago (1541), Rio de Janeiro (1567)—became citadels of colonial control and administration. They were points of penetration into the interior, collection points for the wealth and commerce of the rural hinterland.

These new cities became central also in the mission of the Roman Catholic Church that accompanied the conquistadores. "Even the briefest royal

---

11. Basil Matthews, *Forward Through the Ages* (New York: Friendship, 1951), 59–60.

12. Donald McGavran, *The Bridges of God: A Study in the Strategy of Mission* (New York: Friendship, 1955), 36–41.

13. Hildebrandt, "Church Expansion and Africa's Cities," 40.

directive for establishing towns rarely failed to mention the spreading of Catholicism and that God would be better served as the reasons for building towns."[14] The first parish was always the cathedral. It would be erected in an area thickly populated by the Iberian conquerors and therefore automatically recognized by the pope as a city. In those large metropolitan areas such as Mexico City, Lima, and Bogota, the majority of the population, in fact, was Spanish. There, religious priests lived a community life and owned the church income in common.[15]

The earlier model of mission as a movement from superior to inferior was perpetuated in the social isolations of Iberian priests from their parish and the urban elite from Indian and mestizo. The elite were usually to be found in the cities. "In many instances, religious orders including Franciscans, Augustinians, and, predominantly, Jesuits forcibly resettled Indians into towns, ostensibly to achieve the goals of 'Christianizing' and civilizing them."[16] By 1700, for example, there were said to be thirty such "reductions" (as they were called) in a Paraguay that included a good deal of Uruguay, Argentina, and Brazil. The total population of these numbered around 100,000.

Early colonialism in Africa followed many similar patterns. Defeated earlier by itself and by Islam, the church began its second attempt to reach Africa in the fifteenth and sixteenth centuries. As in Latin America, Portugal generally bypassed the ancient kingdoms of the peoples of Dahomey, Yoruba, Ashanti, and Ewe and the West African cities they had erected long before as the core of their power.[17] As in Latin America, no one saw the indigenous connection of these precolonial cities to their hinterlands and their possible role as launching pads for people movements.

In their place, port cities were built around forts erected by the colonists, cities whose life, as in Latin America, was dominated by foreigners. And central to the economy and politics of port cities in East Africa was the major obstacle to the progress of the gospel in Africa—the "black gold" of slavery.

Criss-crossing Africa by several routes, the trade quickly reached epidemic proportions. Following previous Arab examples and supplied by African tribal leaders themselves, the inhuman exploitation used Portuguese cities as ports of embarkation to the Americas. From the regions of Angola and Benguela alone, about 5000 slaves went annually to South America.[18]

---

14. Eisenstadt and Shachar, *Society, Culture, and Urbanization*, 103.

15. Francois Houtart and Emile Pin, *The Church and the Latin American Revolution* (New York: Sheed and Ward, 1965), 20.

16. Gerald M. Greenfield, ed., *Latin American Urbanization* (Westport, Conn.: Greenwood, 1994), xiii.

17. Peter C.W. Gutkind, *Urban Anthropology* (Assen, the Netherlands: Van Gorcum, 1974), 13–18.

18. Neill, *Colonialism and Christian Mission*, 267–84.

"Some priests traded in slaves. The Church in Angola derived much of its income by instructing and baptizing the enslaved, and the end of the slave trade caused a financial crisis for the Luanda see. Exported slaves were branded as proofs of ownership and of baptism. It was a peculiar irony that only Christians could be sold, and that they could be sold only to Christians. . . . Protestants shared this myopia."[19]

Tied to the foreigner in the African mind and thus to slavery, missionary activity left little lasting impressions of a positive sort. "Missionary activity on the part of other European peoples did not exist, and therefore left no impression at all."[20] Eventually the Portuguese turned their attention to the Far East and the church planted along the west and east coasts of Africa withered. Inadequately taught and organized Christian groups in cities such as Loanda and Mozambique found themselves imitating the earlier history of the church in North Africa.[21]

Later Western Colonialism, City, and Church

Toward the end of the eighteenth century, new motivations stirred this major recession of church growth and effected a change in its mission approach to the city. The wars of the Napoleonic era had moderated European interest in overseas ventures and consumed the capital needed for colonial mercantile trade.

With the emergence of the Industrial Revolution, that ennui disappeared. Factories and new technology reshaped the cities of Europe and North America into crowded arenas of poverty and need. A strong anti-urban spirit developed as the cities of the United States[22] and Europe[23] were overwhelmed by expanding population and accelerated change.

Colonialism began to shift and expand as well. As the need for cheap raw materials grew, Europe looked once more to Africa, Asia, and Latin America to meet those demands. Colonialism began to take on a territorial form that extended beyond its past interest in merely trading port toeholds.[24]

With this new thirst for territorial acquisitions came the newcomer Protestant churches, now stirred to mission by the Second Great Awakening. In China and Africa Protestant activities were confined at first to city ports. In the latter continent, except for West Africa, urban centers in the sub-Saharan

19. Isichei, *A History of Christianity in Africa*, 71.
20. Neill, *Colonialism and Christian Mission*, 271.
21. Cecil Northcott, *Christianity in Africa* (Philadelphia: Westminster, 1963), 59.
22. Harvie M. Conn, *The American City and the Evangelical Church* (Grand Rapids: Baker, 1994), 37–53; Morton and Lucia White, *The Intellectual Versus the City* (Oxford: Oxford University Press, 1977).
23. Andrew Lees, *Cities Perceived: Urban Society in European and American Thought, 1820–1940* (New York: Columbia University Press, 1985).
24. David Drakakis-Smith, *The Third World City* (London: Routledge, 1990), 13–17.

part of the continent had been rare and very small. Thus these ports became the early centers of Protestant mission activity.

In China, government concessions to Western threats and aggressive trading treaties had restricted foreign activity to city ports. Before the Tientsin and Peking Treaties of 1858 and 1860, when doors were opened to full movement, Protestant mission personnel found themselves limited to approximately sixteen urban centers.

But cities were not generally a chief part of missionary strategy, whether Protestant or Catholic.[25] The demographic world of the nineteenth century was a rural world. And though undoubtedly motivated to some part by an anti-urban spirit from their homelands, the bulk of missionary personnel wisely saw that rural world as the place for concentration.

Other reasons shifted attention to the hinterlands. In Asian civilizations like China, cities were not so much independent entities as centers of a more controlled bureaucratic system. Because of that, they had great potential for promoting the gospel, a power base that had been used by Ricci and others. But also, depending on the desires of the ruler, proximity to government bureaucracy could obstruct its progress.

The new towns of the emerging colonial world often provided no better prospects. Aylward Shorter comments on Africa, "In some cases, colonial rulers were hostile to Christianity, or at best uncomfortably impartial, favouring Islam, for example, as a counterweight to the Church."[26]

The same could be said elsewhere also. Missionaries could not exist without government approval. But remaining in the cities and working under a hostile government's close scrutiny was not wise.

Following examples like that of the China Inland Mission (founded in 1865) and stirred by the explorations of David Livingstone (1813–1873), the missionary movement turned from the coastal ports to the interior. Before the turn of the century, other boards were created in Africa with a similar focus (e.g., Africa Inland Mission, 1895; Sudan Interior Mission, 1898).

The mission station emerged as an inland alternative to the cities. These out-stations functioned originally as exploratory mission probes for evangelism and church planting. Often in Africa they were located near royal residences that provided them with authorization and protection, the only moderately dense center of population, and the possibility of a royal baptism that might initiate a people movement comparable to that of the Europe of a thousand years before.[27]

Many of the stations became permanent institutions. Churches emerging from them often resembled gathered colonies. Converts found themselves

---

25. Aylward Shorter, *The Church in the African City* (Maryknoll, N.Y.: Orbis, 1991), 58–59.
26. Ibid., 63.
27. Hastings, *The Church in Africa*, 307.

separated from their own cultural roots and people with the stigma of "foreign." And as first generation became second and third generations, the mission station, McGavran believes, became an obstacle to church growth, not an asset. Converts attaching themselves to the stations were isolated from their traditional societies and the human bridges of kinship and connection broke.[28] The mission station approach became the model and the people movements the exception.

In the end, suggest some, the mission station strategy may have been the instrument that "turned great numbers of workers away from the cities."[29] It was originally created as an outpost addition to urban ministry in a time when cities were still small and rural areas still neglected. But increasingly it became a substitute instead of a supplement. When urban growth began to explode in the post-colonial, industrial world following the 1950s, urban ministry was done more by default than by design.

Urban Expansion and Church Responsibilities

As we have passed through the last half of the twentieth century, massive urban growth has shifted into high gear everywhere except North America and Europe. Africa's urban community has jumped from 7 percent at the beginning of the century to 28.9 percent in 1980. By the end of the 1990s, more than 345 million Africans will be living in cities. Asia's urban population will likely hit 40 percent by 2000, a 665 percent growth over 1920. According to UN predictions, world population in cities will reach 51.3 percent by the end of this century.[30]

A unique feature of this growth has been the "mega-city" phenomenon. At the beginning of this century only twenty cities in the world had a population exceeding 1 million. As of 1980, that figure had reached 235, with some 118 located in less economically developed countries. In 1950, only two cities, London and New York, were over 10 million. As of 1980, ten cities had reached that size. By the end of this century, there will be twenty-five. Six of the ten largest cities in the world will be in Asia.

All this places new demands on a global church that has planted its more recent historical roots outside the city. At the heart of these pressures is the growing size of the non-Christian urban population. The growth of urban cities outside of North America and Europe, coupled with nominalism and the erosion of the church in those former centers of Christianity, has created a significant drop in the percentage of urban Christians. In 1900, argues David Barrett, Christians numbered 68.8 percent of urban dwellers. By 2000, that

28. McGavran, *Bridges of God*, 42–67.

29. Hildebrandt, "Church Expansion and Africa's Cities," 44.

30. Harvie M. Conn, "Urban Mission," in James M. Phillips and Robert T. Coote, eds., *Toward the 21st Century in Christian Mission* (Grand Rapids: Eerdmans, 1993), 319–21.

figure will drop to 44.5 percent.[31] By mid–1995 the number of new non-Christian urban dwellers per day reached 140,000, or 1.6 every second.[32]

To meet this new challenge some clarifications may be helpful and older strategies may need sharpening.

First, participants in missiological discussions need to remember that urbanism is not a phenomenon new to the latter half of the twentieth century. Nor is it simply a one-way street for the gospel that always leads to a dead end. The city, no matter what its size or density, has remained a center of human culture from Cain through Kublai Khan to Clinton. As such, it has exercised its role as a religious way of life. And it has continued to exercise that role, either for God or against him, in its work as socio-cultural innovator, stabilizer, integrator, and power broker.[33] Linking the gospel to that mega-city bridge is no more overwhelming—or easier—than when Paul connected with a first-century Corinth of half a million persons. But linking to it has, in fact, often opened the door to larger movements to Christ, as our brief outline has shown. The anti-urban mentality of the last hundred years of mission strategy has not helped us to remember this.

Second, recent evangelical studies have spent much time on urbanization and its demographic focus. Urbanization as a process remains a rich source of reachable new urbanites who help link church planting strategies to the urban community. The essay in this section on immigration by Rebecca Long is an excellent example of how to make use of that process for mission strategy.

The attention of Donald McGavran to winnable homogeneous movements of peoples offers another way to use urbanization for gospel purposes. Refined by useful criticism, recent writing from the Church Growth School speaks less dogmatically of "homogeneous units" and more of people "mosaics." New emphases on the social dimensions of these urban mosaics, such as class, wealth, and power, are also appearing. Buttressed by supporting research in the strength of ethnicity and the complexity of social assimilation patterns, we now see these mosaics as continuing urban bridges. Further investigation and qualification is needed.[34] Cities are "gateway cities" to the peoples of the world.

31. David Barrett, "Annual Statistical Table on Global Missions: 1989," *International Bulletin of Missionary Research* 13, no. 1 (1989): 20–21.

32. David Barrett, "Annual Statistical Table on Global Missions: 1995," *International Bulletin of Missionary Research* 19, no. 1 (1995): 25.

33. Harvie M. Conn, "A Contextual Theology of Mission for the City," in Charles Van Engen, Dean S. Gilliland, and Paul Pierson, eds., *The Good News of the Kingdom: Mission Theology for the Third Millennium* (Maryknoll, N.Y.: Orbis, 1993), 96–104.

34. Donald McGavran, *Understanding Church Growth* (Grand Rapids: Eerdmans, 1970), 278–95; Harvie Conn, "Unreached Peoples and the City," *Urban Mission* 8, no. 5 (1991): 3–5; Roger S. Greenway and Timothy M. Monsma, *Cities: Mission's New Frontier* (Grand Rapids: Baker, 1989), 112–25.

Third, it is time to tackle the tougher questions revolving around urbanism as a place and a process. Current urban studies are moving in that direction. Scientific research outside the Christian community is looking at networking, the nature of community in the city, and the growing significance of human connections that are secondary to kinship ties. We are becoming more sensitive to cities as nodes within society, a context of networks, of interactive cultural and social systems that link neighborhood to neighborhood, neighborhood to city, city to expanding horizons of hinterland and to world developments. "No Towne is an Islande of Itselfe."[35]

Recent evangelical thinking has often seen the gospel as too compartmentalized, too individualistic, to prosecute this growing understanding. But in some innovative strategies this too may be changing.

Mission studies are beginning to search for new clues, to look as closely at socio-cultural context as we have looked at institutional life. David Britt's essay reminds us of the significance of the church's link, its congruence, with the community. Robert Linthicum points our attention to the missiological use of networking that has long been a theme of the urban social scientist.

Fourth, our missiological paradigms have often defined themselves as taking the gospel from superior to inferior, from powerful to powerless. Colonialism and racism, conjoined with the wealth and power of traditional mission bases in the West, have reinforced these urban paradigms.

Such models are being questioned in circles Catholic and Protestant. The impact of liberation theologies, particularly in Catholic interaction with society, is pressing the church to look again at past definitions of evangelism and mission.[36] Among evangelicals, growing concern for the poor is shaping a more inclusive urban mission agenda that will give more attention to the poor.[37] Viv Grigg's essay is a powerful challenge to connect the city and its concentration of the poor with traditional values of evangelism and mission.

The city is reminding us again of our calling to serve the poor. In that ministry we may find that our past triumphalisms of mission are being reshaped into something more like God's upside-down kingdom of grace and justice. The poor have much to teach all of us.

---

35. Roger Sanjek, "Urban Anthropology in the 1980s: A World View," *Annual Review of Anthropology 1990*, 19 (1990): 151–86.

36. Bosch, *Transforming Mission*, 432–47.

37. *Sharing the Good News with the Poor: WEF-TC Consultation on the Evangelization of the Poor* (Seoul: World Evangelical Fellowship Theological Consultation, 1993).

From Homogeneity to Congruence

A Church-Community Model

David Britt

If we in the church do not yet completely understand how urban churches grow, it certainly isn't for lack of trying. We have expended enormous amounts of energy attempting to dispel the mists that obscure our perspective on urban church growth.

Though significant advances have been made, a stubborn fogginess persists. For example, call after call has been sounded to guide us toward the insights of social science, especially anthropology, in the service of mission. Yet we search through reams of purported efforts to do so and find only descriptive accounts of this or that people or homogeneous group. Theoretical modeling that provides real explanation of the social dynamics involved in urban church growth is rare. Even rarer is the empirical testing needed to discern the adequacy of our models.

The task is daunting. How can we hope to understand the social processes that engender or enable church growth in a context as fluid and apparently random as the pluralism of a modern city? Physicists have developed a fractal geometry to analyze the endlessly irregular variations in the flow of water, the movement of clouds, or the structure of a tree. No one has yet developed a fractal social analysis.

This chapter first appeared in *Urban Mission* 8, no. 3 (1991): 27–41. Used by permission.

Several perspectives, however, have been advanced that hold promise for our understanding of urban church growth. The task of this chapter is to point out some promising approaches and to present an empirically tested model which incorporates some of the insights they provide.

Background

Though growth has always been a high priority for the church, much of the emphasis of the modern Church Growth Movement dates from the efforts of Donald McGavran to understand what he observed in the rural Third World mission field. McGavran brought real insight into the social processes leading up to a people movement. His use of the term *homogeneous unit* to describe a "section of society in which all the members have something in common" showed his awareness of the web of relationships that affects our very self-understanding and sense of destiny.

When McGavran's wisdom was focused upon the American city, however, the results were often less than satisfying. The original version of *Understanding Church Growth* contained a brief concession to the possibility that the homogeneous unit becomes problematic in the city. McGavran recommended in 1970 that urban converts forsake their original language and break ties with their old homogeneous unit as prerequisites for baptism.[1] In the 1980 edition of the book, however, he omitted these prerequisites and spoke of the "mosaic" of homogeneous groupings persisting in the city.

In applying McGavran's insights to the urban American context, some writers have sought to maintain the homogeneous unit as an explanatory or even prescriptive concept. In doing so, they found themselves quite unexpectedly embroiled in theological and ethical disputes, accused of ethical insensitivity at best and segregationism at worst.[2] More to the point here is that the intuitive sociological understandings which seemed to serve McGavran well in rural settings no longer worked as easily when they were carried over into the pluralism of a modern American city. Indeed, some American church growth writers have never seemed entirely comfortable with their urban context. Wagner, for example, classified urban population change as the pathological agent leading to "ethnikitis," a congregational disease without a cure,[3] but one he never analyzed through many pages of church growth literature. Students will look in vain for either an adequate appreciation of the social dynamics affecting urban churches or the rigorous testing of a hypothesis.

    1. Donald A. McGavran, *Understanding Church Growth* (Grand Rapids: Eerdmans, 1970), 214–15.
    2. C. Peter Wagner, *Our Kind of People: The Ethical Dimensions of Church Growth in America* (Atlanta: John Knox, 1979).
    3. C. Peter Wagner, *Your Church Can Be Healthy* (Nashville: Abingdon, 1979).

A major contribution did appear in Dean M. Kelley's *Why Conservative Churches Are Growing*.[4] Kelley wrote that strict churches in America grow because they are able to offer meaning in a society where meaning is an increasingly scarce commodity. A spate of journal articles followed the book, lending partial support for its major assertion.[5] Each of these articles reported structured research efforts to explore church growth.

Some of these articles were contained in an anthology entitled *Understanding Church Growth and Decline, 1950–1978*.[6] The editors, Dean Hoge and David A. Roozen, advanced a simple but elegant concept: the division of church growth factors into contextual and institutional categories. National and local factors were added along a second axis to create a four-cell classification table. The contributing writers presented several empirical studies of membership data on local and national levels, and the result was an important contribution to the understanding of church growth in the urban American context.

Defining the Problem

What does homogeneity mean in the city? It may be that the ethical discussion over the homogeneous unit principle as a strategic ploy, as helpful and necessary as this discussion has been, has side-tracked any fuller discussion of the actual dynamics of social grouping in urban contexts. Perhaps part of the problem is that the word "homogeneity" connotes a thoroughgoing social consistency that is strange to urban memories. If we may bracket the question of oughtness for a moment, do I in fact go to church with my own kind of people? Is that possible? I am not entirely sure which kind my own

4. Dean M. Kelley, *Why Conservative Churches Are Growing* (New York: Harper and Row, 1972).

5. Reginald W. Bibby and M. B. Brinkerhoff, "The Circulation of the Saints: A Study of People Who Join Conservative Churches," *Journal for the Scientific Study of Religion* 12 (September 1973): 273–83; Reginald W. Bibby, "Why Conservative Churches Really Are Growing: Kelley Revisited," *Journal for the Scientific Study of Religion* 17 (June 1978): 129–37; Gary Bouma, "The Real Reason One Conservative Church Grew," *Review of Religious Research* 20 (Spring 1979): 127–37; Dean R. Hoge, "Why Are the Churches Declining?" *Theology Today* 36 (April 1979): 92–95; Douglas McGaw, "Commitment and Religious Community: A Comparison of a Charismatic and a Mainline Congregation," *Journal for the Scientific Study of Religion* 18 (1979): 146–63; McGaw, "Meaning and Belonging in a Charismatic Congregation: An Investigation into Sources of Neo-Pentecostal Success," *Review of Religious Research* 21(1980): 284–301; McKinney, "Performance of United Church of Christ Congregations in Massachusetts and in Pennsylvania," in Dean R. Hoge and David A. Roozen, eds., *Understanding Church Growth and Decline, 1950–1978* (New York: Pilgrim, 1979), 224–47; Everett L. Perry and Dean R. Hoge, "Faith Priorities of Pastor and Laity as a Factor in the Growth or Decline of Presbyterian Congregations," *Review of Religious Research* 22 (March 1981): 221–32; Reginald W. Bibby and M. B. Brinkerhoff, "The Circulation of the Saints Revisited," *Journal for the Scientific Study of Religion* 22 (September 1983): 253–62.

6. New York: Pilgrim, 1979.

kind of people would be. In fact, one of my chief blessings and frustrations as an urbanite can be that I am not entirely sure which kind of person I really am; the answer most likely is that I am many kinds of people at once, depending upon the circle with whom I interact at any given moment.

Sociologists of knowledge such as Peter Berger have demonstrated how inevitably our self-understanding relies upon our social context. Growing up in a pluralistic society means never having only a single model for belief, etiquette, politics, musical taste, intellectual pursuit, or family type. City folks are especially prone to harbor different, even conflicting, loyalties and values simultaneously. It seems incredible that anyone would suggest a homogeneous church in a setting which makes even psychological consistency itself a struggle.

Actually, however, as knotty as the question seems, there is evidence to support the idea that churches grow best in settings where their values are shared. Certainly it has been documented that community context affects a church's growth; Hoge and Roozen's 1979 volume contained several studies to document this fact. In one of them, William McKinney found that contextual factors accounted for more than 90 percent of the variance in growth explained in Congregational churches, and 50 percent of the variance in Evangelical and Reformed churches.

In a separate article, C. Kirk Hadaway argued that demography places "adaptive constraints" upon the church; further, he said, these constraints "may be much more important to institutional survival" than the institutional factors of meaning and belonging.[7] Hadaway employed U.S. Census data for the neighborhoods of churches in five denominations in four metropolitan areas. Other information such as church size was also included from other sources. In all, 586 churches were included in his study.

Hadaway, a Southern Baptist researcher, found that population change is positively and strongly correlated to growth. Several contextual variables could be used to predict growth with some reliability. The presence of minorities in a neighborhood did not affect growth, but the displacement of whites by blacks adversely did so in white churches.

Using sophisticated statistical analysis, Hadaway found that six of his explanatory variables together explained 22 percent of the variance in church growth. A previous study of Presbyterian church growth that had used only questionnaire items to assess the community explained 7 percent less variance. Hadaway concluded that contextual variables were a significant influence.

In another article appearing the following year, Hadaway used the typology of churches advanced by Douglas Walrath[8] and found that "for the most

7. C. Kirk Hadaway, "The Demographic Environment and Church Membership Change," *Journal for the Scientific Study of Religion* 20 (March 1981): 77–89.
   8. Douglass A. Walrath, "Social Change and Local Churches: 1951–1975," in Hoge and Roozen, *Understanding Church Growth*, 1979.

part, churches are still locally based organizations, dependent for their membership on the neighborhoods that surround them."[9] Churches in downtown or inner-city neighborhoods were highly unlikely to grow, while those in areas with new housing often fared quite well.

The work of Hadaway and Walrath is important for urban missiologists. It assumes and demonstrates the validity of the homogeneous unit principle as a sociologically descriptive concept. Churches become "structured around the class character, values, and actual residents" of their neighborhoods.[10] This leads inevitably to a lack of "fit" between a church and neighborhood undergoing significant change. Hadaway objected to the homogeneous unit principle on ethical grounds. However, his anticipated norm of a stable church, based on his research, was the embodiment of a single cultural group and its values.

How Many Factors Can You Count?

We are led to ask a basic research question: which kinds of factors tend to form the basis for a church fellowship in urban America in the latter half of the twentieth century? Which variables of interest, to use the sociologist's jargon, are most powerful in explaining the variation in urban church growth? And how many do we have to consider before we can sum up our discussion?

Some of the values used in congregational studies are demographic. *Education* and *income* still provide two of the best handles for distinguishing one type of congregation from another. By way of an example that is only a little bit whimsical, church visitors probably begin to get their first feel for its membership by subconsciously figuring the ratio of pickups to Volvos in the church parking lot. If the ratio is similar to the one they know in other significant parts of their lives, their first impression of the church may incline them to remain.

Other values that seem to form a basis for identification are *ideological*. Wade Clark Roof has suggested that a fundamental value differential in urban life may be the local cosmopolitan continuum.[11] Those who value the life of their immediate community over a more global perspective tend to view a broad range of issues in similar ways, while those whose concern extends far beyond their city limits form a separate pattern of belief. Are localism and cosmopolitanism important stackpoles for congregational identity? If so, might a clear articulation of one or the other lead a church to grow? Kelley's writing about

---

9. C. Kirk Hadaway, "Church Growth (and Decline) in a Southern City," *Review of Religious Research* 23 (June 1982): 372–86.

10. Ibid., 373.

11. Wade Clark Roof, *Community and Commitment* (New York: Elsevier, 1978); Wade Clark Roof, et al., "Factors Producing Growth or Decline in United Presbyterian Congregations," in Hoge and Roozen, *Understanding Church Growth*, 179–97.

"strict" and "intolerant" churches and their penchant for growth also represents a claim for the importance of ideological factors in church growth.

A third group of values with the potential for affecting church growth is *relational*. Claude Fischer, for example, has documented the networking of friendships in urban settings.[12] Fischer argued that friendships in the city do not become less numerous or less important; they simply are no longer tied to geography and tradition as they might have been in a rural locale. Of course, McGavran emphasized family and friendship ties long before Fischer, styling them "bridges of God" in an early book by the same name.[13] Kennon Callahan has written of the importance of "significant relational groups" in effective churches.[14]

Yet another group of factors may have only recently come under consideration. James F. Hopewell wrote about the place of narrative and story in a congregation's *self-perception*.[15] It may be that the particular telling of a congregation's story, with the unpredictable twists of plot that make every church unique, may be well worth studying for its effect on church growth.

The Implicit Model of Church Growth

Still, there is something rather unsatisfying and messy about piling up single church growth factors like so many grains of sand, as though we can bury the problem if we keep at it long enough. Diagramming the process in this manner produces a model that is both unwieldy and overly simplistic.

Much of the discussion about church growth has in fact proceeded from just such a model. Church growth is the dependent variable of interest, while other factors are set up as independent variables that influence church growth. The Church Growth Movement has strongly emphasized institutional factors, such as pastoral leadership style, involvement of the laity, spirituality, and planning. Some mainline researchers have focused more on contextual and demographic factors. Whichever emphasis is adopted, however, the basic theoretical model used is that of Figure 11.

This model, though cluttered, has a decided advantage in any research endeavor: It is simple. It has engendered a great deal of excellent investigation and learning; for example, it provided the basic framework for Hoge and Roozen's work, though they did not diagram it in this way.

---

12. Claude S. Fischer, *To Dwell Among Friends* (Chicago: University of Chicago Press, 1982).

13. Donald A. McGavran, *The Bridges of God* (New York: Friendship, 1955).

14. Kennon L. Callahan, *Twelve Keys to an Effective Church* (New York: Harper and Row, 1983).

15. James F. Hopewell with Barbara G. Wheeler, *Congregation: Stories and Structures* (Philadelphia: Fortress, 1978).

However, it suffers from several problems. First, it fails to account for a coherent relationship between the independent variables. They appear in the discussion as though they act independently of each other; in reality, *independent* variables never are. In fact, some factors have meaning only in relation to each other. A contextual factor of "percent black" may produce one effect upon a minority church but quite another on a majority church. It can be fully understood only in conjunction with the "institutional factor" of congregational ethnicity.

Second, the model in Figure 11 makes no allowance for the impact of social factors upon the makeup of institutional variables themselves. It essentially assumes that a congregation is created *ex nihilo*, apart from any social context, and that the community around it exerts its influence from a separate point of origin. Such is, of course, never the case.

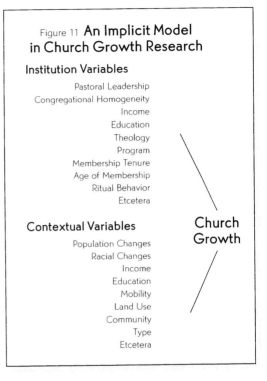

Figure 11 **An Implicit Model in Church Growth Research**

Institution Variables

Pastoral Leadership
Congregational Homogeneity
Income
Education
Theology
Program
Membership Tenure
Age of Membership
Ritual Behavior
Etcetera

Contextual Variables

Population Changes
Racial Changes
Income
Education
Mobility
Land Use
Community
Type
Etcetera

Church Growth

Missiologists commonly speak of ethnic churches, southern churches, or rural churches; what is such talk except an acknowledgment that all congregations build their character and story from a cultural base which precedes them?

A third difficulty is that the model in Figure 11 leaves no clear room for the discussion of personal relationships in church growth. Is the friendship between a church member and a community resident a contextual factor or an institutional factor? Neither category seems to contain such relationships easily, though a friendship between two community residents might be said to be contextual, and a bond between two church members might be considered institutional.

A more refined model for understanding church growth would seem appropriate. Such a model should account for the interrelationship of congregation and community context, and allow study of specific variables of interest as well. It must be at least as capable of generating specific hypotheses for testing as the earlier model has been, but it should also generate hypotheses in areas that the first model has ignored.

Figure 12 contains a church–community congruence model for understanding church growth. Here, church growth remains the dependent variable, or that which we are trying to predict or understand. However, the primary independent (predicting) variable is *the degree of congruence between the values of the institution and those of its context.* Congruence may be measured in many ways. Four have been suggested in this article: *demography, ideology, relationships,* and *narrative.* Demography has been the focus of research to date, probably because data on geographical segments of metropolitan areas are

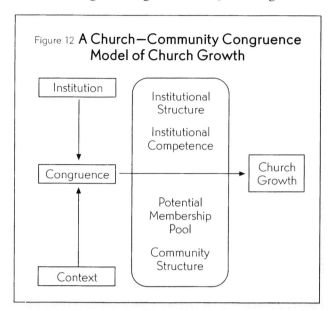

Figure 12 **A Church–Community Congruence Model of Church Growth**

most readily available in the form of census data and market research. Single institutional or contextual characteristics act as constraints on the effect of congruence.

The reader who is familiar with Church Growth literature will notice that the term "homogeneous" does not appear in the second model, and only briefly in the first. It does not figure prominently in Figure 11 because homogeneity within a congregation can be treated as an institutional variable. Indeed, this is the way that McGavran and others have generally employed it. A congregation that is made up of one kind of people will prove attractive; a diverse congregation will embody too many differing cultures to attract new members comfortably. This kind of variable might be quantified with an index showing homogeneity in race, ethnicity, state of origin, or whatever characteristic constitutes a homogeneous grouping for that particular congregation. In any case, homogeneity would be subsumed under institutional variables.

Homogeneity does not appear as a major feature of Figure 12 because the concept of congruence between congregation and community is intended to develop it a step further. Congruence is similar to homogeneity in that congruence also assumes that most of us are attracted to others who share like values. Congruence differs, however, from homogeneity in that it refers not only to a characteristic of the congregation, but to a relationship between the congregation and its community context. My adoption of the term stems from my understanding of social theory, especially that of Berger.[16]

Theoretical Background

Berger writes that the construction of meaning is basic to the human enterprise, and that the lack of stable meaning constitutes an unbearable threat to one's sense of the reliability of the world and one's place within it. To ward off the sense of threat from values that seem precarious and unreliable, people engage in ritual, shared versions of everyday reality in order to reinforce the values and meanings that define who they are.

The presence of different or conflicting values is threatening. They make our own values seem arbitrary and, to use again Berger's word, precarious. Pluralism in urban life, by definition, quickly brings city dwellers into contact with different values and points of view. Though people in the city may assimilate many different or conflicting values, even city folks tend to gather around shared values. No one is immune to the need to maintain and reinforce his or her beliefs; this is best done in groups whose members share their beliefs. That is why church attendance is as important as most pastors intuitively know it to be, and why regular, frequent church attendance is better than sporadic visits. Without the regular, frequent, and social reaffirmation of Christian values that is provided in worship and Sunday school, most of us in the church begin to lose something of the certainty of our religious meaning. Regular church attendance does not guarantee certainty, but it does tend to reinforce our belief.

Churches inevitably celebrate and interpret the symbols of the gospel by attaching to them the cultural symbols of their own members. For example, a wealthy German-American congregation expects a different style of worship than can be found among the faithful in a poor African-American church. The symbols of the gospel are generally the same, though they may be emphasized uniquely by both groups. Many of the differences in worship and the congregations' perceptions of purpose are due to the separate cultures represented.

It may actually be that the idea of preaching the gospel without the contaminating influence of culture is more than just unrealistic. If it were actually possible to strip away all cultural symbols from a congregation, some of the basis for the group's identity and ritual would thereby be removed as well. Whatever values remained would have less symbolic support as the group came together; belief in the midst of a pluralistic context would become even more difficult, not less so.

16. Peter L. Berger, *The Sacred Canopy* (Garden City, N.Y.: Anchor, 1967); Peter L. Berger and Thomas Luckmann, *The Social Construction of Reality* (Garden City, N.Y.: Anchor, 1966).

City folk bring their knowledge of other values with them into worship. If the values they see celebrated in worship are congruent or consistent with those they know elsewhere, the gospel message seems more familiar and acceptable. They are inclined to believe and to return. If, on the other hand, the cultural symbols that accompany the gospel are alien, visitors may not want to return because worship in that place creates a threatening cultural discrepancy for them.

Hence the need to understand congruence: *Where the cultural symbols of a congregation are congruent with those of a local community, the gospel will receive an easier hearing.* Church–community congruence forms the backdrop for church growth or decline.

Adaptive Constraints

The model in Figure 12 lists four other groups of factors which affect church growth. *The ability of the congregation and its leaders* to carry out their normal tasks affect growth, too. However, institutional competence is best seen as a constraining variable, not a primary independent one. In this regard, much of the writing in Church Growth literature is based upon an unfortunate error. One reads often that if the pastor can lead a church in this or that manner, or if the laity can respond in this way, then growth will follow. The basic flaw in this logic is that it takes social congruence between the church and the community for granted. Indeed, many of the examples of fast-growing churches are located in suburbs, usually areas of great homogeneity. For a church in such a situation, the advice offered by church growth experts may prove helpful. For churches in other areas, however, the same advice can lead to frustration.

It simply will not do to pass off these latter cases as failures or exceptions, the unfortunate results of some rare and unpredictable disease. Even less satisfactory is the more frequent tendency at the congregational level to blame the pastor, the staff, or other leaders for the lack of growth.

Of course, there are incompetent pastors and staffs. There are even incompetent congregations. Just as pastors can lapse into defensive, unhealthy behavior that alienates them from their congregations, so too can congregations develop destructive patterns of relationships, or procedures and policies that prevent the adequate expression of the symbols upon which the church was founded. But incompetence is best seen as a constraining factor which filters the effect of congruence upon church growth.

In other words, a skillful pastor in an incongruent church–community situation usually will not be able to achieve numerical growth. By the same token, a less skillful pastor in a highly congruent church may actually find himself or herself presiding over a growing congregation. Perhaps the more skilled pastor might achieve an even higher growth rate. Focusing on institutional competence alone, however, misses a prior and more basic phenomenon: the degree of symbolic congruence between a congregation and its context.

A second set of factors has to do with *institutional structure*. This area has been the focus for some church consultants who have concentrated their attention on removing visible sources of visitors' dissatisfaction. A barely visible church sign, a shabby building, or inadequate parking may make subtle impressions that prevent the fellowship within from getting a fair hearing from potential visitors. Suggestions for physical improvements to the church facility are highly pragmatic and often effective. But again, factors of institutional structure such as these are best seen as institutional constraints on growth rather than primary causes of it. They are worth consideration, but taken alone they cannot provide an adequate understanding.

The last two types of constraints on church growth were contextual in nature. The third is a concept I have chosen to call *the pool of potential members*. It might be thought of as the contextual counterpart of institutional competence: how many members is this community context able to contribute to any church? The pool of potential members includes such factors as population change; a local community losing half of its population due to economic decline will be hard pressed to support several growing churches. True, a congregation might articulate the gospel in a way that is particularly sympathetic with the plight of those remaining in the community. Thus it may attract church members who might otherwise have gone elsewhere. Such a practice often means smaller attendance at the remaining churches, who then must deal with worse leadership shortages than before.

The final group of constraints on growth deals with the *physical structure of the community*. Are the roads to the church facility passable? Will they accommodate increased traffic? Is the facility of the church easily accessible, or is it tucked away in an area traveled only by a few? Probably the most that a congregation can do about these factors is to be aware of them when deciding the location of a new facility or mission.

Testing the Model

The congruence model is offered with two hopes in mind. First, it may help provide conceptual clarity for discussions of church growth. Second, it can generate specific hypotheses which can be tested to determine the model's validity. The model involves factors that can be time-consuming and thus expensive to measure; the testing done so far has been quite limited. I believe that the results achieved so far warrant further exploration, however. If nothing else, the model represents a synthesis of much writing in the field that has yet to be tested in a rigorous manner. Additional testing will help determine the validity not only of the model but of much that passes for common knowledge among practitioners of church growth.

Method

We turn now to a brief account of one effort to test the model in Figure 12. A full reporting of the method and results from this test is beyond the scope of this article; those desiring such information are directed to the source.[17]

In 1985, seventy churches in Jefferson County, Kentucky, agreed to participate in a study designed to test an earlier version of the congruence model. Most (55) were Southern Baptist, fourteen were United Methodist, and one was an independent Church of Christ (more than thirty independent Churches of Christ were invited to participate, but only one of these congregations agreed). Pastors gave names and addresses of active lay leaders in their congregations so that questionnaires could then be mailed to them. In all, 729 out of 1070 persons responded for a response rate of 68 percent.

In addition to the questionnaire, the census tracts containing each congregation were analyzed. On-site visits were conducted so that influences peculiar to each church might be pinpointed. Zoning categories and distance to the central core of the city of Louisville were also recorded.

Two computer data sets were created. The first simply contained the 729 responses of individual church leaders. The second set contained congregational data: the average or median scores for each congregation, a variety of contextual data for each congregation, and the pattern of growth or decline for each. In this way both contextual and institutional factors could be compared to church growth figures. Then a number of congruence estimates for each church and its community were created and added to the data set.

Congruence was measured in different ways. First, the percentage of high school graduates in the church neighborhood (census tract) was compared to that reported by the congregation's leaders. Congruence in family income and ancestry (as defined in the 1980 U.S. Census) was compared to that reported by the congregations' leaders. Congruence in family income and ancestry (as defined in the 1980 U.S. Census) was also measured. Finally, congregational scores on a localism index were compared to the educational levels of the community, based on prior research showing education and localism to be strongly correlated in a negative direction.

Of the seventy churches whose pastors agreed to take part, only sixty-four did so in a way that meaningful conclusions could be drawn. Thus, the second data set contained information pertaining to sixty-four congregations.

Results

Institutional variables that proved to be most related to growth included age of the church leadership (the older the leaders, the less likely the church was

17. David T. Britt, "Local Factors in Urban American Church Growth" (Ph.D. diss., Southern Baptist Theological Seminary, 1985).

to grow), length of membership of the leaders (the longer the leadership had been members, the less likely the church was to grow), and family income (wealthier churches grew more). Doctrinal orthodoxy on such items as belief in a seven-day creation, the virgin birth, and the necessity of Christ for salvation tended to be associated with growth. Growing churches also tended to be more intolerant.

Several institutional variables were interesting for their lack of correlation to growth. Religious rituals such as prayer and Bible reading did not affect growth significantly. Even more intriguing was the total lack of a relationship between church growth and the perception of the pastor's style and competence. Perceived homogeneity within the congregation did not correlate with growth.

As expected, contextual variables affecting growth included population change. Churches also tended to grow more when they were farther away from the city's core.

Churches were more likely to grow in areas with more education and income. At first blush, this is somewhat surprising in that education levels within the congregations' leadership did not affect growth. However, education becomes quite important when we view the "match" or congruence between the educational level of the congregation and that of the community context.

Church–community congruence variables predicted church growth to a significant degree, especially congruence in education and ancestry. In addition, the congruence between localism in the church and education in the community was quite significant in predicting church growth. Of these factors, congruence in ancestry was most strongly related to growth. The theoretical model in Figure 12 thus found support.

Discussion

Perhaps one of the most significant findings of this study was that conservative churches tended to grow, but only when they were congruent with their community contexts. This runs counter to Kelley's argument that conservative groups have grown by being distinctive. The church–community congruence model argues, contrary to Kelley's, that conservative congregations grow best when they articulate the values already present in their cultural contexts. Those values may be different from the values assumed to be dominant in the national culture, but they are community values in a local sense. What a mainline Protestant sees as culturally dissonant may in fact be quite congruent with local culture but insulated from the dominant national culture.

Also significant is the nearly complete lack of correlation between growth and pastoral leadership, at least as perceived by the congregation. These findings argue for a redirection of much church growth dialogue, especially that which focuses on a fairly simplistic attention to pastoral authority and congregational orthodoxy. While pastoral competence is both intuitively and demonstrably related to church growth, the amount of attention it has received in many quarters has probably exceeded that which the data would require. The relationship of the congregation to its community setting, however, needs more understanding by all of us.

No testing has been attempted to determine the effect of two potentially important dimensions of congruence upon church growth, relationships and narrative. The methods necessary for such a study would be significantly different from those used for demographic analysis. To my way of thinking, this constitutes an important omission, but also fertile ground for future research.

Conclusion

> Of course, the entire effort is to put oneself
> Outside the entire range
> Of what are called statistics.
> > (Stephen Spender, quoted by James Gleick in
> > *Chaos*)

Francis DuBose criticized the Church Growth Movement in 1978 for omitting "the transcendent dimension."[18] That critique is, if anything, even more applicable to this chapter (a fact I acknowledge with some trepidation). The model advanced here is an attempt to carry the social study of church growth further, but no mention of transcendence has yet been given.

For the record, I have no quixotic intention of banishing theology from the discussion of church growth or urban mission. But if we are to use sociology or anthropology in the service of the church, we must do so fairly and thoroughly, without retreating to doctrinal truisms just as things begin to get interesting. The ultimate purpose of church growth studies, at least by those of us within the church, is to get beyond statistics and on to the church's mission and purpose.

Rather than view social research with suspicion, we would do better to use it as groundwork for our theological understanding. Social science does a good job of telling us that which is: What is happening in this or that congregation or community? How did this come to pass? Mixing in theological preferences at this point can result in confusion. When faced by the complex social phenomenon of community transition, for example, rather than pressing on to understand its social dynamics thoroughly, we may react prematurely by giving it an emotionally charged label such as "ethnikitis" because

---

18. Francis M. DuBose, *How Churches Grow in an Urban World* (Nashville: Broadman, 1978).

our own particular view of the church's mission becomes problematic in a transitional setting.

Using the congruence model of understanding church growth (and decline), a troubled church in a transitional community might view itself in this way:

"Our congregation began in a particular place and time that are alien to the place and time we now face. Whereas in earlier years we felt comfortable with the church's surroundings and knew them intimately, we now feel strangely out of place. We are frustrated with the increasing drain on our leadership and financial resources. More than that, we grieve over the memory of the vibrant and exciting program of ministry that we once were able to perform.

"Rather than vent our grief unfairly and destructively, however, we choose to recognize the reality before us. Though we enjoyed the ministry of an excellent pastor in the years when our membership grew, we realize that our fit with our community provided us with another luxury of God's overflowing grace: It enabled us to do the work of the kingdom of God without encountering significant cultural obstacles. Rewards were visible then, and things often seemed to fall into place, because of our faith, because of our leadership, most of all because of the leadership and providence of the Spirit of God; but also because of the cultural fit our congregation enjoyed with its community.

"Membership and attendance are lower now and declining, and we confess that at times it is difficult to retain that sense of excitement that the best in our faith can provide. We are tempted to shorten our tempers, scale back our commitment, throw up our hands, and seek a quick solution to the threat we sense for the congregation we have worked so hard to support.

"However, we continue to be stewards of God's mission to the world. We pledge ourselves to continue to carry out that commitment as God leads us. We no longer have the luxury of a cultural fit with our neighborhood, and thus our work has become significantly more difficult. We commit ourselves to carrying out God's mission in this place, realizing that our work now is as important as it ever was, even if tangible rewards are fewer. We call upon the depths of God's grace for strength, for courage, for creative innovation, and for the understanding necessary to carry out the work of the unchanging kingdom in an ever changing world."

I submit that the church–community congruence model is a useful conceptual framework. Testing so far has found support for its major assertions. However, more testing is necessary. Congruences in friendship networks and narrative types especially comprise areas which warrant further study. Certainly, refinements on the methods used here are needed. For example, church communities will rarely coincide with census tract boundaries; a more precise measurement should provide more illumination.

Cities are the fastest growing and most challenging locus of mission today. Urban church growth is increasingly a complicated phenomenon. However, our task is worth all the rigor and care that we can muster. May our energy and commitment be no less applied to our understanding as to our action.

Sorry! The Frontier Moved

Viv Grigg

It was a Marxist city of 10 million. Two and one-half million lived in the *bustees* (slums). Most of the middle-class families are poorer than the street people of Los Angeles. Sixty-six percent live one family per room. And the church? In the bustees there are only two house churches. Some of the middle-class families from the bustees are involved in the fifty-eight middle-class churches. But the poor of the slums, the 500,000 poor in the refugee camps, the 200,000 poor on the streets[1] had never known a poor people's movement or their own churches. No one had ever proclaimed Jesus to them. No holy man had ever lived among them to show them Jesus in word and deed, in acts of mercy and deeds of power.

It was a joy to find such a man. The government had imprisoned him for working with the poor. He clearly couldn't face talking about it. Quietly, he had gone back to the ragged, wretched orphans, widows, and beggars whom he loved and for whom he labored. He was a man who took Jesus' pattern of ministry to the poor seriously.

In my book, *Companion to the Poor,* a theology and praxis was developed for establishing the kingdom in the slums in a Catholic-animistic setting. In the process of preparing teams for other Asian mega-cities, it seemed prudent to discover whether the principles and practice developed in the slums of Manila were equally valid elsewhere, to find out if anyone in Asia has generated a movement of fellowships among the urban poor.

This chapter first appeared in *Urban Mission* 4, no. 4 (1987): 12–25. Used by permission.

1. Figures on numbers of churches are from an extensive survey of the church in the city. Figures on numbers of street people are a conservative estimate between the 1971 government estimate of 48,800 and various estimates of up to 400,000 from more general news articles and researchers. Numbers of bustees and refugees are documented from the Metropolitan Planning Office of this city.

This is a report on two years of walking the slums of the great cities of Asia, looking for God among the poor, seeking to know how effectively the great mission surge of the past decades has established the church in these areas of greatest need.

The sad news is that, after thorough research in eight cities, I found only two embryo movements. The conclusion: The greatest mission surge in history has entirely missed the greatest migration in history, the migration of Third World rural peasants to great mega-cities.

I wanted to find answers to two major questions: (1) Where are the men and women who, like Jesus, choose to live as poor among the poor, establishing and tending newly formed churches day and night? (2) Is the incarnational approach necessary to establish the kingdom among the poor? Is it the wisest approach?

Assumptions

Two assumptions in mission seem self-evident. The first is that Jesus is our model for mission. Did he not say, "As the Father has sent me, even so I send you" (John 20:21)? And did not his first declaration of his own great commission tell us: "The Spirit of the Lord is upon me, because he has anointed me to preach good news to the poor. He has sent me to proclaim release to the captives and recovering of sight to the blind, to set at liberty those who are oppressed, to proclaim the acceptable year of the Lord" (Luke 4:18)?

Did he not with these words model the gospel as primarily good news for the poor? Did he not focus his ministry on the poor, declaring that the ministry to the poor is holistic, involving preaching, healing, deliverance, justice, and doing good deeds, though initiated by proclamation (and reception) of the kingdom?

The second assumption is pragmatic missionary strategizing: (1) Urban is the direction of history. (2) The poor are the most responsive target group, according both to Jesus' teaching and to missions history, research, and sociological analysis.[2] (3) The migrant poor are the largest, most responsive group on earth today. I have found this to be true of Muslims in Karachi, Hindus in Calcutta, Buddhists in Thailand, and Catholics in Manila. All are in a state of rapid socio-economic and worldview change and are hungry for the reality of a relationship with a god.

Jesus commands a focus not so much on the least unreached, and mostly unresponsive, people groups in the world, as on major unreached or partially reached groups that are responsive. The first five years following a person's

---

2. Donald McGavran, *Understanding Church Growth* (Grand Rapids: Eerdmans, 1980), 269–94.

or family's migration is the time of greatest responsiveness to the gospel, for peoples and for individuals. Roger Greenway speaks of his conversion to ministry to the urban poor with the phrase: "If the streets are paved, move on." Jimmy Maroney, speaking of his experiences strategizing for church planting in Nairobi, tells us:

> Finally, a national pastor pointed out to me that they [new migrants] were the most responsive to the gospel. In fact they proved to be more responsive to the gospel in the city than back in their villages. The traditional guardians of custom and culture do not exist in the city. People away from home are "off balance" and willing to listen to what they considered strange back home. I would certainly have spent more time with this group if I had it to do all over again.[3]

How wise the analysis; how sad that last line! If missions deliberately directed their strategies to the poor, there would be no need to "rediscover" the receptivity of the poor every few years.

The Frontier That Moved

The experience of seeing hundreds of thousands of squatters in destitute poverty is devastating. As history moves toward its climax, the wound in God's heart for this migration of people must make it difficult for him to hold back his judgment.

If the destitution of the urban poor is staggering in itself, their numerical growth is just as devastating. Since the Second World War, there has come an endless convoy of buses into the mega-city capitals of the Third World city-states, disgorging impoverished farmers and teenage adverturesses into their next step toward affluence (or more likely, poverty) in the slums, squatter areas, favelas, barrios, and bustees.

Between 1950 and 1980, the urban growth in Third World mega-cities rose from 275 million to just under 1 billion. It is expected to double by the year 2000.[4] Wherever land can be found, the huts and plywood shacks will go up and few governments will have the capacity to prevent it or to service the people arriving. The majority of the new arrivals will remain in the squatter areas. Each capital city will continue to grow exponentially as it exploits the resources of its rural hinterland.

Some of the most destitute live in mud homes on the streets of modern Dakha city, a new city with 3 million people in the 1980s. It will grow to 20 million by the turn of the century. The 730,000 people in the 771 squatter

---

3. Larry Rose and C. Kirk Hadaway, eds., *An Urban World* (Nashville: Broadman, 1984), 117.

4. *Patterns of Rural and Urban Population Growth, Population Studies No. 68* (New York: United Nations, 1980).

areas (1983)[5] will, by the year 2000, make up the majority of the population. There is little possibility for the city's industrial growth to keep pace with the migration influx.

In most cities, industrial growth ranges from 1 to 4 percent annually. The population growth ranges from 12 to 15 percent. Shanty towns (slums, squatter areas) are expected to double in six years.[6] Those unable to enter the industrial life of the city remain trapped in lives of service and patronage, without ever being able to secure their own land or housing. The squatter and slum areas range geographically from 19.6 percent (Bangkok)[7] to 66 percent (Calcutta).[8] For those trapped in continuing poverty, the reproduction rate remains undiminished. About half of the population growth in these cities is due to a high birth rate in the resident population.

Rarely a Pastor; Seldom a Missionary

More nightmarish than the poverty and its staggering growth is the fact that there are no more than a handful of God's people ministering among these poor.

I don't mean that there are no relief and development agencies. They are many, and most are doing good work in their defined diaconal roles. But the church has given the poor bread and kept the bread of life for the middle class. The search has not been for aid programs but for people who are living among the poor to establish the kingdom of God.

Yet in the midst of the darkness there are heroes—in each city a handful of people who have followed Jesus fully in his calls to renunciation and involvement with the poor. One pastor in a west Asian city wears the sandals and blanket of the poor, walking as holy men do. God has used him to mobilize and deploy 300 aid workers into the slums. A doctor ministers on the streets of one city to the sick. The government has tried to deport him for ministering to the poor. For four years he has remained in the country by bringing a court case against the government and quietly continuing.

There is a pastor who for some years has chosen to live among the poor in a relocation area of Manila. He helped build houses for the poorest in his community. The housing manager and gang leaders were curious about this man and his concern for their people. They decided to work with him on the housing. They were converted because he incarnated the love and justice of God among them. There is excitement in Bangkok, where a new generation

5. Center for Urban Studies, *Slums in Dakha City* (Dakha: University of Dakha, 1983).

6. The U.N. predicts 15 percent annual growth in shanty towns worldwide. See *The Aging of the Slums and Uncontrolled Settlements* (New York: United Nations, 1977), 10.

7. Sopon Pornchockchai, *1020 Bangkok Slums: Evidence, Analysis, Critics* (Bangkok: School of Urban Community Research and Actions, 1985).

8. United Nations Center for Housing estimate.

of creative church leaders is seeing breakthroughs for the gospel. There are now ninety-seven churches[9] in this city of nearly 6 million. Hidden in these figures is an old, highly successful, Finnish, Pentecostal church planter. At seventy, he has gone back to spending his days in a slum area, quietly establishing a church.

Nevertheless, in the 1020 slums, there are only two churches and two house groups. That is, 2 percent of the churches are among the migrant poor. For the 600,000 prostitutes[10] in Bangkok there are only two ministries. For the 500,000 drug addicts, the first ministry was initiated by some Malaysians in early 1986. These figures are not given to shame us but to compel us to a new focus.

Examples of men and women who are following Jesus in his ministry to the poor should not be the exception but the rule if we as a church are following Jesus. We must refocus our energies and make the urban poor the primary thrust of missions.

In an otherwise excellent article on the urban poor, Francis M. DuBose makes an unusual series of conclusions: "Like the poor who have long gathered in their urban store fronts in America, the Christian communities are proliferating among the urban poor in the wake of an impressive advance of the gospel and are gathering in 'shop churches' and in 'house churches' in all major areas of the world."[11]

This statement is simply not true. Perhaps it is a misunderstanding of the word "poor." To Americans, all the world is poor, including the middle class of the Third World. Or perhaps he is inaccurate because he is using Latin American Catholic categories for the church among the poor. Perhaps his statement may be true of some African churches. But missionaries from those countries say that, though there is more activity than in Asia, the percentage and focus of activity is about the same.

Is Incarnation Necessary?

Some have said to me, "Don't be too fixed on the idea of incarnation as the key." So I talked and visited with those who had tried various things with the poor: missionaries and pastors, evangelists who would go in and preach, and churches that have aid programs. My conclusions certainly have been modified—but come out essentially the same. Rarely have they been successful beyond establishing one or two families long-term into the middle-class church.

9. Figure from Bill Smith, Church Growth researcher on Bangkok.

10. Figures for prostitutes and drug addicts have been discussed and checked with a number of sources and appear to be conservative and are generally accepted. These numbers reflect government, church leadership, and media estimations.

11. Rose and Hadaway, *An Urban World*, 70.

One significant movement in Asia is generated by a dynamo of a friend in Hong Kong through a ministry to drug addicts.[12] As they are freed from addiction, many who go through the program move back to the poorer areas where their families live. Out of this ministry has come a movement of disciples, many linked in small fellowships. The key? Jackie Pullinger has for years lived among these people in the destitution of the Walled City. She lives much of her time on the streets. After eighteen years she still has no room to call her own.

A life lived among the poor as one of them is the key to a movement. That is part of what Jesus was talking about when he discussed grains of wheat.

In Latin America, statistics are more encouraging than in Asia because of Pentecostal growth. Many Pentecostal pastors have little choice but to work in the slums because of the economic situation. Some years back, Roger Greenway was able to establish significant numbers of slum churches in Mexico City working from outside of the slums and sending workers in.[13]

Musing on this excellent case study, the question arises as to whether it negates the need for emphasis on incarnation. Success in this case came through a strategic focus on the slums from the outside. To refocus mission agencies even to this extent would be a major achievement. Yet even within this approach of training and sending workers into the slums, the churches that took root did so when leaders emerged from within the community. It seemed that incarnational leadership, not the missionaries or the trainees in church planting, was the key to long-term establishment of the church in these city slums also.

In Manila, a YWAM (Youth with a Mission) training school has established another model that runs counter to incarnational theory. They have planted a slum church by sending in, every few months, a new short-term team without much language or cultural orientation. They live in a house just outside of the slum. The work has the expected problems related to a lack of indigeneity but it has been successful. Despite the problems of short-term missions and the cultural lacks, there has been enough identification with the poor for the gospel to take root and bear fruit into a church.

Based on these examples, the question moves from a question of the necessity to a question of the extent of incarnation. Linked to it is one of the major issues facing missions in the next decades: how to develop slum church leadership so that multiplying movements can be developed.

One of the problems involved is that it is rare to find a natural leader in a slum community who can develop a church beyond seventy people. There are several apparent reasons. Lack of management skills within the culture

---

12. Jackie Pullinger, *Chasing the Dragon* (London: Hodder and Stoughton, 1970).
13. Roger S. Greenway, *An Urban Strategy for Latin America* (Grand Rapids: Baker, 1973).

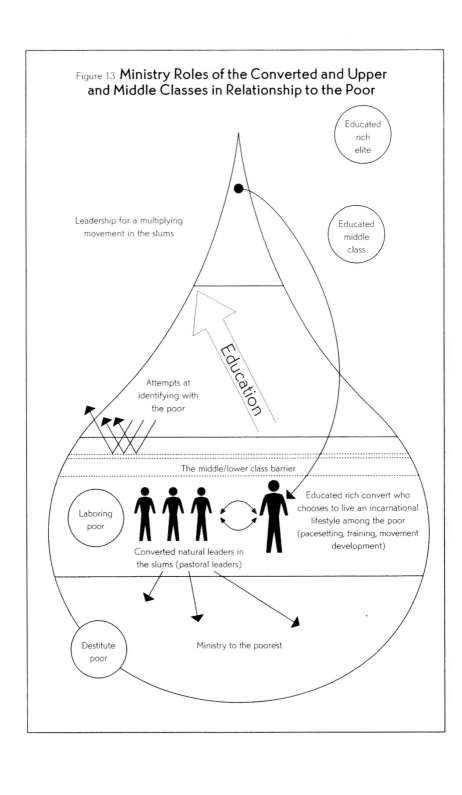

Figure 13 **Ministry Roles of the Converted and Upper and Middle Classes in Relationship to the Poor**

Educated rich elite

Educated middle class

Leadership for a multiplying movement in the slums

Education

Attempts at identifying with the poor

The middle/lower class barrier

Laboring poor

Educated rich convert who chooses to live an incarnational lifestyle among the poor (pacesetting, training, movement development)

Converted natural leaders in the slums (pastoral leaders)

Destitute poor

Ministry to the poorest

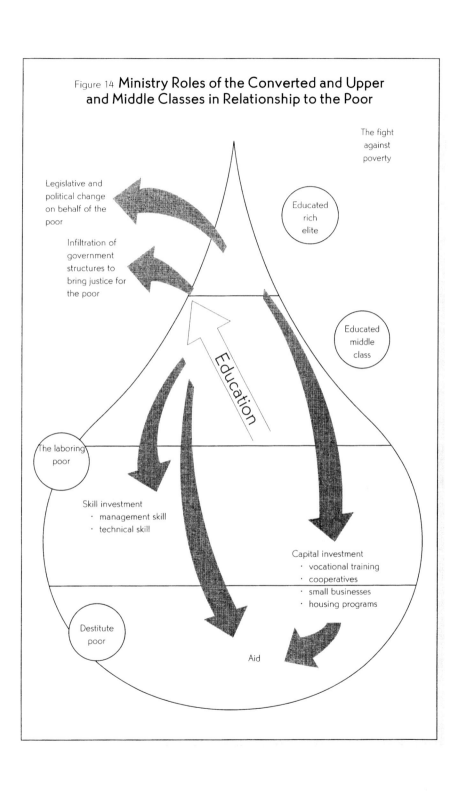

Figure 14 **Ministry Roles of the Converted and Upper and Middle Classes in Relationship to the Poor**

The fight against poverty

Legislative and political change on behalf of the poor

Infiltration of government structures to bring justice for the poor

Educated rich elite

Educated middle class

Education

The laboring poor

Skill investment
· management skill
· technical skill

Capital investment
· vocational training
· cooperatives
· small businesses
· housing programs

Destitute poor

Aid

of poverty is one. For a church to grow beyond seventy requires administrative as well as pastoral skills. The extent of pastoral problems and the inability of the poor to provide financially for full-time pastors limit the use of time for broader ministry. Family dynamics tend to limit churches to three extended families, which then get cut off from their religio-cultural context.

It appears from the available data that the extent of incarnational modeling and pastoral leadership from within the communities determines whether the church will be established. My own conclusion is that there are two levels of leadership that must be given: an educated catalyst, with a broad perspective and managerial skills, leads a score of squatter leaders who function as pastors. That catalyst may be a foreigner or may be one of the converted, educated rich who chooses to renounce all.

The development of Pentecostal and charismatic superchurches for the rich elite in places like Manila, Bangkok, and Kuala Lumpur may provide the opportunity to call the rich to follow Jesus in his renunciation of wealth to minister to the poor. Historically, the leadership of the Catholic orders to the poor has come from the rich elite who have taken Jesus seriously at this point. Unfortunately, present imported Western theology encourages people to keep their wealth, ignoring the gospel teachings on using wealth on behalf of the poor by choosing simple lifestyles, or, for many, renunciation of wealth.

Middle-class leadership is useful in initiating a work, and as a backup in areas of economic development, legal and medical help, or political issues. But it is threatening to a middle-class family to have one of its sons choose the lifestyle of poverty among the poor which seems necessary to establish churches. These families are valiantly struggling to stay out of the poverty from which they have come. Thus it appears unwise to invest large amounts of time seeking to develop leadership for squatter churches from this class. Only the leadership that lives in the community can effectively develop the church.

As such, it is unwise to presume that student movements will be the key to the task ahead of us. They may provide some backup, and certainly, if they are trained in a poor-focused, holistic theology, may significantly affect government structures toward justice for the poor. But they should not be the focus of our time and energy if we are to reach the poor (perhaps with the exception of recruiting, while at university, the scions of the rich, elite families into incarnational approaches).

Biblically, we must encourage all people, at whatever level of society they are working, to have a focus of ministry to the poor. We must call all people at all levels of society to lifestyles of simplicity so that others may simply live. We must call all to the patterns of renunciation we see in Jesus' teaching. This does not imply that all should live among the poor. But we must also hold out to our people the further call of Jesus to take up an apostolic lifestyle of identification with the poor in order that the poor people's church might be established.

Is incarnation essential? For church planting, the leadership of the church in the slums must be incarnate in the community. The missionary, in order to train others in such pastoral work, must set the patterns of identification and model the incarnational lifestyle.

On the other hand, as development work in the slums has been observed, incarnation does not appear to be essential. However, even development work is greatly advanced by people who work with people from their own perspective rather than work for them. And if developmental work is to be done from a kingdom perspective where the goal is more than projects, incarnation appears necessary.

In Thailand, I spent time with some Buddhist community organizers who have captured from a Christian this concept of living among the poor in order to serve them. They are paying a price for enabling the people. Why do the Christians pay a lesser price? Incarnation is more effective. It gives the poor a greater sense of dignity. It is more just. It is more loving. But no, it is not essential for development workers.

The Great Misconnection

When faced with the sad failure of the great mission thrust to reach these poor, one must ask, "Why?" and, beyond the why, "What can be done to rectify the failure?" The following appear to be some factors:

First, as mission leaders, we have failed to foresee both the urban growth and the fact that most of the urban growth will be in squatter areas. The opportunity to save the cities from many traumas associated with this development, the opportunity to establish a church in every squatter area as it has formed, has been lost almost entirely. As Tom Sine says, we have in our long-range planning unconsciously assumed a static view of the future.[14]

People are being thrust out to the last frontier, but the last frontier has moved. Perhaps we could encourage the U.S. Center for World Mission to revise their charts of unreached peoples. Instead of dividing them by religious groupings alone, perhaps they should also be divided into urban/rural and rich/poor. We may find that the largest grouping for truly "unmissionaried" people is the urban poor.

Second, some missions have made a deliberate strategy to go for the rich, believing in a sort of religious "trickle-down" theory. "Trickle-down" no more works in the kingdom than it does in the economic realm. This strategic mistake lacks both biblical exegesis and sociological analysis and has already been refuted.

The gospel "trickles up." Any man or woman who would follow Jesus to walk among the poor will affect countless among the middle and rich classes. They come because they are curious. They hear of good deeds and, like

14. Tom Sine, *The Mustard Seed Conspiracy* (Waco: Word, 1981), 17.

Nicodemus, they know that this is reality. The converted rich come because, despite the failure of affluent missionaries to preach the Scriptures about repentance for unjust wealth or to live simply themselves, these new believers can read the Bible. They come searching for the person who has chosen the poor because here they know is a true answer to their problems of wealth. They come because they are concerned now for the uplift of those they have previously exploited. Jesus has an answer for the rich man. The rich middle-class missionary often has only words.

Third, for the same strategic reasons America failed in the Vietnam War, the church has failed in this spiritual war. Depending on affluent and high-powered programmatic approaches, the mission force has been out of touch with the realities of the Third World poor. A missionary living on $2800 a month in an American-style house, sending his children to an American-style school, trying to reach people who live on $200 a year, is like a B–52 bomber attacking guerrillas.

Fourth, this failure in the great American mission thrust is, at its roots, not a strategic but a spiritual failure. An American church trapped by cultural perspectives on affluence rather than biblical opposition to the American "god of mammon" has exported this into missions. We must return to the pattern of Jesus, who chose non-destitute poverty as a way of life, who took the time to learn language and culture and who refused to be the welfare agency king. We must return to the way of the apostles and of the wandering friars who have been the key to the conversion of the world in generations before us. Non-destitute poverty and simplicity must again become focal in missions strategy.

Fifth, some have concluded that the poor are unreachable. This is a culturally logical conclusion for those of European descent who grew up in the capitalism of the United States. David Claerbaut, in an excellent analysis of urban ministry, has some penetrating insights into American cultural attitudes about the poor:

> The truths of stratification and self-perpetuation of the socioeconomic system are not widely known or accepted. As a result, negative attitudes towards the poor persist. To argue that poverty is a self-perpetuating condition in a capitalistic society is to attack the nation's sacred civil doctrine of the self-made person. To suggest that one is poor because of an unequal distribution of opportunities is to suggest that riches are as much a matter of good fortune as virtue.[15]

However, the poverty of the Third World urban poor is a direct result of social forces and oppression, not personal sin. Such oppressed poor in the

15. David Claerbaut, *Urban Ministry* (Grand Rapids: Zondervan, 1983), 69–70.

Scriptures are considered to be rich in faith and the ones for whom the kingdom is particularly to be preached.[16]

Sixth, the propensity for the American church to accept the agenda of the aid organizations as focal to the Great Commission has seriously skewed mission. Mission to the middle class is seen as proclamation. To the poor it has become giving handouts or assisting in development as defined by Christianized humanitarian perspectives. It is far easier for churches to give thousands of dollars than to find one of their members who would walk into the slums for a decade.

A Proposal: Protestant Orders with Vows of Non-Destitute Poverty

My convictions have deepened and changed during these months of research, wandering, and preaching to the poor.

The central conviction remains: We must thrust out groups similar to the Catholic devotional communities of preaching friars. In our case, we must send communities of men and women, marrieds and singles, with commitments to live poor among the poor in order to preach the kingdom and establish the church in these great slum areas. Westerners and upper-class nationals who choose such lives of non-destitute poverty will be catalysts for movements of lay leaders among the poor in each city. The spearhead of such a thrust will be those who accept the gift of singleness for some years. We must set up new mission structures. The key is older couples who will choose to be recycled into this kind of ministry lifestyle and can give leadership to these communities of pioneers.

Orders

We need men and women who will commit themselves to lives of simplicity, poverty, devotion, community, and sacrifice in areas of marriage and family. We need orders that free men and women for pioneering, apostolic, prophetic, church planting, and mobile roles, rather than an order that limits people to a rigid structure.

Devotional Communities

Most mission teams are not communities, but teams. The focus of most teams is to work. On the other hand, traditional communities in the church are, by definition, primarily committed to relational caring, worship, and a devotional pattern. These emphases are essential if workers are to survive in the slums. Working and living two by two in various slum areas, they need to come together every two weeks for a day of ministry to each other, of worship and relaxation.

16. Viv Grigg, *Companion to the Poor* (Sydney: Albatross, 1984), 47–50.

Poverty, Chastity, Obedience

The needed commitments to non-destitute poverty are similar to the older Catholic orders, without the legalism. So too are the commitments to singleness, not as vows of celibacy, but for periods of time. As Protestants, we have lost the concept of the gift of singleness. Marriage has been seen as the only ideal. The biblical blessing on chosen or given singleness has to be recovered. Part of the blessing of that gift is the freedom to pioneer in difficult and dangerous places.

New Structures

Historically, movements among the poor have consistently been thrown out of the middle-class churches. It is traumatic for one missionary living on $2800 per month to be in the same mission team with one who is willing to receive only the $300 for his own living expenses and all his ministry and travel costs. To avoid such traumas, it would be wise for mission agencies to create orders of men and women called to the poor. These could be within or without their old mission boards. Ultimately, this will enhance effectiveness and prevent disharmony.

However, these orders should only be under the authority of persons who have lived, for long periods, this kind of sacrificial and incarnational lifestyle. They should never give authority to administrators who have not lived out this lifestyle. Incarnational workers do not want protection. They want pastoral care from leaders who have been on the front line and who will keep them at the front line and take the bullets out when the workers are shot up.

Later-life Vocation

May God touch the heart of some older, experienced couples with these cries of the poor. May he raise up couples who are willing to take on a harder missionary task than they have faced in the past. Then perhaps we may redeem ourselves from failure.

An Opportunity Lost?

God is offering the opportunity to American missions to return to the biblical commitment to the poor and to incarnation as the primary missionary role model. The need is urgent for several thousand catalysts in the slums of scores of Third World cities who can generate movements in each city. Two billion people cry out!

If the American mission leaders, boards, and pastors do not heed this call, God will sidestep them and turn to the emerging Latin American and Third World missions to meet this focus of mission in the next decades. How sad to miss the focal call of the Scriptures to preach the gospel to the poor! For the God who sent his Son to a manger will find a way to send other sons and daughters to those poor for whom he particularly came. He will not leave their cries unheard.

Some Large Mega-Cities in the Third World

City	Total Estimated Population by Year 2000 (Millions)	Percentage Living in Slum/Squatter Communities in 1980
Mexico City	31.6	46
São Paulo, Brazil	26.0	
Calcutta, India	19.7	67
Rio de Janeiro, Brazil	19.4	30
Shanghai, China	19.2	
Bombay, India	19.1	45
Beijing, China	19.1	
Seoul, South Korea	18.7	29
Jakarta, Indonesia	16.9	26
Cairo, Egypt	16.4	
Karachi, Pakistan	15.9	23
Buenos Aires, Argentina	14.0	
Delhi, India	13.2	36
Manila, Philippines	12.7	35
Lima, Peru	12.1	40
Bangkok-Thonburi, Thailand	11.0	18
Baghdad, Iraq	10.9	29
Madras, India	10.4	25
Bogota, Colombia	9.5	60
Kinshasa, Zaire	9.1	60
Istanbul, Turkey	8.3	40
Caracas, Venezuela	6.0	42

Networking
Hope for the Church in the City

Robert C. Linthicum

Networking—it has become a popular term lately, a technique newly discovered for city ministry. But networking has actually been around a long time. "Why, we Africans have been networking for thousands of years," one African Christian said to me. "It is just that we didn't know that's what you call it."

I would concur with that observation. I first heard the word about six years ago. But I've been doing networking since 1955, when I began my first urban ministry among children and teens in a black Chicago housing project. If you are successfully doing urban ministry, the likelihood is that you, too, have been doing a great deal of networking—whether you call it that or not.

What is networking? The term itself comes from the world of business, and it simply means the creation or maintenance of a "net" of contacts, through which one more effectively carries out an enterprise. That net can be a human net or a corporate net or an electronic net (as in the internet telecommunication computer system). But whatever sort of net it might be, it is only as effective as are the net's contacts in their ability to carry out a given activity.

Urban Christian networking builds and maintains contacts which will enable those in that network to more effectively carry out ministry to the ex-

This chapter first appeared in *Urban Mission* 4, no. 3 (1987): 30–51. Used by permission.

ploited, the lost, and the unchurched. Superficially, networking is simply a strategy by which people get in touch and maintain contact with each other. In a way, forming urban networks creates an identifiable "community" in which to work.

But networking is far more profound than that. If built upon biblical foundations, it will enable the urban church to reorder and prioritize its life and mission so that it will be able to effectively join with the poor and exploited of its city in their liberation. By so joining in common cause, the church will gain the credibility to proclaim the gospel to those who formerly despised it.

Underlying the biblical concept of networking is the essential assumption that all human beings, however uneducated, exploited, and beaten down by life, have a greater capacity to understand and act upon their own situation than has the most highly informed or sympathetic outsider. Every human being, no matter how deprived, is created in the image of God and is no less innately capable of determining his or her future than the most highly educated and self-determined individual.

To understand urban networking at its most effective, therefore, we must begin with its biblical foundations.

The Biblical Framework of Networking

"The kingdom of heaven is like a dragnet cast into the sea that brings in a haul of all kinds. When it is full, the fishermen haul it ashore then, sitting down, they collect the good ones in a basket and throw away those that are no use" (Matt. 13:47–48).[1] Through the image of a fisherman's net, Jesus described the kingdom of God. All are gathered in to eventually be brought before God, where judgment will occur.

Biblical Networkers

One way to approach the biblical framework for networking is to examine the lives of key biblical leaders. Invariably, a pivotal ingredient in the practice of their vocation was their capacity to network. Two examples will illustrate.

Moses, the Hebrew Egyptian Desert-dweller

As he met with God at the burning bush (Exod. 3:1–4:17), Moses was a person most carefully prepared by God for the task awaiting him. "Who am I to go to Pharaoh and bring the sons of Israel out of Egypt?" Moses incredulously asked God (Exod. 3:11). But God knew why he had chosen this apparently forgotten shepherd on the backside of the desert. As the son of a Hebrew slave, Moses had been miraculously delivered from Egyptian infan-

---

1. All Scripture quotations in this chapter are from the Jerusalem Bible.

ticide (Exod. 1:8–2:7) and had been subsequently taught in the ways of Abraham, Isaac, and Jacob (Exod. 1:8–10). His commitment to the Jews and to their liberation was so great that he would later risk his own life and career in order to rescue an Israelite in distress (Exod. 2:11–15). It could truly be said of Moses that he was a Hebrew of the Hebrews.

But Moses was also an Egyptian of the Egyptians. "When the child grew up," Exodus 2:10 tells us, "[his Hebrew mother] brought him to Pharaoh's daughter who treated him like a son; she named him Moses because, she said, 'I drew him out of the water.'" Moses was, according to Josephus, considered a prince of Egypt, a member of the royal family. The treasures of Egypt and its political influence as the world's most powerful nation were all available to him (Heb. 11:24–26). Tradition has it that Moses was one of Egypt's most competent generals, and he successfully led a campaign against the Ethiopians. This was a man who understood the Egyptians—how they thought, their priorities, how they organized themselves. Even as a shepherd on the backside of the desert, he had access to the pharaoh, whom he could later confront and declare, "Let my people go!" And once the Israelites had been let go, Moses would have the Egyptian education to organize this great host for a march across the desert.

Finally, Moses was a man of the desert. For forty years he had lived in the desert, herded sheep and made a livelihood on it, married and raised a family there. As well, he had entered into the family of Jethro, the priest of Midian who had taught him more about the Israelite God than he had known or experienced in captivity (Exod. 2:16–22; 18:1–12). Jethro taught him to survive in the desert and later helped him to organize and administer the vast company of freed slaves from Egypt (Exod. 18:13–27). From his desert associates, Moses was spiritually taught and strengthened so that he was prepared to lead his people through the forty years of wilderness wanderings.

Once Moses met God at the burning bush and received his vocation for the remainder of his life, it is intriguing to note how Moses used the network he had built over the years. Aaron, his brother and a Levite leader of the slaves, provided him credibility and entree to the Hebrew people. He used his contacts in Egypt to do what no other Israelite could do—enter the pharaoh's presence at will. Moses used Joshua and Caleb as lieutenants to organize the people. And he used his father-in-law to train Israel's leaders in desert survival. Without the network Moses had built unknowingly over the years, and without his continuing ability to network during his confrontation of Pharaoh and to lead the people during their forty years in the desert, Israel's exodus from Egypt could never have happened.

Paul, the Roman Pharisee

A second example of remarkable networking is found in St. Paul. Like Moses, Paul was a man magnificently prepared by God for the vocation to which God had called him. He was a man who thoroughly understood and was totally devoted to the Jewish faith and nation. In his own words, he testified, "I was born of the race of Israel and of the tribe of Benjamin, a Hebrew born of Hebrew parents, and I was circumcised when I was eight days old. As for the Law, I was a Pharisee; as for working for religion, I was persecutor of the Church; as far as the Law can make you perfect, I was faultless" (Phil. 3:5–6).

But, at the same time, Paul was a man who understood and appreciated the Gentiles. Born and raised in the Gentile city of Tarsus, Paul was a Roman citizen—a political lever he would use often for the sake of the church and his vocation. He understood the Greek culture, Roman law, Gentile society, and pagan religions; he therefore knew profoundly the people to whom he had been called to minister. No wonder Paul could write, "I made myself a Jew to the Jews, to win the Jews. . . . To those who have no Law [the Gentiles], I was free of the Law myself . . . to win those who have no [Jewish] Law. For the weak I made myself weak. I made myself all things to all men in order to save some at any cost" (1 Cor. 9:20–22).

When Paul was converted to Christ, God sent Ananias to him with these words: "You must go, . . . because this man is my chosen instrument to bring my name before pagans and pagan kings and before the people of Israel" (Acts 9:15). This was exactly what Paul did. For the remainder of his life, Paul became a tireless evangelist, spreading the gospel not only throughout Judah but primarily into the Gentile world. Paul's three successful missionary journeys into the pagan Roman Empire transformed Christianity from a Jewish sect into a worldwide faith for Jew and Gentile alike. A primary tool Paul used to accomplish this task was networking.

Consider Paul's missionary methods, which can be gleaned rather easily from Luke's careful record in Acts. When he entered into a city, Paul did not enter alone but rather brought with him lieutenants who were trained both to evangelize and to build a community of believers. His first visit in each city would be to the local synagogue where he would proclaim the gospel; normally, he met with scorn and rejection, but there were always a few Jews who listened and responded to his message. Paul would then go to a gathering place of the Gentiles in that city (the site of which would likely have been identified by his team). He would proclaim the gospel to the Gentiles, and, most often, would again be met with scorn and rejection. But, again, the few would listen and respond.

Gathering those responsive Jews and Gentiles, Paul and his lieutenants would withdraw from public ministry to begin the intensive discipling of these new Christians. The new believers would learn about the Christian faith and how to develop and maintain a church (which, incidentally, was modeled upon the Jewish synagogue). As Paul and his team would work with these new converts, he would particularly encourage the Christian community to call forth each other's gifts, that each might contribute to the building of that local body of Christ (1 Cor. 12:1–14:40; Eph. 4:7, 11–13). Out of that process, the leaders of the church would be chosen, and they would receive the intense attention of Paul and his team.

Finally, it would be time for Paul and his team to leave the fledgling church. But the foundation had been built for the church to develop and grow strong. And even though the church had to make its own way in their pagan city, it was not alone, for it continued in contact with the church in Jerusalem and sister churches throughout the region. Paul and his disciples maintained a continuing written dialogue with each church and often returned for visits.

Networking as a Biblical Principle

Perhaps the clearest statement about networking is given by Paul himself in Ephesians 4:1–16.

"I, the prisoner of the Lord, implore you therefore to live a life worthy of your vocation" (Eph. 4:1). Paul begins this critical passage on networking with the insight that each Christian has been called by God to serve him and humanity in a particular way. That is our vocation. Paul instructs us to live our lives in conformity to our vocation. It is our vocation that shapes how we are free and how we are constrained to live. Our lives are to be a consistent display of our vocation, so that our lives don't defame but rather support the work to which God calls us.

But our vocation can be practiced only within the community of faith. Therefore, in verses 2–6, Paul presents the way life is to be lived together in the church. We are to charitably tolerate one another, to deal gently and patiently and even selflessly with each other. The Christian is to have, as a primary objective, to do everything in his or her power to preserve the unity of the church given by the Holy Spirit (v. 3), and that unity is to be preserved by cultivating the peace that binds us together. That unity is to be built upon the recognition that oneness centers, not in our liking of each other, common nationality or background, or theological oneness. Rather, that unity is built on the recognition that we bear common devotion to "one Lord, one faith, one baptism, one God who is Father of all, over all, through all and within all" (v. 6).

"Each one of us, however, has been given his own share of grace, given as Christ allotted it" (v. 7). Each member of the church is to actively work to maintain the peace and unity of the church, Paul teaches. Each of us is, at the same time, to recognize and call forth the vocations to which each person in the church has been called by God. Consequently, it is critical to recognize that each of us is "graced" or gifted by God to practice that vocation to which we have been called.

With this setting of the stage, Paul is now able to move to the heart of his teaching on networking. It is found in Ephesians 4:11–16:

> And to some, his gift was that they should be apostles; to some, prophets; to some, evangelists; to some, pastors and teachers; so that the saints together make a unity in the work of service, building up the body of Christ. In this way we are all to come to unity in our faith and in our knowledge of the Son of God, until we become the perfect Man, fully mature with the fullness of Christ himself.
>
> Then we shall not be children any longer, or tossed one way and another and carried along by every wind of doctrine, at the mercy of all the tricks men play and their cleverness in practicing deceit. If we live by the truth and in love, we shall grow in all ways into Christ, who is the head by whom the whole body is fitted and joined together, every joint adding its own strength, for each separate part to work according to its function. So the body grows until it has built itself up, in love.

The person whose gift is to be an *apostle* is one who, in the proclamation of the gospel, exercises authority over the church (bishop, elder, deacon). The *prophet*, in the proclamation of the Word, calls the church to accountability for its life and ministry. The *evangelist*, in proclaiming the good news, calls listeners to receive and accept Jesus Christ. The *pastor* shepherds and nurtures the people of God and takes part in proclamation. The *teacher* instructs the Christian community in the faith, building in them the knowledge by which they can effectively live their Christian lives.

Exercising authority in governance, calling to accountability, introducing people to Jesus Christ, shepherding and nurturing the people of God, and teaching the faith are all ministries needed in the life of a church. The critical point, however, is that these "pastoral" gifts are exercised in the church as preparatory gifts. These gifts exist to prepare the other members of the church to undertake their respective vocations and to perceive their respective gifts. These are not the only gifts of the church, nor are they the most critical. The most critical gifts are to be exercised by all the members, gifts that sustain the church, maintain its peace and unity, and reach out to the world in compassionate service and in proclamation of the gospel.

What happens in a church which assumes that every member is called and gifted by God to a vocation of service in the world? Paul asks. What if the clergy of that church practice the vocation of preparing its members to exercise their vocations of service, rather than be the sole ministers themselves? Then, Paul states, the congregation exhibits: (1) comprehensive doctrinal understanding; (2) spiritual sophistication capable of discerning theological deceit; (3) a tremendously effective Christian network. Properly prepared and sustained Christians, Paul tells us, become a spiritual body governed by Christ as its head, with each person both doing ministry and encouraging the ministry of others.

In such a scenario, the church becomes a giant Christian network, capable of communicating the gospel effectively to the lost, able to minister in transforming ways to the poor and exploited and to the rich and exploiters, and practicing an authentic life together in the Spirit. By so practicing both the preparatory and sustaining vocations, the church creates the conditions in which the practice of the church's unity and peace becomes inevitable. And the church will grow and build itself up in love—not by concentrating upon growing or by making itself a loving fellowship, but as each person discovers vocation, doing a unique work of ministry both in the church and to the world, and supporting brother and sister Christians as each undertakes their respective vocations.

This is networking at its best.

Networking with One's Peers

The essential sin of the city church is parochialism. Churches and pastors often become so absorbed in the maintenance of that congregation's internal ministry and its institutional existence that they lose perspective on the life of the city around them. Even evangelism can easily degenerate from the sharing of the gospel into new member recruitment, perceived as necessary to sustain the membership and the income of the congregation.

The typical city church is caught in a survival mentality. As such, it often has a difficult time perceiving how God is at work in that city, particularly through groups different in focus, purpose, or theology. Worse, the parochialism of the typical city church prevents it from confronting the depth of evil in that city.

Paul was careful to instruct his churches not to underestimate the power of evil in their cities. He wrote, "It is not against human enemies that we have to struggle, but against the Sovereignties and the Powers who originate the darkness in this world, the spiritual army of evil in the heavens" (Eph. 6:12).

I find that the church seems consistently to underestimate the enemy. C. S. Lewis observed that the way Satan has his way is to either get people to ignore him or to make light of him. The liberal Christian community most often ignores the Prince of Darkness, believing that good community organizing or education or enlightenment will somehow transform their cities. The evangelical Christian community often makes light of Satan. Fixated upon their own congregations and their consignment of evil to the individual, they don't perceive the extent of the power of Satan or of his principalities. Consequently, they really don't appreciate how the Prince of Darkness possesses the structural powers of the cities and uses those powers for corporate and even systemic political, economic, and social evil.

To be effective Christians in the city, I believe that we must free ourselves from the constraints of our own institutions, for those constraints are them-

selves demonic. We must become deeply concerned about our neighborhood, our larger community, and our city. In those settings of human habi-
tation, God is already at work—and calling us to join him in the ministry. But
also in those settings, the powers of darkness are at work, seeking to control
all the city's individuals and every political, economic, educational, judicial,
social, cultural, and ecclesiastical structure for their own ends. This is the
transcendent urban battlefield to which God calls every Christian and every
church.

How can the church, pastors and people, overcome insularity and parochialism, and begin to respond to God's call to minister to the city? Our response needs to begin with networking.

When I am asked for advice by a pastor who is about to begin an urban
ministry, I respond,

"For the first year of your pastorate, commit 20 percent of each week to
preaching, sermon preparation, and research, 20 percent of your time to getting to know the members of your congregation, 20 percent of your week to
the administrative and maintenance functions of your church, 20 percent of
your week to teaching your congregation about vocation and mission and preparing yourself to teach, and 20 percent of each week out in your community.
Make sure your church officers concur (or at least acquiesce) with this division
of time—especially the one day a week spent in the neighborhood. And above
everything else, begin no new programs!"

I am suggesting a concentration upon the unique preparatory ministry of
a pastor (preaching and teaching) and upon building a community and congregation network—a network among the pastor's peers.

In both these functions, the pastor is modeling New Testament ministry
to the congregation. By concentrating on preaching and teaching, the pastor
is modeling to the congregation the scriptural limitations of the ministry
while introducing the congregation to the potential in their ministries. By
committing time each week to community networking, the pastor sets an example for the congregation of commitment to that neighborhood. Essential
to effective urban ministry must be a willingness on the part of the congregation and pastor alike for the pastor to be involved in community ministry;
one must not ask the congregation to do what the pastor is not willing to do.
On that personal commitment the credibility of the church and the pastor
will stand.

How does a person network among peers in an urban community? First,
define the geographical parameters of the "parish" area of the congregation.
It is best to let the congregation define those parameters. Then, begin visiting
in that area. Obviously, the pastor can do this visiting one-on-one, but it is
more effective to include the congregation in the building of this network. To
have teams of parishioners call with the pastor, or in their respective teams,

opens the congregation to an awareness of their community and a desire to serve it, an awareness which all the biblical study or sermons in the world can never give.

In building these networks with one's peers, it is critically important to keep a right attitude. One must approach the task with the recognition that God is already at work in this community, and your task as a networker is to discover how he is at work. As one wise community resident put it to me when I was an inexperienced and excitable young pastor, "Son, God was at work here before you arrived; he will be working here in spite of you while you are here; and he will even survive after you've left." So one approaches networking with an expectant and open attitude, ready to learn from the accumulated experience and wisdom of both the Christians and the pagans of that neighborhood.

Perhaps the best place to begin is with other pastors. When I arrived in my Chicago parish eighteen years ago, I visited the Protestant, evangelical, and Roman Catholic pastors and Jewish rabbis in our community. I went to each, asking them to share with me what they had learned from their years of ministering in that community and how they had seen that neighborhood change from a relatively wealthy to an impoverished community. I was received everywhere with open arms. And out of those original contacts grew an informal network of pastors who began addressing that community's problems in creative ways.

Four years later that network had grown into an ecclesiastical tax-exempt corporation—a cooperative body of twelve evangelical, Protestant, and Roman Catholic churches, one Christian social service agency, a seminary, and one Christian university. Together we undertook joint ministry of community and parish education, conducted a community-wide Festival of Faith, coordinated efforts with the local community organizations, sponsored a vocational and career guidance service for youth, and had programs for the elderly. These were all ministries far beyond the capabilities of any one of our congregations to develop.

Begin then with the pastors; visit every one of them. Then call on the pivotal people in your community who provide the human and social services (education, health care, and vocational training). Follow those visits by next calling on those who make the political decisions of your community. Include among these leaders both those elected by the people and those who organize the elections and operate the party machinery—the unelected political organizers who often exert more political power than those who are elected. Then call on the shop-keepers and business people in the community—those who earn their livelihood by servicing the residents of that neighborhood.

With all these people, ask the same questions. Find out how the community has changed over the years, the people's greatest needs, and the greatest joys and frustrations of living or working or ministering or serving in this community. At the same time, take the opportunity to tell who you are, a little of your background, and your interest and commitments to this neighborhood. They will not forget you, and you will have uncovered the critical people who can get specific jobs done, who can be a resource to you, and with whom you will need to build relationships.

The final group of people with whom you should visit in the community (and the ones on which you will spend the most time) ought to be residents—particularly the "old-timers" who hold in their memory an extended history of the community. Again, your questions need to be similar to those you asked of others, but particularly how it feels to live in that neighborhood right now.

Of particular importance to ask of the residents are these questions: "If you had a problem getting a service of the city that is rightfully yours, to whom would you go for help?" and "If you had a real crisis at two o'clock in the morning, to whom would you turn in your neighborhood—outside of your family?" If these questions are asked of enough people, certain names will begin to emerge repeatedly. The repeated names given in response to the first question will reveal the implementors or "gatekeepers" of the community (the can-do people). The repeated names given in response to the second question will give you the compassionate "caretakers" of the community. These are the pivotal people you and your church leaders will need to know, those with whom you will need to build strong and trusting relationships, who will be the people most critical to the redevelopment of that neighborhood.

While meeting all these people in your community, gather and maintain accurate records. Create a standard form for your visits and/or the team visits. Be sure to fill out a form on each person you visit and catalogue those forms for later retrieval. Develop, as well, a system for indexing these forms for easy access by you and your church later on. One important point—don't fill out the form while interviewing a person. Rather, develop the ability to retain the information in your memory, and then fill out the form promptly after you leave.

How much time should one give to building these initial networks among peers? If you are doing this as an individual, I would commit one day a week (20 percent of your time) for at least one full year. If a group of people from your church is sharing in this task, I would commit one day/evening a week for three to six months (depending on the size of the group and the immensity of the task). This may seem like an inordinate amount of time, but nothing can later replace the importance of this investment in building the critical contacts with the people of your community. Along with building your congregational network, it will be the most valuable investment of your time in your ministry at that church.

The importance of networking with one's peers is seen in the recent development of the Madras (India) Committee on Urban Evangelism. The Christian church in southern India is a vital body, but it is also a splintered one. The church of South India combines the former Episcopal, Methodist, Presbyterian, and Congregational denominations. The Roman Catholic Church is strong and active there. Chief among smaller denominations is the Evangelical Church of India; there are, as well, many Baptist, Lutheran, Pentecostal, and charismatic fellowships, as well as a number of indigenous churches which do not trace their origins outside India. Many of these churches are strongly evangelistic and some are involved in creative ministries of social justice. Yet, like so many in the body of Christ in cities throughout the world, these churches tend to exist independently and even be essentially unaware of each other.

In July of 1984, Raymond Bakke, professor then at Northern Baptist Theological Seminary of Chicago and an expert on urban ministry, held an Urban Consultation in Madras on behalf of the Lausanne Committee for World Evangelization. At this consultation, pastors and para-church leaders of Madras "discovered" each other. With their decision to keep in touch, these pastors were taking the first steps toward creating an urban network. After the consultation, these pastors and Christian leaders formed themselves into the Madras Committee on Urban Evangelism (MCUE).

The MCUE met regularly under the leadership of Sam Thanaseelan, an executive in Madras Youth For Christ. Out of these meetings, a second consultation was held on March 8–9, 1986, with 120 Christian workers and leaders from Madras city. Specific groups were identified as being critical to reach with the gospel.

At a third consultation on July 23–27, 1986, the Madras Committee on Urban Evangelism developed specific plans for reaching out to the railway porters in Madras city, a particularly needy and ignored group. Representatives of the committee went to the railway stations, met with porters and did specific data gathering. From that research, a wide spectrum of problems were catalogued, and goals were set in literacy training, schooling, insurance protection, counseling, and evangelism. A five-step strategy for a project that would last through December of 1987 was developed, needed resources for this ministry were determined, and the means for raising those financial and volunteer resources among the churches of Madras was set.

As one participant in this planning and networking process put it, "While working on a strategy to reach the railway porters, I realized how much we need to and can do to uplift this neglected community, not only spiritually but also socially and economically. Hitherto, I was thinking only of their spiritual welfare." This is the power of networking—for it not only provides new ways of developing ministry, but it expands the minds and spirits of those involved, as they interact and learn from each other.

Networking with the Poor

Networking with one's peers is only a preliminary step to a more important act of networking: networking with the poor and exploited and with the rich and powerful. The goal is to bring them together in community-transforming and life-transforming ministry.

Underlying networking with the poor is the biblical concept of the dignity of the individual and the consequent necessity for each person to be free to assume responsibility for the future. A number of Scriptures speak to this concern (e.g., Ps. 127; Isa. 66; Acts 14–15; Titus 1:5), but perhaps the clearest is Isaiah 61:1–4, the passage used by Jesus Christ to introduce his own ministry (Luke 4:14–21). In the verses not quoted by Jesus, Isaiah says of those who had been deprived, oppressed, and cast down:

> They are to be called "terebinths of integrity,"
> planted by Yahweh to glorify him.
> They will rebuild the ancient ruins,
> they will raise what has long lain waste,
> they will restore the ruined cities,
> all that has lain waste for ages past.
>
> (Isa. 61:3b–4)

In this passage, the defeated and cast down of the city will become the rebuilders of that city; their healing will enable them to assume responsibility for their city's future. It is significant that, in this passage, neither God nor the prophet will assume responsibility for the city. Only its people can assume responsibility for dealing with their own condition.

But what will enable them to be freed of their attitude of defeat, which prevents them from assuming responsibility? It is the ministry and presence of the prophet. And what does the prophet do to free these oppressed people and to enable them to take charge of their situation?

According to Isaiah:

> The spirit of the Lord Yahweh has been given to me,
> for Yahweh has anointed me.
> He has sent me to bring good news to the poor,
> to bind up hearts that are broken,
> to proclaim liberty to captives,
> freedom to those in prison,
> to proclaim a year of favour from Yahweh.
>
> (Isa. 61:1–2a)

First the prophet and later the Messiah speak and act in ways that liberate people. He ministers to their deepest felt need, their immediate pain ("to bind up hearts that are broken"), and he presents a message that is good news to them in their poverty. He shows them that they can be freed from that which spiritually and psychologically imprisons them.

And what is that good news? He "proclaims the year of Jubilee." The message of Jubilee—that the social order will be changed so that economic and political equality is accorded to all—is presented, not as an ephemeral, pious hope, but as a specific political, economic, and religious reality for the reordering of a nation's and city's priorities, which enables people to stand on their feet and do something about their own situation.

Networking That Liberates

It is upon such a biblical perspective that these insights of networking with the poor are based. Operating out of this perspective, networking then becomes the means to enable an oppressed, exploited, or alienated people to discover each other and to mobilize successfully. Three conditions must exist in order for the networking described below to work. First, circumstances in that urban neighborhood or community must be seriously injuring the quality of life there. Second, the people who are living in that community feel helpless to do anything about those circumstances. Third, concerned Christians have done peer networking in that community.

Out of the "peer networking" described above, a few committed Christians gather together and decide that this neighborhood condition can no longer be tolerated. These few determined individuals gather the community residents identified as the neighborhood gatekeepers and caretakers, together with other people perceived in the peer networking as being pivotal to that community's future. Frankly, I would recommend that no elected or self-appointed political leader or strong economic leader in the community be included in that gathering. Such people tend to seek to control the group and to use it for their own purposes.

The group of committed Christians, the natural leaders of the resident poor, and other local concerned people begin meeting together. They spend time exploring the circumstances that are injurious, especially to the poor and those who lack access to the political and economic power systems. The exploration examines the forces which have created, maintain, and/or benefit from these conditions. Possible ways to confront the issues are explored. With that exploration will come the inevitable realization that individually those meeting can do very little about the issues, but that together they can make a profound difference. When that realization occurs, the group passes a critical point. The people have begun to own the problem and their strategy to deal with it. And the primary network has been born.

It is critical in this early stage of networking that this fledgling group get used to winning. An essential problem for the poor and exploited is that they have lost at the hands of the system all their lives. Therefore, victory is imperative in order to gain a sense of success and to communicate to the poor residents that, together, they can win. Consequently, the group should select initial actions that cannot fail. At the same time, these projects should be ones for which the network assumes full responsibility.

The network succeeds at its first projects. With the confidence born of success, they should then move on to address more difficult substantive issues. As they examine those issues, they may realize that they can't successfully address those issues alone. They may identify people and groups from the larger community or throughout the city who can be of strategic help. They call these people together and form a secondary network.

The primary network now begins to address more critical issues of the community, using people and groups from the slowly developing secondary network to help achieve goals. As the primary network continues its community organizing, it tackles progressively difficult and substantive issues, for it can now afford occasionally to lose. With each new project, the primary network adds people and groups to the secondary network, taking care that power is not transferred to those new people, but remains with the primary network. People added to the secondary network should, in due time, include the political and economic leaders. They should be added where they can make a contribution, but where it would be difficult for them to take control. They may need to receive an excessive amount of public recognition for their participation, which, from my perspective, is a price worth paying for their support.

As increasingly influential and powerful people and groups are added to the secondary network, those exploited people of the poor community discover that almost all the resources they need—people-power, money, expertise—are available within that city network. But the people and groups of that larger network help only when asked. The rich and the powerful of the city (and even of the neighborhood) participate at the behest of the primary network (i.e., the church, the poor, and the exploited), because it is imperative that the poor be responsible for their own situation.

One might ask why the rich and powerful of a city would cooperate with the poor? For some, it might improve their image in the city, garner more public support for their companies or more votes for their candidacies. It might assuage their guilt or deflect criticism. For others, there can be deep pride for and strong commitment to their city. If they can see that support for specific actions of the poor and the church will bring about observable neighborhood improvement, they will support that action with their time and money. Many middle-class and upper-class people feel a genuine concern about the plight of the poor. If practical and concrete means can address that concern, they will do so.

Among Christians and the church, an essential commitment to justice for the poor and oppressed can be tapped. It has been my experience that most church groups do not lack commitment to justice; they need practical ways to express and act on that commitment. A critical task of the primary network—and especially of the Christians and churches in the network—is to perceive and communicate the motivation that will influence each person or group it contacts.

One example of networking involved me as a pastor of a suburban church. This network, called "People In Faith United" (PIFU),[2] was built by the churches and people of one of Detroit's most deteriorated neighborhoods.

In 1981, a group of clergy and community leaders in this Detroit slum began to gather to talk about its future. Over fifteen years, this neighborhood had received various rehabilitation projects, but all of these efforts had left a devastated neighborhood of decaying, rat-infested homes, deteriorating businesses, untenable apartment buildings, and whole blocks of the community razed.

Out of those meetings in 1981 and 1982, a primary network was born. The network decided to initially tackle an issue which could be addressed with some certainty of success—the isolation of the community's senior citizens. PIFU was formed as a legal entity, and the first program was birthed— a senior citizens luncheon program. It was staffed and funded entirely by the people and churches of that neighborhood.

In 1982, I was invited to introduce PIFU to suburban churches as a secondary network, and my suburban congregation joined. We were ready now, as a network, to tackle more intensive problems—the needs for emergency help and for youth programming. An emergency food pantry and counseling center was developed in cooperation with the Episcopal diocese. A youth ministry was begun in cooperation with the Presbytery of Detroit, which provided the first opportunity for members of suburban churches to join with community people and network churches in working with youth in this neighborhood. A Lutheran church began a soup kitchen. Two major suburban churches joined the PIFU network.

By 1983, the people were ready to tackle the major issues—housing and unemployment. We opened a job placement service, which in its first year of service placed more than 120 community residents. We formed a housing corporation, and my congregation, recognizing the potential of the housing ministry of PIFU, granted me a four-month leave of absence so that I might become its full-time interim housing director.

We created an initial housing and community reformulation plan, purchased our first houses, and began to build another network. This informal network consisted of pivotal people and organizations in Detroit—large

2. The description of the ministry of People In Faith United is taken from the article "How You Can Make A Difference," by Robert Linthicum, published in *Concern* magazine (September 1986).

businesses, major Detroit fiduciary institutions, a national housing network, and all strategic governmental agencies. Access to many of these Detroit leaders came through the contacts of the three major suburban churches now participating in PIFU. With the assistance of this auxiliary network, PIFU employed permanent housing staff, and actual housing development began.

Projects and Networking

A critical part of the networking process is the introduction of projects by the network. It is imperative that projects not be introduced too soon, nor by outside groups.

The natural tendency of churches, foundations, government agencies, and other institutions is to identify or define a community problem and then create a project or a program to meet that need. There is no strategy more designed for failure in the city than this approach. Such a project, while it may be successful as long as the sponsoring agency continues to invest money and human resources in it, will not endure because it is not a project created, maintained, or supported by the people whom it serves. Projects introduced from the outside are artificially maintained by outside financial and material support and will continue only as long as that external support continues.

Projects endure by being introduced at the right time by the right people. In a networking model of urban ministry, the neighborhood or the community network must first be carefully and quietly built, churches must be pulled behind the emerging organization, and leadership must be developed. Sometimes this occurs quickly (as in the PIFU example), and sometimes it is agonizingly slow. But nothing substitutes for a carefully constructed and nurtured foundation, built upon the people who are assuming the decision-making authority for the projects which will profoundly establish their own future.

Earlier I mentioned that when a network of the poor develops its first projects, it is critical that it "win." The way that projects are organized is critical. The initial projects in particular need to be small-scale, with their resources (even if hidden) coming from within the community and the community's churches. "Don't get into a project unless you can succeed" is the essential creed at this stage of organizing. For this must be the people's project done without outside aid and done successfully.

Once the network has become used to winning, it is then possible to move to more substantive projects which require the expertise, staff, and/or funding of organizations outside that immediate community. But even in those projects, the outside organization enters at the behest of the community network and under the network's direction. The outside organization is a "guest" in the organizing of that community and must act like a guest. Inevitably the network's confidence and capability to handle increasingly larger projects will grow. With that growth the involvement of the funding and support organizations can also grow. But it is imperative that the network not permit the outside organizations to become policy-setters.

Networking and Evangelism

Perhaps a word needs to be said about the relationship between evangelism and networking. When the church builds networks between the poor and people of power which result in the observable improvement of the life of the poor, the gospel gains a credibility all the preaching by the church cannot provide. When self-confidence and self-respect of the poor are raised by networking to solve their own problems, the gospel gains a new hearing. It is a hearing based upon the respect the church has shown the poor. They are not objects to be ministered to, but people capable of taking charge of their own lives.

An example of this principle is the credibility that the churches in the PIFU neighborhood have gained as they have sought to be a liberating influence in that Detroit community. The growing commitment of the community to the gospel represented by the PIFU churches was expressed several months ago when the young priest of the local Roman Catholic Church died of cancer; the people of the neighborhood—Roman Catholic, Protestant, and pagan alike—packed that massive church as a sign of solidarity with that man who had so compassionately incarnated the gospel in his life and work in that neighborhood. It is in that kind of a context that the good news of Christ's redeeming love can be naturally and lovingly shared, because it is built upon the credibility of the Christian lives and the sacrificial work of the churches practiced there.

Thus have I always experienced it. A gospel which has won respect both by identifying with the poor and enabling the poor to take charge of their own problems is a gospel heard and received!

"We Can't Save the City, But . . ."

Fifty years ago, four of the five largest cities in the world were cities of the Western world—New York, London, Paris, and Berlin. Today, four of the five largest cities are in the Third World—Tokyo, Mexico City, Shanghai, and São Paulo. These Third World cities are growing at a phenomenal speed. Fifty years ago, the world's largest city was 8 million. Today the largest city— Tokyo—is 22 million. Sometime during the next twenty-five years, four cities—Mexico City, Shanghai, Beijing, and São Paulo—will approach 30 million apiece.[3]

---

3. David Barrett, *World-Class Cities and World Evangelization* (Birmingham, Ala.: New Hope, 1986), 48–49.

The dilemma of the rapidly expanding cities of Asia, Africa, and Latin America was well expressed by Rafael Salas, executive director of the United Nations Fund for Population Activity: "In about nineteen years, the world will undergo a momentous change: for the first time in recorded history a majority of the world's people will live in cities—cities of enormous size, plagued by unemployment, overcrowding and disease, where basic services such as power, water, sanitation or refuse disposal will be strained to the breaking point."[4] In a report to the United Nations, Salas stated that many Third World cities are "cardboard structures supporting an empty process incapable of self-sustaining industrialization. . . . [There,] the poorest have worse health problems than their country cousins. They suffer more from malnutrition and live in poorer housing in worse locations, which increase the risk of disease and reduce the chances of recovery."[5]

Whether in the slowly decaying cities of North America, Europe, and Russia or in the burgeoning, overburdened cities of Asia, Africa, and Latin America, the church can make a difference. It is critical that the church approach its urban mission—both its strategy and its practice—with a sober awareness of the overwhelming predicament of the mammoth cities of today. No strategy guarantees that, in some magical way, Christianity will be able to transform the sin, darkness, and injustice of the city. Such evil will resist all attempts to exorcise it. But there is a different way to do city ministry—a way that will place ownership of ministry in the local church, that will allow the projects of the poor to emerge from the poor, and that will enable evangelism and community action to lie in the hands of the churched who live among those poor and lost. It is, therefore, a particularly biblical strategy, for it affirms that God is already active in the city and calls his church to play a servant role there among his poor and lost ones. Following this strategy, the church can make a difference as it lives out some ancient Chinese wisdom:

> Go to the people,
> Live among them.
> Learn from them.
> Start with what they know.
> Build on what they have.
> But of the best of leaders,
> When their task is accomplished,
> Their work is done,
> The people all remark
> "We have done it ourselves."

4. Rafael M. Salas, "Meeting the Challenge of Urban Explosion," *Indian Express* (April 5, 1986).

5. Rafael M. Salas, "1986 State of World Population Report" (United Nations Fund for Population Activity).

Rural Roots and Urban Evangelism

Rebecca Long

Harvie Conn reminds urban workers of the strong links that exist between the rural and urban areas of Third World countries.[1] He argues, first, that numerous churches have been established in urban areas by migrant groups who were Christians in their rural place of origin, and second, that urban Christians have returned to rural homelands to expand evangelism there. This pattern of returning to evangelize suggests an appropriate rural/urban strategy for missionaries. One might spend the first term on the field in a rural area known for its heavy migration patterns to the city and then move to the city, building on the relationships established in the rural area.

Though not by design, my co-worker and I have participated in this phenomenon and have come to see that, while leaving the rural area at first looked like a hindrance to our work, it has proved an asset.

This chapter recaps our ministry history and examines the interrelationship of our rural ministry to a later urban experience. We found that rural contacts were not only useful but essential to our urban ministry, and that without them, our efforts would have encountered insuperable barriers. This chapter will examine our relationships to people in the city, trace the rural origins of those relationships, and investigate the linkages noted by Conn.

This chapter first appeared in *Urban Mission* 8, no. 5 (1991): 25–34. Used by permission.

1. Harvie M. Conn, *A Clarified Vision for Urban Mission: Dispelling the Urban Stereotypes* (Grand Rapids: Zondervan, 1987), 48–50.

Background

In 1974 we began living in the rural Mexican village of Pueblito[2] in order to translate the Scriptures into the Zapotec language under the auspices of the Summer Institute of Linguistics. Because of my co-worker's translation work in a nearby town where a church has been established, the people have always associated us with "the evangelicals." By their definition this is a sect that opposes their religion and has the potential to undermine the existing community structure in which their folk Catholicism is a significant institution. When we began living in their town, the majority of people were guarded in their interaction with us, perceiving us as a threat to their faith. It took us years to build a few relationships of trust.

Our intention was to remain in that area until we finished the translation and accompanying activities, but in 1985, due to a problem with our visas, we had to leave Mexico. Providentially, nearly one-third of the Zapotecs from Pueblito (about 400 out of approximately 1300) had migrated to Los Angeles, California, in search of work. Before we left the rural area we asked our Pueblito friends for names and addresses of their relatives living in Los Angeles so that we could look them up.

We found that the majority of the Pueblito people lived within a few miles of downtown Los Angeles. It was not difficult to locate a number of others once we made the initial contacts. The friendships we had made in Pueblito enabled us to establish relationships and showed us that people did indeed maintain strong ties with their home community. However, finding people and reaching them with the gospel are two different things. Furthermore, though we could speak the Zapotec language, which broke down some of the barriers of our "outsider" status for many very positive initial contacts, identification through language alone was an insufficient basis for continuing and deepening relationships. Some people were open, but others were not, and we struggled to understand why.

Research Plan

As a field worker in linguistics, I soon realized that getting a firm grasp of a language required more than listening to, recording, and reproducing the speech I heard around me. Although many an individual has learned to speak a second language well without linguistic analysis, the production of literacy materials and the translation of such difficult material as Scripture demands an understanding of the rules behind the spoken language. However, I did not realize the importance of the study of social factors. My urban experience led me to discover that, just as thoughtful analysis of the features

---

2. Pueblito (Spanish for small town) is a fictitious name for a small, rural Zapotec town located in the mountains of Oaxaca, Mexico.

of the spoken word yields insights into the target language of translation, so analysis of social features can yield invaluable insights into the target culture.

In an attempt to answer the question of why we had good relationships with some individuals and not with others, I decided to examine the relationships we had with Zapotecs. First, I made a list of all the unbelievers from Pueblito with whom we had repeated contacts in Los Angeles. We have some Christian friends as well, but since our interest was in reaching unbelievers I limited the list to that group. I came up with fifty adults from Pueblito and three from nearby towns related by marriage. I did not include children because access to children is only through adults.

Next, I sorted the list into three groups: (1) those open to us and to the gospel; (2) those open to us and not to the gospel; and (3) those closed to the gospel and to us because of our association with it.

I then examined our relationship to each individual on the list in terms of how we met them. This netted six categories: (a) those we had frequent contacts with in Pueblito before they moved to Los Angeles; (b) those whose close relatives we had frequent contact with in Pueblito; (c) those we met through a friend or relative who also lives in Los Angeles; (d) those we met once or twice in Pueblito before they came to Los Angeles; (e) those whose close relatives we had occasional contact with in Pueblito; and (f) those we met by making a first-time contact from a list of names we solicited from our friends.

Data Analysis

Table 7 shows how openness to the gospel in this target group related to the basis on which our contacts were established. I have concluded from the data that in this set of relationships, a long-standing history with an individual or close ties to the individual's social network significantly increase that person's openness to the gospel.

All of our relationships with those open to the gospel were established either through extensive contact with those individuals themselves in the rural setting, or through our relationship to a relative or friend in either the rural or urban setting. Over two-thirds of the people who were at least open to friendship were established in these ways.

The remaining people who were open to friendship but not the gospel were those with whom we had one or two contacts in the rural setting before they came to Los Angeles or whose close relatives we had met occasionally. About 80 percent of the people who were closed to friendship and to the gospel were met for the first time in Los Angeles without reference to their personal social networks. The most dramatic contrast is between that group, at the lower right-hand corner of the table, and those in the upper left-hand corner.

Table 7

Correlating Degree of Openness with Type of Personal Contact

Degree of Openness

Basis of personal contact in Los Angeles	Group I Open to friendship and to gospel	Group II Open to friendship but not to gospel	Group III Closed to gospel and to us because of our association with it
(a) Frequent contacts before the person came to Los Angeles	6 (3 also b)	2 (2 also b)	
(b) Frequent contacts with close relatives in Pueblito	6 (2 also c)	5 (2 also c; 1 also d)	
(c) Met through a friend or relative in Los Angeles	6	11	2 (1 also d, e)
(d) Met the person once or twice before he or she came to Los Angeles		3 (2 also e)	1
(e) Occasional contact with close relatives in Pueblito		4	1
(f) Met through other Zapotecs in Los Angeles without personal ties			17
Total by Group*	14	18	19

*The total of the numbers in the table exceeds the total number of people by group because some individuals are counted in more than one place—those with whom we had multiple social ties. For example, the six people in box b under Group I are all people with whose relatives we had frequent contacts in Pueblito. However, we also had frequent personal contacts with three of them; we met two others in this group through a friend or relative in Los Angeles.

Category c (relationship through others in Los Angeles) is the only one which includes people from all three classifications of "openness." In examining that list of individuals, I find that in many cases, though not all, the depth of our relationship with the friend or relative through whom the contact was made could be a factor in their response.

What the table does not show is how an outsider establishes these relationships. In reviewing the list of people open to us and to the gospel, I found that in every case the relationships with the person or with relatives were based on purposeful contacts that were both natural and useful to the individual. Four people in this group are close relatives of families from whom we rented houses during our stay in Pueblito. Two of these people and two others were relatives of language helpers who worked with us extensively. Another was a woman we met each week in the market. She sold cold drinks, and we sold books and tapes nearby. Another became our friend during her late husband's illness, as we visited their home to encourage him and offer what help we could.

It was this socially relevant interaction that enabled us to maintain a continuing relationship that could be deepened and then extended to others. Likewise, in the Los Angeles setting we have found that, in order to have a basis for repeated visits, there needs to be a mutually understood purpose that makes the visit a normal form of social intercourse. Among our best friends are two families we offered to tutor in English. Since giving instruction in English was the purpose of our visits, interaction was natural and comfortable. These families have also been happy to accept a brief Bible study with the English lessons. Perhaps this approach could be used with less open people to establish a bridge for communicating the gospel.

Zapotec Social Organization

An explanation for the difficulty in reaching Zapotecs with the gospel is found in the basic social organization of the Pueblito Zapotecs. The importance of social ties and the instrumental nature of interpersonal relationships are basic to the system.

Social Ties and Social Control

Pueblito is a rather tightly controlled, face-to-face corporate community where individuals establish multiple ties.[3] Social networks formed through kinship and pseudo-kinship ties of the compadrazco system make up the fabric of society. Relationships are rarely limited to two individuals, but extend in some way to the individual's social network. The sense of corporate community looms large. The will of the community mandates conformity in its members; individual identity is defined by the corporate group, and the individual is subordinate to the group.

Extensive migration and a strong belief in education as a means for economic advancement have made them a more open community than they might otherwise be. This does not, however, mean that the corporate community is open to the outsider. Rather, it is open to whatever the outside has to offer that the community perceives has the potential to advance its goals. What prosperity exists in Pueblito has come largely as a result of migration of community members who maintain their ties with the community by sup-

---

3. Eric R. Wolf, "Kinship, Friendship, and Patron–Client Relationships," in Michael Banton, ed., *The Social Anthropology of Complex Societies* (Cambridge: Cambridge University Press, 1968), 1–22. See also Eric R. Wolf and Edward C. Hansen, *The Human Condition in Latin America* (New York: Oxford University Press, 1972).

porting family members and village projects. The continuance of that prosperity depends on the stability of those ties.

One of the evidences of the corporate nature of the community is the recurrence of the theme of social unity and harmony in descriptions of the town system or other aspects of life in Pueblito given by its citizens. For instance, people will often mention that Pueblito is not like some of the other towns in the area where political factions have resulted in division and even violence. In public speeches, solidarity is lauded as a major reason for community progress and well-being. This does not, however, suggest an absence of conflict and strife within the community.

Several internal mechanisms of social control exert power over the individual community member. Formal control is exercised through the political-religious system, in which all members of the community are required to participate. Similar to other Mexican towns, Pueblito's political system consists of a series of town hall posts to which the local men are appointed yearly by their fellow townsmen. No one is exempt from the obligation to serve the town in this way.

The formal religious system is bound to the political system in that there is also a series of posts in the Catholic Church to which men are appointed. Those who occupy these posts are responsible for various religious fiestas, for the care of the church, and for directing formal religious activity.

Men who migrate are not exempt from these town duties. They may pay someone to serve in their place in a few of the less important posts. But for most of the civil and religious posts they must return to fulfill their obligation if they wish to remain a respected member of the community. The person who fails to fulfill these obligations will experience difficulty in securing the assistance of town officials in matters such as procuring official documents.

Formal control also extends to the Zapotecs in Los Angeles through a village association which cooperates with the home community or town improvements. Officers for the association are elected yearly by the Pueblito people living in Los Angeles, just as the town officials in Pueblito are chosen by the resident population. However, the jobs are considered voluntary activities and do not count toward town service. The Los Angeles association collects an obligatory yearly quota from migrant villagers which is used for community projects in their hometown, and collects voluntary contributions toward the major town fiesta.

A certain level of equality among community members is achieved because all must cooperate, and all are subordinate to the system. All who are outside the system or who refuse to submit to the system are regarded with suspicion.

Although making a living is the task of the nuclear family with some extended family involvement, the claim that the political-religious system makes on the time and labor of members of the community impacts the individual economically as well. The obligation to hold town office (without pay) or to sponsor one of the church fiestas serves to maintain a degree of economic equality among members of the community.

Informal control is facilitated by the fact that people desire personal prestige and respect. Such control may take the form of gossip and ridicule. In a small community such as Pueblito, where it is difficult to maintain privacy in one's personal affairs, these are powerful tools. Fear of ridicule and loss of status motivates a high degree of social conformity. Criticism and gossip are motivated by envy for anyone who noticeably prospers. Beyond any control which is externally manipulated, there is the heavy weight of tradition which dictates appropriate behavior for every sphere of life.

The exposure to other cultures and the additional personal freedom that migration provides has lightened this load somewhat. However, since ties with the home community are still important to most Zapotecs in Los Angeles, they are still vulnerable to slander. If a person sends money back to build a new house, people expect him to contribute to community projects and celebrations as well. If he doesn't "share" with the community, or if he doesn't give as much as people think he can, he may be slandered. Even if there is no visible evidence of prosperity, people may assume that, because a person has worked in the United States, he has money and they may hold it against one who doesn't "share." Conversely, by such sharing, one can achieve a measure of prestige back in the hometown that is not possible for the migrant to achieve in Los Angeles.

The Instrumental Quality of Social Relations

The instrumental nature of interpersonal relationships may be observed in daily activities, in which reciprocity plays an important part. Zapotecs rarely visit one another without a purpose in mind. It may be to borrow something, to negotiate work arrangements, or to visit a sick friend, but there is usually a specific transaction involved. The success of the transaction is dependent on the reciprocal relationship between the two parties. In the case of a loan or labor arrangement, a person who is socially indebted to the one making the request will most likely grant it if it is within his power to do so. Likewise, when one has a need, he goes to one who is obligated to him. There is an interdependence between the individuals in a network through which needs are met and through which individual behavior is, to some extent, controlled.

Reciprocity in both goods and labor is somewhat formalized through *gwzon,* a system that includes cooperative labor at various stages in the agricultural cycle and cooperation in providing food and labor for celebrations which will later be reciprocated when it is the giver's turn to sponsor a celebration. Economically, participation in *gwzon* is a means of saving for one's own future needs, or of meeting present needs when one lacks resources. Socially a certain confidence, established between participants, provides another network of ties to bind members to the community. This system has been described as a way in which people build up what is called social capital. Security is established more through multiple interpersonal ties than through the meager economic resources available to the individual community member.

Even though economic resources have increased significantly in recent years, security still lies more in social ties than in economic resources, which people recognize to be unstable and unpredictable. These ties remain important to Zapotecs living in Los Angeles because they do not always have jobs, and few jobs offer benefits for sickness, or any security. They still need the safety net of their social network.

This tight social structure makes it difficult for a Zapotec to consider an ideology that differs from that accepted by the community. When all of one's social security is bound up in a closed system, it is most threatening to consider the kind of change the gospel brings. If mere consideration of the gospel causes social disruption, an individual will not even be open to listen. But if there are shared ties through which some trust has been established, the person is free to dialogue, especially if in the added social space that urban living allows.

Conclusions

Other factors are, of course, crucial to an individual Zapotec's coming to know Christ, the most important being the sovereign work of the Holy Spirit in the person's heart. But I believe the conclusions we can draw from this brief analysis offer, first, some specific guidance for ministry to Zapotecs, and second, some general guidance for any urban ministry among people of rural origins. I believe it also gives insight into the broader plan of God for reaching unreached peoples.

This study leads to three very specific conclusions regarding the Zapotecs: (1) Establishing relationships with Zapotecs in the city is greatly enhanced by prior contact with the individual or with members of the social network; (2) instrumental contacts are essential to developing continuing relationships; (3) the positive correlation of these data with what is known of Zapotec social organization in general show that the nature of our relationships with individuals was to a large extent prescribed by the culture. Development of continuing relationships can be significantly enhanced by understanding the social system.

This study supports two premises that also may apply to other rural peoples engaged in urban migration, regardless of their specific form of social organization. The first premise is that people carry rural boundaries of relationships to the city. Therefore, to understand them in the city, one needs to know their rural social boundaries. The second general premise, closely related to the first, is that rural contacts will carry over to the city. Although the results of this study are by no means dramatic, they do show the importance of grasping the social dynamics of ministry when working cross-culturally, and that a clear understanding of the individual can only be obtained through knowing rural roots. To begin working with people of such a group in an urban setting without understanding the social environment that has patterned their social behavior and shaped their worldview is less than desirable.

Looking at the major features of Zapotec social organization has made me see the migration of Zapotecs to Los Angeles as part of God's plan for reaching them. On the one hand, urban migration has made them more free to listen to the gospel, while at the same time they still maintain social ties through which the gospel may reach other Zapotecs. Furthermore, since the missionary is a member of the migrant's host culture, there are opportunities to serve that did not exist when the missionary was the outsider. The Zapotec case illustrates Paul's sermon to the Athenians in Acts 17, where he states that God has set the times and places where we should live in order that we might seek him (vv. 26–27). Though in some Zapotec groups there has been response to the gospel, the people of Pueblito as a group have remained singularly unresponsive to it. It appears that urban migration is a key factor in bringing change to this closed system and thus opening the door to the transformation that the gospel brings. This undoubtedly has broader application than to the Zapotecs.

Finally, this case is a reminder that the world's cities are made up of numerous people groups representing great cultural diversity. If we want to reach these groups with the gospel of Christ, we must be sensitive to their uniqueness.

Resources for Linking Church to City

Bakke, Raymond J., and Samuel K. Roberts. *The Expanded Mission of 'Old First' Churches.* 1986. Valley Forge, PA: Judson Press (P.O. Box 851, Valley Forge, PA 19482–0851). An examination of the ministries of those U.S. churches which had historically been in the power and life of a community. Using extensive case studies, the authors explore the histories of the churches for clues to understand their context and structures and to revitalize their ministries.

DuBose, Francis M. *How Churches Grow in an Urban World.* 1978. Nashville, TN: Broadman Press (127 Ninth Ave., North, Nashville, TN 37234). Systematic, structured look at the urban world. From a comprehensive sketch of the history of the church in the global city and theological perspectives, suggested strategies are developed for the urban church. Excellent introduction.

Ellison, Craig W., and Edward S. Maynard. *Healing for the City: Counseling in the Urban Setting.* 1992. Grand Rapids: Zondervan Publishing House (5300 Patterson SE, Grand Rapids, MI 49530). Groundbreaking evangelical study of the counseling and family needs encountered in U.S. urban ministry by two professional practitioners. Following an introductory section on the distinctive elements of the urban situation for counseling, separate chapters deal with the specific needs of Asians, African Americans, and Hispanics. The final part offers chapters on particular problems (addictive behaviors, divorce recovery, sexual abuse, stress, etc.). Full case studies illustrate this helpful, one-of-a-kind work.

Greenway, Roger S., and Timothy M. Monsma. *Cities: Mission's New Frontier.* 1989. Grand Rapids: Baker Book House (P.O. Box 6287, Grand Rapids, MI 49516). Reflective, balanced discussion of various issues of urban church growth and planting, with attention to settings in both North America and the world. With a wide use of sample case studies, the authors touch on such questions as ethnicity, urban people movements, raising families, and pastoring in the city. There is a fifty-three-page bibliography. The standard text in the area.

Greenway, Roger S., ed. *Discipling the City: A Comprehensive Approach to Urban Mission.* 2nd ed. 1992. Grand Rapids: Baker Book House (P.O. Box 6287, Grand Rapids, MI 49516). Eighteen chapters of urban potpourri form a reader that is less comprehensive than its subtitle claims. Topics range from the very practical (doing research; mapping a city; youth ministries) to the more historical, technical, and theological. The authors are a veritable "who's who" of evangelical experts on urban mission.

Grigg, Viv. *Cry of the Urban Poor.* 1992. Monrovia, CA: MARC (World Vision International, 919 W. Huntington Drive, Monrovia, CA 91016). A global analysis of the mega-city phenomenon, followed by an outline of various church planting models for urban squatter communities. Some very practical advice is given on such issues as pastoring the poor and developing leadership for slum churches. Fine blend of practical and theoretical.

Schaller, Lyle W., ed. *Center City Churches: The New Urban Frontier.* 1993. Nashville, TN: Abingdon Press (201 Eighth Ave., South, Nashville, TN 37203). Eleven brief case studies of contemporary urban churches in the U.S. The closing chapter by Schaller sketches thirty recurring themes that run through the case histories, seeking a conceptual framework for analyzing an urban congregation. Interesting clues but the brevity of the treatment may frustrate.

Tillapaugh, Frank R. *Unleashing the Church: Getting People Out of the Fortress and Into Ministry.* 1982. Ventura, CA: Regal Books (2300 Knoll Drive, Ventura, CA 93003). Exciting model for urban ministry, built on the author's experience as an urban pastor in Denver, Colorado. Part One develops the philosophy of ministry out of which the church must operate. The second part focuses on the methodology, with chapters highlighting specific peoples—singles, international students, seniors, street people, middle-class families.

Part 4
Samples:
Linking Strategy to Model

Introduction

Harvie M. Conn

We now open a sample case of urban mission wares. In the chapters that follow there will tumble out in exciting array stories of megachurches and house churches, team ministries, and congregations mono-ethnic and multi-ethnic.

How should we evaluate these samples? How do we decide what will work in a particular setting? The copycat mentality can be very strong. The megachurch sample worked in Willow Creek; why won't it work in Westchester? House churches have proven their worth in Cranston and Canton; surely we can try them in East Providence and Beijing.

The essays by Fred Smith and Dick Scoggins provide quiet warnings against any assumption that samples are models. The megachurch beginning in Lima, Peru, needs many modifications before it can emerge again in Guayaquil, Ecuador. The house church pattern in one part of Rhode Island doesn't quite transfer with ease to another part of the state.

More strident warnings are also emerging. Recent critics use the megachurch sample as an occasion to look for larger socio-theological flaws—gospel marketing, the dangers of modernity, evangelical blurring of the distinctions between Christ and culture.[1]

1. Os Guinness, *Dining with the Devil: The Mega Church Movement Flirts with Modernity* (Grand Rapids: Baker, 1993); John Seel, *The Evangelical Forfeit: Can We Recover?* (Grand Rapids: Baker, 1993); David Wells, *God in the Wasteland: The Reality of Truth in a World of Fading Dreams* (Grand Rapids: Eerdmans, 1994).

These larger concerns, we affirm, are healthy ones worthy of an attention not always given to the megachurch phenomenon. But one sample (usually of Willow Creek) is not a model. And we find ourselves wondering if the focused interest is not such a model anyway, but rather on a larger worldview paradigm.

Evaluating the final usefulness of these samples of megachurch or mini church, of mono-ethnic or multi-ethnic congregation, of various leadership styles, raises a wide diversity of questions. These questions link institution to context over many terrains: What will be our strategy for church growth and planting? How is that strategy affected by our theological perceptions of church and city, reinforced by the experience of our histories? What presuppositional model is interacting with our strategy? How does the urban setting in which we labor shape our commitment to strategy and modeling? How ought the church to develop biblical structures appropriate to that urban involvement?

The Formation of Evangelical Samples

Fundamental to all evangelical urban models and strategies are two biblical convictions. One affirms that the city, with all its people and interlocking systems, has been touched by the perversity of human rebellion against God; nothing is left undisturbed by that defilement. The other conviction affirms that for urban life thus defiled there is a divine remedy in the saving work of Jesus Christ.

However, the paths diverge as these convictions are shaped by other theological commitments.[2] How do we understand sin? Are personal sins primarily in view? Or must we also represent Christ against unjust social structures and oppressive societal systems? Should we understand people primarily important as souls? or as soul–body unities? On what level do people touched and changed by Christ touch and change the city? Should gospel interaction focus on a personal level as individuals are converted? Or is our responsibility also as persons-in-community touching society-in-community? How is the gospel to be shared in the city? By words or also by actions? by charity or also by justice? How do we see the city? As a sinking ocean liner from which we must rescue as many souls as possible? or as a lighthouse whose burnedout beam needs replacing?

As important as are the answers to these theological questions, other pressures influence our strategies and models. The history of various eschatological points of view illustrates this complexity. Tracing the roots of church–city

---

2. Dealing with the issue of the relationship between evangelism and social responsibility, Ronald Sider offers a helpful list of ten theological questions that make an impact on this issue. We see many parallels here with our question. Consult: *One-Sided Christianity? Uniting the Church to Heal a Lost and Broken World* (Grand Rapids: Zondervan, 1993), 26–32.

relationships too simplistically to millennial formulations does not always work well. "Without doubt, our understanding of the millennium affects the way in which we view the world," observes one Lausanne report. "The degree of hope which we sustain seems to be proportionate to the degree to which we see the Kingdom of God as an already present reality or as a largely future expectation."[3]

Yet it is also true that particular eschatological points-of-view do not always shape history as much as they are shaped by it. "Time and again," Stanley Gundry reminds us, "there seems to be a connection between eschatology and the Church's perception of itself in its historical situation. Eschatologies have been a reflection of the current mood or *Zeitgeist* or response to historical conditions. In other words, in many cases eschatologies appear to have been sociologically conditioned."[4]

Gundry is not trying to diminish the role of exegetical and theological considerations in formulating our eschatologies. He is simply saying something of the realities that shape city–church patterns. Those patterns, even evangelical patterns, are not exclusively theological constructs. They are also conditioned by the history of the socio-cultural world in which we do our formulating.

In terms of our discussion, Gundry's warning should encourage humility in supporting some purist role for theology in building our city–church patterns. Life is too complex for such easy answers. And so is theology. We cannot ignore such formulations. But we cannot overdo them either.

The Function of Models

Urban patterns for church growth and planting are largely determined by our models of how to proceed. And, though these models also demand the judgment of biblical perspective, sometimes balanced judgments are not so easy to get at.

A model, says Louis Luzbetak, is a "particular perspective from which the real world is being examined and described."[5] Models are human, conceptual arrangements of reality, more than abstract theories and less than empirical observations. In the world of grammar, we call them analogies—the church as the body of Christ, the Christian life as a pilgrimage, the city as a haven of refuge.

They do more than simply inform or explain reality; they reinforce, they stimulate, they shape. Through the model, the user can find imagination aroused, with resulting new ideas deepening the model even further.[6]

---

3. *Evangelism and Social Responsibility: An Evangelical Commitment, Lausanne Occasional Papers, No. 21* (Wheaton: Lausanne Committee for World Evangelization, 1982), 37–38.
4. Stanley Gundry, "Hermeneutics or *Zeitgeist* as the Determining Factor in the History of Eschatologies?" *Journal of the Evangelical Theological Society* 20, no. 1 (1977): 50.
5. Louis Luzbetak, *The Church and Cultures* (Maryknoll, N.Y.: Orbis, 1988), 135.
6. Charles Kraft, *Christianity in Culture* (Maryknoll, N.Y.: Orbis, 1979), 31–33.

With a model, General Motors builds its cars, a lover creates an image (sometimes true, sometimes false) of the object of his or her love. A local congregation dreams of its modeled ministry in an urban neighborhood and then plans and prays and works according to the consensus model.

Models by their very nature are risky; viewed from another angle, their assets can be liabilities. Because they are open-ended creations, they are only approximations of the truth, even biblical truth. They build on what is perceived. And sometimes we do not perceive key facts. The model can then go off kilter and lead us astray. Because they are simple, they can reduce the complexities of reality to simplistic alternatives. They become too neat. Because they tend to conserve, they can close us off from what needs to be changed. And, similarly, because they stimulate, they can close us off from what needs to be conserved.

Our social perceptions of the city provide us with a good example of what I mean. Edward Krupat points out that a large part of how we respond to cities lies in pictures, the images that we create of cities. Out of these images, he contends, flow the models by which we see.[7] When we look at the city, we see what we want to see. If you're wearing dark glasses, cities look very bleak, without light. Cities take on different meaning, depending on the personal or subjective filters through which they pass. Our mental maps of cities are shaped by more than objective criteria or even biblical balance; they are shaped also by our social and human presuppositions.

How then have contemporary evangelicals constructed their models and, in conjunction with their strategies, produced their samples?

In his classic work, *Christ and Culture*, H. Richard Niebuhr surveys the history of Christianity's perceptions of human culture and draws a rich and stimulating typology of five models.[8] While we may feel some reservations regarding Niebuhr's methodology and his choices, his models can be transposed into our discussion.[9] My assignment now is even narrower than was Niebuhr's: I center my focus only on the contemporary evangelical models.

Niebuhr's spectrum of models moves between the two extreme poles that I have re-named the "Christ of the city" model and the "Christ against the city" model. Between these are scattered other perspectives, some closer to one end of the spectrum and some to the other. Closer to the positive side of the typology he places what we now call the model of "Christ and the city in paradox." We suggest that evangelicalism in the city wavers among these three models but not in mutual negation. Especially in the past two decades, these models can even intertwine and sound very similar.

7. Edward Krupat, *People in Cities: The Urban Environment and Its Effect* (New York: Cambridge University Press, 1985), 3–4.

8. H. Richard Niebuhr, *Christ and Culture* (New York: Harper, 1956), 39–42.

9. Some of my reservations and modifications are treated more fully in: "Christ and the City: Biblical Themes for Building Urban Theology Models," in Roger Greenway, ed., *Discipling the City*, 1st ed. (Grand Rapids: Baker, 1979), 222–27.

All three models within the evangelical orbit have a common goal, to practice the presence of God in the city. But they differ both in how they see the city and in how they see their practice of the presence of God in terms of the city.

The Model of Christ Against the City

The evangelical model of Christ against the city has been growing in the United States for at least a century. Alarmed by the rapid growth of American cities in the nineteenth century and identifying that growth with poverty, crime, and ethnic migration, the evangelical turned more and more against the city in a "blame-the-environment" mentality.[10]

Early academic research outside the church supported the mentality. Scholarship saw the cities as a chaos of size, density, and heterogeneity. And out of this chaos, the argument went, flowed competition, alienation, exploitation, anonymity, stress, and personal and social dislocation.[11] As the decades passed, academic corrections were offered that led to greater balance. But the stereotypes were forming. *Rural* was sacred . . . communal . . . natural . . . friendly . . . stable; *urban* was secular . . . individual . . . unnatural . . . unfriendly . . . chaotic.[12]

Mission strategies reflected these polarizations. Eschatological perspectives turned negative toward a darkening world of the future. And the city became the symbol of that decaying future. The church's approach to the city tended to be individualistic, moralistic, and short-term. "[These believers] know that they cannot change things permanently. But they believe that there are some things that they can do."[13]

The biblical proof texts used in support of the Christ against the city model revolve selectively around the apostasy of the city—the first recorded building of the city by Cain the murderer (Gen. 4:17); the raising of Babel by the tyrant Nimrod and its razing by Jehovah (Gen. 11:1–9); Abram's flight from the city (Gen. 11:31–12:4); Sodom and Gomorrah (Gen. 19:1–29); Babylon "the great harlot" (Rev. 17:5).

Some of the current writing on spiritual warfare seems to follow this pattern, underlining the darker satanic side of a demonized city that can be broken only by "strategic-level" intervention. The marks of God's common grace and general favor on the city are blurred at best.

10. Harvie M. Conn, *The American City and the Evangelical Church: A Historical Overview* (Grand Rapids: Baker, 1994), 59–73.

11. David A. Karp, Gregory P. Stone, and William C. Yoels, *Being Urban: A Sociology of City Life* (New York: Praeger, 1991), 30–43.

12. John Gulick, *The Humanity of Cities: An Introduction to Urban Societies* (Granby, Mass.: Bergin and Garvey, 1989), 8–10.

13. Timothy Weber, *Living in the Shadow of the Second Coming: American Premillennialism, 1875–1982* (Grand Rapids: Zondervan, 1983), 236.

198 Harvie M. Conn

Some samples of this mind-set come close to a survivalist perspective, seeing the church as a fortress, its gates closed, "occupying till Jesus comes." Where this perspective dominates the model, the church sees itself as under siege and turns to an introverted exclusivism.

In the North American context there is a strong pull in this attitude toward always looking back, clinging to a mythical ecclesiastical past, purified of spot or struggle. The style of ministry such a view encourages can become one of an older individual piety, the cultural defense of a rural, small town America.

America's "Old First Churches" can exemplify this mind-set. Once the centers of power, stability, and continuity in the emerging city of the early and mid-nineteenth century, they served the conscience of the rising middle class.[14] They rose to welcome the immigrants of Ireland and Scotland, Norway and Sweden.

Now they struggle with identity questions. The Swedish and Dutch neighborhoods they once served in Chicago and Paterson, New Jersey, have become Puerto Rican and African American. Church buildings constructed for 800 now serve fifty to seventy-five. The average age of the membership is now in the sixties, with most of those at worship driving in from the suburbs. Disillusioned by an uncertain economic future, overwhelmed by change and ethnic diversity they cannot understand, they return to what they imagine was their past.

Samplings outside the United States hint at a similar mentality. A socio-political history of Mexico City's evangelicals from 1964 to 1991 concludes that "the isolationist heritage of fundamentalism" has been a critical factor in maximizing interest in such areas as family life and minimizing reflection on the city's social and political life. Church life and urban socio-political life are unrelated.[15]

Another author underlines this same tendency toward introversion in Mexican evangelical churches. "Historically, this can partly be explained by Mexican cultural factors, the anticlerical Mexican government prohibiting social ministries by the church, the militant hostility of the Catholic church, . . . and the competitive and divisive attitudes of U.S. and Protestant missionaries of an earlier generation."[16] It may also be part of the reason why those who have been won from Islam do not find easy acceptance into the fellowship of such churches. And also why the churches that set out to evangelize Muslims have, with few exceptions, merely drawn their members from other churches.

---

14. Raymond Bakke and Samuel Roberts, *The Expanded Mission of 'Old First' Churches* (Valley Forge, Pa.: Judson, 1986), 13–33.

15. Lindy Scott, "Salt of the Earth: A Socio-political History of Mexico City's Evangelical Protestants (1964–1991)" (Ph.D. diss., Northwestern University, 1991), 224–28.

16. Richard Gollings, "Planting Covenant Communities of Faith in the City," in Charles Van Engen and Jude Tiersma, eds., *God So Loves the City: Seeking a Theology for Urban Mission* (Monrovia, Calif.: MARC, 1994), 135.

Evangelism still remains a key part of this model. But in some samples it is carried on more as a "remnant" activity. Any larger agenda of urban concerns is limited and often highly selective.

In Third World countries faced with rapid urban growth and a huge influx of rural migrants, even the commitment to evangelism can become problematic for the smaller churches that make up the bulk of the urban congregations. The demands created by urbanization are overwhelming for such a congregation busy with varied internal problems. So, as in India, they develop a "maintenance mentality" and "show practically no interest in expanding their ministry beyond their own members."[17] Even evangelism is cut back; the outsider is neglected.

The Model of Christ and the City in Paradox

The Christ and the city in paradox model, and the third we will look at shortly, offer a different way of seeing the city and its churches. They incorporate more urban-affirming metaphors into their strategy for church growth and planting. They do not forget what the city has become under Cain and Nimrod and Nebuchadnezzar. But neither do they forget what the city can become under the sovereign rule of King Jesus. Unlike the model of Christ against the city, the answer of Christ and the city is not either/or, but both/and. Those who hold this view are against the city for the city. They do not avert their eyes from the urban darkness. The city and its people can be altered, and Jesus and his people must do it.

The model we examine now, that of Christ and the city in paradox, is a dualistic one as its name indicates. In this model, like the wandering hero of Bunyan's *Pilgrim's Progress*, the church becomes a pilgrim passing through the city toward the Gates of Light. The pilgrim has no illusions about what to expect from the corruption of the city. But, unlike the model of Christ against the city, the dualist, to use Niebuhr's words, "knows that he belongs to that culture and cannot get out of it, that God indeed sustains him in it and by it."[18] This dualist knows that God can do something about things now. In the face of the awesome reality of sin in the city, the pilgrim remembers also the awesome reality of the grace of God in the city.

Using another verbal analogy, this model acts out its dualistic mind-set something like triage in the medical world. Here, outside the mobile operating tent, this M*A*S*H* unit model comes alive. Christians make reactive decisions propelled by the immediacy of the urgent.

Its mission strategy is built around the model's self-understanding as a restraining force, a dike against sin, a preventer of anarchy.

17. Atul Aghamkar, "Family Coherence and Evangelization in Urban India," in Van Engen and Tiersma, *God So Loves the City*, 151.
18. Niebuhr, *Christ and Culture*, 156.

It wants to do more than first-aid in the city; triage is not first-aid. It is the first step in the path of conserving life. It evaluates the seriousness of the wound needing treatment. And the seriousness of God's response—the death and resurrection of our Lord Jesus Christ.

This reactive, conserving nature of the model sometimes makes it hard to distinguish from the earlier model we outlined. Richard Mouw recalls the person who said to him, "I don't mean to suggest that it is wrong to pay attention to some of these social issues—but I do wish we would spend more time talking about the things of the Lord!" Which model—survivalist or pilgrim—was speaking to him?

Mouw saw no need to attack his brother's fundamental premise; it is, of course, of the utmost importance that we talk about the things of the Lord. He was also aware that his partner in conversation was not totally turned off by social issues.

But the triage question now becomes: What are the "things" of the Lord? Doesn't Jesus agonize over racist stereotypes destroying the dignity of those made in his image as well as over racists who need to repent? Doesn't he grieve over the injustice of police brutality in the name of law and order as well as over police officers whose very brutality shows their need of Christ? Are we to provide only tracts and sandwiches for a homeless population of at least 200,000 to 600,000 people in the richest nation in the world? Are not these "social issues" also part of that agenda we call "the things of the Lord"?[19]

The paradox model does not dismiss the validity of any of these sets of questions. This is where this pilgrim model stands in sharpest contrast to that of Christ against the city. It does not retreat from the city in concern for its own health. Borrowing again the language of Niebuhr, it does not ask "what profit for the self may be gained; but rather what the service of the neighbor in the given conditions demands."[20]

But it is a dualistic model embracing Christian membership in two kingdoms, the kingdom of God and the kingdom of the city. And, combined with its desire for preventive care, this mind-set can sometimes lead to ossification in the church and less than radical change for the city.

Is the contemporary appearance of the religious right and the Christian Coalition in the United States a sample of this evangelical model? It has come out of the social and political closet in a way one could not expect from a Christ against the city model. It has not retreated from the public obligations of a Christian citizen. But its agenda, as wide as it is, is dictated more by its desire to protect what it perceives as a lost moral past than by the radical demands of a more holistic Christian perspective. In the process, has the

19. Richard J. Mouw, *When the Kings Go Marching In* (Grand Rapids: Eerdmans, 1983), 71.
20. Niebuhr, *Christ and Culture*, 186.

dualism of the pilgrim metaphor domesticated urban transformation into shortfall improvements?

Are there signs of this same dualism in the continuing discussions among evangelicals of the relationship between evangelism and social responsibility? David Bosch suggests this dualism can be heard in the echoes of a "primacy to evangelism" or in some suggestions of "separate but equal" views of the relationship.[21]

The Model of Christ Transforming the City

There is a third urban direction evangelicals take. With the model of Christ and the city in paradox, it shares a clear picture of the self-destructiveness of the city and its hopelessness without God. And with the pilgrim model, it is also a model of hope and urban affirmation: it knows that God can change cities.

It is also clearer and more hopeful about its holistic mission in the city. Nicholas Wolterstorff writes, "The responsibility of the saints to struggle for the reform of the social order in which they find themselves is one facet of the discipleship to which their Lord Jesus Christ has called them. It is not an addition to their religion; it is there among the very motions of Christian spirituality."[22]

Where specifically are its differences with the pilgrim model? At least in two areas. First, the pilgrim mind "tends so to concentrate on redemption through Christ's cross and resurrection that creation becomes . . . a kind of prologue to the one mighty deed of atonement. . . ."[23] To put it another way, the pilgrim owns no real estate in the city. And that lack of ownership defines the model's vague sense of strangeness with things urban.

On the other hand, the model of Christ transforming the city sees a clearer link between creation and redemption. Redemption means putting on the "the new man" (Eph. 4:24; Col. 3:10). And that means putting on "the new Adam," and a new start for a new creation (Gal. 6:15; Eph. 2:10). This is the attitude of a property owner, of earth's inheritors (Matt. 5:5). The church has begun to exercise creation rights of urban ownership before the closing papers of the final eschaton are signed. All things are now ours, because we are Christ's and all things belong to him (1 Cor. 3:21–23).

Second, the two models differ in how they see the present history of God's work in the city. The pilgrim mind-set tends to see that history as a spiritual

---

21. David Bosch, "In Search of a New Evangelical Understanding," in *Word and Deed: Evangelism and Social Responsibility*, Bruce J. Nicholls, ed. (Grand Rapids: Eerdmans, 1986), 76–79.

22. Nicholas Wolterstorff, *Until Justice and Peace Embrace* (Grand Rapids: Eerdmans, 1983), 3.

23. Niebuhr, *Christ and Culture*, 191.

parenthesis, a great interruption, between the first coming of Christ and his second coming. The orientation of the pilgrim model is more toward the final "not yet" and less toward "between the times." By comparison, the urban transformation model sees the "not yet" transforming the period "between the times" into something more than an urban waiting room for the final day. The urban "now" has become the "already" of the new creation, the new urban beginning.

Perhaps the best analogy to describe all this is that of a model home. We are God's demonstration community of the rule of Christ in the city. On a tract of earth's land purchased with the blood of Christ, Jesus the kingdom developer has begun building new housing. As a sample of what will be, he has erected a model home of what will eventually fill the urban neighborhood. Now he invites the urban world into that model home to take a look at what will be.

The church is the occupant of that model home, inviting neighbors into its open door to Christ. Evangelism is when the signs are put up saying, "Come in and look around." We live in the first erected home of a kingdom housing project, built by the Creator. "He has made us to be a kingdom, priests to his God and Father" (Rev. 1:6).

As citizens of, not survivalists in, this new city within the old city, we see our ownership as the gift of Jesus the Builder (Luke 17:20–21). As residents, not pilgrims, we await the kingdom coming when the Lord returns from his distant country (Luke 19:12). The land is already his, and so are the cities. We have no need to forage or beg for leftover crumbs. Our model home is intended as a preview of coming kingdom attractions.

In this model home we live out our new lifestyle as citizens of the heavenly city that one day will come. We do not abandon our jobs or desert the city that is. We are more than mannequins on silent display in the living room window. We wait, but we wait actively, not passively. Our calling, like that of the Israelites in exile, is to "seek the peace and the prosperity of the city to which" God has carried us in exile (Jer. 29:7). And our agenda of concerns in that seeking becomes as large as the cities where our divine development tracts are found.

Samples of what we mean are found in the pages that follow. The ministries of New Song Church in Baltimore and Harambee Christian Family Center in Pasadena give you small previews. Other chapters spend more time on the initiating steps in moving in that direction. Enjoy the kingdom view.

Church-Planting Strategies
for World-Class Cities

James E. Westgate

The global village has exploded into the global city. The global village, which was held together by a network of relationships, is now replaced by the global city, which is held together by a network of technology. This dramatic, worldwide change is having an impact on missions both at home and overseas. New strategies are necessary to cope with the realities of urbanization.

The birth and growth of world-class cities is a new frontier for the evangelist and church planter. The world's population has migrated to the cities and this migration has given birth to cities larger than have ever before existed. They are called world-class cities because they are tied technologically and economically to other major urban centers around the world. The economics of the nations of the world depend greatly on what happens in these world-class cities. There are those in the financial sectors who prophesy that if one major banking institution collapses, it will set up a domino effect with other institutions around the world, and the world economy may collapse. The scare of the Continental Bank in Chicago brought some of these possible scenarios to the surface.

World demographers project that by the year 2000 we will see the emergence of sixty cities of more than 5 million people, twenty-five cities of more than 10 million people, and five cities of more than 20 million people.[1] These statistics are startling when we consider that between 1950 and 1980 the

This chapter first appeared in *Urban Mission* 4, no. 2 (1986): 6–13. Used by permission.

1. Elaine M. Murphy, "World Population: Toward the Next Century" (Washington: Population Bureau, 1981), 2–3.

urban population of developing countries more than tripled, increasing from 275 million to just under 1 billion.[2] By 1983 the world had become 42 percent urban, up from 25 percent urban in 1950 and 33 percent urban in 1960.[3] By the end of this century the world, for the first time in its history, will have a majority of persons living in cities. Raymond Bakke projects that "the 240 world class cities of December 1982 will increase to 500 by the year 2000."

Strategies for these world-class cities will need to cope with the intense pressures created by a multiplicity of cultures, languages, classes, religions, and political structures. What then are some of the possible church planting strategies that will have an impact on this kind of city? Currently five major types of strategies for church planting seem to be emerging. These models seem to have the flexibility to penetrate diverse and complex urban structures and to utilize the technology and transition in world-class cities.[4] I will define and give a capsule description of each of these strategic models.

The Team Church Planting Strategy

The Eastern Model

The Eastern model is currently being developed by Ben Sawatsky of the Overseas Department of the Evangelical Free Church of America. He developed this model in Malaysia and is now exporting it to ten world-class cities. He defines this strategy as "a team of missionaries (and eventually nationals) representing a constellation of complementing gifts, skills, training and experience, [who] will plant a plurality of local churches." This strategy calls for a team of trainers equipping teams of church planters. The primary role of the team is to train others.

> First, the team will teach Leadership Assistance Program courses (LAP). A series of twenty courses spread over a five-year training cycle will form the team's basis for a teaching curriculum. Second, the team will model the Christian life and the Christian home. This requires a transparency of lifestyle before the church planting teams. Third, the team is to demonstrate ministry skills. They must be able to show how to lead evangelistic Bible studies, and present the gospel as well as lead a worship service or a Bible message. Fourth, the team must foster team unity. The goal is to bring the church planting team to the place where they experience mutual understanding, love, etc. Fifth, the team must promote church growth by sharing biblical church growth princi-

2. Population Information Program, "Migration, Population Growth, and Development," *Population Reports* (September–October 1983): M–247.

3. *The World Population Situation in 1979* (New York: United Nations, 1980), 55.

4. Larry Rose and C. Kirk Hadaway, eds., *An Urban World: Churches Face the Future* (Nashville: Broadman, 1984), 77.

ples. The goal is to train eighty . . . church workers and spawn twenty churches in ten years.[5]

This model demonstrates the awareness of the need to develop a mini community in the midst of an urban pressurized society. Instead of sending one lone couple to face the difficulties and adjustments of complex urban culture, this model provides a network of supportive and complementary relationships to deal with the diversity and complexity of an urban setting. The focus of this team is not only to plant a church but to reproduce themselves by training others to plant reproductive churches. This method has the potential of saturating a city with local reproductive churches.

The Western Model

The Western model is similar to the Eastern model in that it consists of four to six couples with complementary gifts and abilities who work with a church planter. The team members may be seminary couples who have had training in church planting or lay couples from sister churches who have demonstrated leadership skill through service in their local church. The couples are chosen carefully in relation to evangelism, discipleship, small group Bible study, Christian education, and worship. The leader of the team, the church planter, organizes and unites the team for the specific tasks in the church planting project.

The team is committed to a bi-vocational approach to church planting. The primary goal of the team is to plant a church in a strategic place in the city. The primary focus of the team is evangelism, with each team member committed to disciple five to ten people during the first year, a potential of fifty people for the beginning of the church. The second year, the church is organized and the couples concentrate on training the new converts to share their faith while achieving their goal of leading ten more people to Christ. This effort has the potential of doubling the size of the church. During the second year the couples also choose someone to be trained in their own particular areas of skill, such as Bible study, or Christian education.

The third year is a transitional stage for the church. Team members turn their responsibilities over to those whom they have trained. The team members also move to carefully chosen areas which will be the sites for sister churches. The density of the city allows for geographic proximity without infringing on the mother church. Each team member then becomes the church planter for a new sister church and calls for four to six new couples to join them from a seminary or denominational sister church.

The potential multiple progression in this strategy is one church the first year, five churches by year four, twenty-five churches by year eight, 125 by

---

5. Ben A. Sawatsky, "A Church Planting Strategy for World Class Cities," *Evangelical Beacon* (February 4, 1985): 3–4.

year twelve. This strategy is designed to be lay intensive, recruiting couples from sister churches in a given denomination, or students from seminaries who have church planting training and experience. Trinity Evangelical Divinity School already has a church planting residency program functioning in which students are placed in a church planting project while they are taking church planting courses. They work as a team and gain experience in demographics, evangelism, Bible study, and organization of a new church. From an urban perspective, these two models take into consideration the density of the city as well as the need for relationships.

The House Church Planting Strategy

The Linear Model

The linear model faces the critical need for a place to meet. Often in the city, especially overseas, costs for renting a facility are prohibitive. The cost of a half acre in 1980 was $41,000 in most areas of Nairobi. Some one-third acre lots sold for $87,000.[6] The linear house church model develops a small congregation, usually in the home of one of the converts. As the congregation outgrows the home, another church is started in the same manner. These congregations are usually pastored by a trained layperson who is bi-vocational and therefore requires only a small salary. Each new house church is a separate entity and supports its own lay pastor. Donald McGavran cites the Disciples of Christ in Puerto Rico as an example of this kind of strategy. He notes that many house churches carry on with no financial outlay at all.[7] This strategy works best in an area responsive to the gospel where converts can be quickly absorbed into small relational and training units. Some of these house churches emerge as large congregations. Others remain small and move from location to location until a building or larger meeting place becomes available.

The Network Model

In the network model each new house church is integrally tied to the others. When enough house churches are formed, they can merge and buy a suitable facility. The key in this strategy is one coordinating pastor or leader, with trained leaders ministering in the house churches with the intent of merging in the future. Ralph Neighbour recently developed this type of strategy through the Baptist Center for Urban Studies in Singapore. The Baptist Center has created the Baptist Training Institute to supply the need for trained lay leadership for these house churches.[8]

6. Rose and Hadaway, eds., *An Urban World*, 126.
7. Donald A. McGavran, *Understanding Church Growth* (Grand Rapids: Eerdmans, 1980), 323.
8. Rose and Hadaway, eds., *An Urban World*, 143.

Both of these models focus on the critical problem of land and meeting places in the city. They also address the issue of homogeneous groupings. Nairobi, for example, has seventy vernacular languages with the dominant languages being Swahili, Kikuyu, and English.[9] The house church provides a flexibility for penetrating the mosaic of such an urban culture.

The Wholistic Church Planting Strategy

The Community Center Model

The community center model addresses the felt needs of an urban community. In areas of poverty or intense needs, the community is often resistant to groups who do not show their concern for the needs of the community. A wholistic ministry has proclamation at the heart of its strategy and authenticates that proclamation through acts of reconciling love.

There are numerous models of this strategy both in the United States and abroad. One of the best developed models is Circle Community Center in Chicago, which is affiliated with the Evangelical Free Church. Circle Community Center has developed a medical clinic, legal clinic, counseling center, housing program, youth leadership program, and job training program in a depressed black community with the goal of leading men and women to Christ. A new black church was started in the Center, and this church reaches out to the nearly 5000 men and women who flow through these programs.

The critical point in establishing this kind of program is discovering felt needs and not imposing an outside agenda. This procedure takes a good deal of exposure and time. Also the goal of church planting must be kept in the forefront lest the ministering agency become the focal point for existence.

The Community Living Model

The community living model differs from the community center model in that those involved in the ministry share in a community lifestyle. There are a variety of arrangements in this model, from shared housing to shared finances. By pooling money, a community living group can set an individual or several individuals free for ministry. Circle Community Center was initially started through Austin Community Fellowship, as a group of young professionals covenanted to share housing and finances in order to free a director, a medical doctor, and a lawyer for ministry. Eventually these individuals and the ministries they represented became self-supporting, and the Fellowship could channel support to other mission projects.

This model also indicates a deep commitment to living and ministering in a given community. Manuel Ortiz effectively developed this strategy in a

9. Ibid., 119.

Hispanic community on the west side of Chicago. Spirit and Truth Fellowship started with a group of dedicated couples who were committed to a holistic ministry in their community. The Fellowship has started a thrift shop, family counseling center, and youth work dealing with justice issues. The original group has now divided by design into four smaller churches using indigenous leadership.[10] The shared lifestyle of the groups and a willingness to support each other have provided the dynamic to impact their community for Christ.

Both of these models address felt needs in the community and provide a testimony of Christ's love in word and deed. The spirit of community lifestyle in these models helps prevent urban burnout and fatigue. The greatest danger these models face is becoming ingrown rather than outward-oriented in their ministry and mission.

The International Network Church Planting Strategy

The Local Church Model

The local church model is the newest model I see forming on the horizon. This model focuses on the internationalization of the world-class cities. The ministry centers on internationals who are in the city studying or working and who have family members and relationships in other countries. The International Evangelical Free Church is a pioneer in this strategy. Samuel Mall has been a church planter in the Medical Center of Chicago. The church has reached many internationals with the gospel of Christ. These new converts have been brought into the church and discipled so that they may be involved in the church as soon as possible. The goal is to help the converts gain a real appreciation of the benefits of a local church so there is a desire to be involved in church planting when they return home. The strategy then is to use those returning to their own countries and their network of contacts for the planting of a new church in their country. Mall has already had contacts from members who have gone back to their own countries and are starting Bible studies with the purpose of planting a new church. Some of these individuals are from countries closed to missionaries, and therefore the plan provides a new approach to church planting. Mall is in contact with mission agencies which have works in some of these countries and wants to network with them to train these new converts. The network also functions from the other end in that believers who are coming to Chicago to study can be channeled into the International EFC and help in the ministry and evangelization of their people group while in North America.

---

10. Manuel Ortiz, "A Church in Missiological Tension," *Urban Mission* 2, no. 1 (1984): 13–14.

The Mission Center Model

The mission center model is also in the beginning stages. A new organization called the Midwest Center for World Missions is formulating a strategy focusing on internationals in the United States and a network with other mission agencies in training for church planting both in the United States and in other countries. The Midwest Center for World Missions sees itself as a networking agency to assist in linking up key leadership to strategize for evangelism and church planting among people groups both here and abroad. The unreached peoples are not hidden in the bush only, but also in the world-class cities around the globe.

These models focus on the technology and the smallness of our world. The need for networking and the unification of home missions and overseas missions is a must in the very near future. Our denominations and mission agencies must develop a new strategy that takes advantage of the internationalization of our cities and moves away from the great separation of overseas and home missions. Emerging models need to be examined for this purpose.

The Superchurch Planting Model

The Eastern Model

There is some ambiguity as to whether the superchurch is a church planting strategy or a church growth strategy. If the multiplication of cell groups is seen as new mini congregations, almost like house churches, then it is a church planting strategy. Also if one would take seriously the building of a megachurch as a means of reaching a world-class city, then it could be a church planting strategy. The best model of this kind of strategy is the Full Gospel Central Church, Seoul, Korea, pastored by Paul Yonggi Cho. This church had a small beginning and was built on prayer, a focus on needs and home cell groups. The church, with its 350,000 to 400,000 members, by 1986, one of a kind.

The superchurch can provide many things that a small church cannot because of its financial resources and the multiplicity of leadership, and it can influence a city in powerful ways. Central Church's development of the World Mission Center could be a vehicle to export a whole new church planting strategy. Mission strategists might give a second look at this kind of church and weigh its importance in world-class cities.

The Western Model

The city of Houston is the fastest growing city in the United States. The Second Baptist Church has a strategy similar in design to that of Cho's in Seoul. Ralph Neighbour is forming care and share groups involving every member of the congregation. The church already ministers to 400 internationals as well as a congregation of 4000. Their goal is 20,000 in a facility that can meet all of the needs of the urban family. Their philosophy of ministry is to reach the "up-and-outer as well as the down-and-outer." The staff plans to use technology heavily. Houston is the wealthiest city in the nation. If this wealth could be channeled toward evangelism and church planting, there is no limit to what could be accomplished.

The five strategies discussed in this chapter are shared with a view to stimulating interaction and discussion. Many other models or classifications of models could be given. Through dialogue and unification of overseas missions and home missions, world-class cities can be more effectively evangelized.

Megachurches for Christian Minorities: Hope of Bangkok

Kriengsak Chareonwongsak

As the church of Jesus Christ develops strategies to reach the continent of Asia with the gospel, we cannot ignore the Buddhist bloc, which forms a major portion of the Asian population. Thailand is probably the most strategic country in Buddhist Asia. The World Fellowship of Buddhism and its president are found in Thailand, where 94 percent of the population confess Buddhism. Many believe that "to be a Thai means to be a Buddhist."

Protestant missionaries first entered Thailand in 1816, and by 1978, 162 years later, there were only 58,953 Thai Protestant Christians.[1] By 1988 the Protestant population probably stood at around 80,000 at the most,[2] an insignificant portion of the bulging population of 56 million. With its population of over 6 million people, over 1020 slums, and a population growth of over 750,000 per annum,[3] Bangkok makes an ideal site in which to test and apply strategies for urban mission in a highly resistant area.

This chapter first appeared in *Urban Mission* 7, no. 3 (1990): 25–35. Some updating revisions have been made. Used by permission.

1. David Barrett, *World Christian Encyclopedia* (New York: Oxford University Press, 1982), 664.

2. This is a figure reported by Reverend Charan Ratanbutra, chairman of the Evangelical Fellowship of Thailand in *Asia Christian* (March 1988), p. 8. A common problem in compiling figures from various missions is that one believer is counted by two (or more!) missions due to unreliable membership rolls. My own guess is that active church attendance of Protestants in Thailand in the late 1980s did not exceed 25,000.

3. Ray Bakke with Jim Hart, *The Urban Christian* (Downers Grove, Ill.: InterVarsity, 1987), 35.

The Hope of Bangkok Church is the largest and fastest-growing single Christian church in the history of Thailand. It was born out of a God-given vision. It was started in September 1981 with five members and in September 1995 had more than 10,000 members in Bangkok alone. It has become a church planting movement within the past eight years, and has planted over 300 daughter churches in Thailand and overseas.

Being a Thai indigenous church and not a branch of any foreign denomination, the Hope of Bangkok seeks to be a biblically and culturally relevant, contextualized Thai church. In so doing, it has challenged many traditional Thai concepts. One of these is that Christianity is Western-owned. The walls of prejudice are slowly breaking down, and people have become more open to the gospel.

Moreover, programs and activities catering to the needs and spiritual development of the members have been carefully designed to be culturally sensitive. This has enabled members to grow spiritually and to be equipped for ministry in a unique cultural setting, though the efforts have been at times misunderstood by Christian onlookers who want only conventional ministry. It has not been easy to pursue this path in evangelizing this nation. The challenge is enormous, and without God's help, the task of reaching this city and country would be a mere dream.

The Vision for a Resistant City

In all church activities, the Hope of Bangkok Church has carefully defined goals and monitors them with strategic, administrative planning. The God-given vision for the church is to plant a church in each of the approximately 685 districts of Thailand. Even before the church began, our vision was to saturate this country with churches by the year 2000.[4] The history of missions in Thailand makes it clear that without God's help, this is an impossible task.

With clear goals and vision, we shared the value and urgency in serving Christ and in accomplishing this vision with church members from the outset of congregational life. Our church planting vision has been shared clearly and constantly with the members at every practical opportunity, such as corporate prayer meetings, small gatherings, and celebration worship services. This has encouraged active participation and made the vision a part of individual lives. The level of involvement and participation of members varies with the depth of their maturity and commitment. But constant prayer and encouragement has allowed the church to work corporately in great unity, pressing ahead tirelessly.

---

4. See details of the vision of the Hope of Bangkok Church in the summary of Kriengsak Chareonwongsak's message at a plenary session at Lausanne Pastor's Consultation, in *World Evangelization* 15, no. 52 (1988): 30–32; "Lessons from the East," *People of Destiny* (January–February 1987): 6–10; "Church That Won't Stop Growing," *Renewal*, no. 134 (1987): 6–11.

Church Growth

The rapid membership growth of the Hope of Bangkok Church can be seen in our need to move several times to accommodate the expanding congregation. We rented a hospital room for our first meeting in September 1981 with five members and a few onlookers. About six months later, the room became too small, and the meeting was moved to the hospital's chapel. Fourteen months later this too became overcrowded, and we moved to the Crystal Ballroom of the Sheraton Hotel. Growth continued, and in November 1984 we signed the lease on the Oscar Theater, the largest available auditorium in town. In December 1988 our membership was 4500. In January 1992 we were able to move to our own premises at Hope Place, allowing us to expand further with a larger auditorium and multiple services. Services were also held on other days of the week and recently have met in other locations around Bangkok to cater to the ever-increasing number of people coming to church. In September 1995 over 10,000 people regularly attended the Hope of Bangkok Church.

This kind of growth is unprecedented in Thailand. Obviously, God gave the increase. We believe he blessed our corporate and personal prayer, along with an appropriate application of biblical principles and strategies for church expansion.

One principle important in the growth has been our emphasis on local church-centered evangelism. This approach enabled us to enfold new converts into church life. As a local church, we can integrate evangelism, follow-up, and nurturing with sensitivity to personal and community needs. The Thai concept that "to be a Thai is to be a Buddhist" is steadily being eroded as the larger community senses that a viable, strong, and thriving Christian church is here for good. The sincerity of the movement to live and bring Christ's love to the Thai people has also helped to shift people's attitudes toward Christianity to a more favorable perspective.

Strategies

Donald McGavran summed up the difficulty of urban mission by saying, "No one yet knows what modes of mission promise most for communicating Christian faith to urban man."[5] Answers to McGavran's riddle can only come as Spirit-led, biblical insights are applied to a variety of mission circumstances. The principles described below have proved effective in the Bangkok situation and may be helpful in urban mission elsewhere.

Urban Church Planting: A Bridge to Rural Areas

Because cities are the centers of complex social interaction, they are home to the nation's social, commercial, political, military, artistic, entertainment,

---

5. Donald McGavran, *Understanding Church Growth* (Grand Rapids: Eerdmans, 1970), 285.

educational, and mass media life. To evangelize a whole nation requires us to use these resources and concentrate on the cities first.

Targeting for a Larger Urban Church

Thais by nature enjoy big, exciting, festival events. They call this *sanuk,* which means "fun." In this culture, a church must be perceived as being big enough to warrant their interest. A big urban church is necessary to work in Bangkok successfully. We need to make the church visible so that it can attract people's interest and confidence.

There are many benefits in having a large church. For instance, people can be ministered to in a holistic manner. The church can cater to felt and real needs. Also, the membership can function in the specialization of their gifts and talents when the church is of a sufficient size.

The Hope of Bangkok Church has been able to bring a large number of converts into it. Its membership is drawn from around every subdistrict in Bangkok. The larger the church, the more spiritual impact it can assert on society.

Mass Evangelism

The purpose of mass evangelism is not solely to incorporate people into the church. At the Hope of Bangkok it is used primarily as a tool to stimulate personal evangelism. It also serves as a means of secular public relations for the church and creates a "dynamic equivalent" festivity for members to enjoy. These replace Thai celebrations, which are thoroughly Buddhist and animistic in origin, content, philosophy, and practice.

The Hope of Bangkok uses every possible opportunity for mass evangelism. Special occasions draw people best; therefore the church often holds mass meetings on Valentine's Day, Father's Day, Mother's Day, and Christmas. One recent event, "Miracle Christmas '88," illustrates our method.

Prior to the event, all members were asked to list at least four people they would invite to the program and to pray specifically for God to prepare their hearts. Attractive posters announcing the event and highlighting special programs were posted on city buses, in public places, at universities, and in office complexes. Member involvement at this grassroots level encourages their interest in inviting people to attend these programs. Full-scale advertisements draw the involvement of business and celebrities to participate in the event, which attracts further interest from the public.

Miracle Christmas was a time of great excitement for the members. The atmosphere of festivity, together with the spiritual eagerness in preparing for new believers to join the church, created a refreshing spirit in outreach. As a result of Miracle Christmas '88, the Hope of Bangkok Church was able to present a gift of over 500 new believers to our Lord Jesus Christ on Christmas Day, and the spirit of evangelism was once again rejuvenated.

Personal Witnessing

Witnessing is a way of life for members of the Hope of Bangkok Church. It is taught, emphasized, modeled, and encouraged; members are continually equipped and mobilized to witness with confidence. Emphasis is placed on reaching out via webs of friends and relatives, who have proven to be most responsive. Almost all of the members of the Hope of Bangkok Church have been led to the Lord through these relationships. "Faith is not usually spread among strangers but among persons who know and trust each other."[6]

Members of the Hope of Bangkok Church have been trained to look for small and large units of responsive people to evangelize. They consciously watch for people's needs and invite them to be exposed to Christian solutions, as well as to attend church-related activities. Concentration on outreach is crucial if the church is to grow. Members are taught to depend on the Lord and pray for his preparation of hearts. Statistics show that 49.33 percent of our members pray for those they want to lead to the Lord.[7]

An incredibly high proportion (95 percent) of the growth of the church has been due to conversion. The burden for lost souls has been instilled into the membership by encouraging them to take advantage of every available opportunity for reaching out with the gospel message. This includes, for example, printing personal testimonies as tracts and distributing them at engagement ceremonies, birthdays, funerals, and weddings.

Follow-up

Having new believers join the church will not lead to church growth if proper follow-up strategy is not well executed. Data collection for statistical analysis plays a vital role as a diagnostic tool for leaders by revealing problems as well as enhancing systematic follow-up. Hope of Bangkok keeps precise records of all visitors and new believers. Correct names, addresses, important dates, maps, and convenient places of contact are filled out when these people first enter the church.

These forms are computerized and a copy of the printout is given to the pastoral leader overseeing that given geographical area. Follow-up within twenty-four hours of the conversion decision is emphasized. This helps to ensure that all doubts can be dealt with and proper spiritual nurturing and encouragement can be given from the start of their newfound faith. Thereafter, the person is visited once or twice a week to lay proper biblical foundation for faith in Christ.

---

6. C. Peter Wagner, with Win Arn and Elmer Towns, eds., *Church Growth: State of the Art* (Wheaton, Ill.: Tyndale House, 1986), 71.

7. Witoon Sinsirichavang, "Communication Characteristics in Evangelism Employed by Christian Organizations in Thailand" (Master's thesis, Chulalongkorn University, 1988), 145.

Care and Mini-Care Groups

A key thrust of the Hope of Bangkok Church is its care group structure. In December 1988 approximately 1000 care groups in Bangkok served as bridges into every subdistrict of the city. Care groups offer a non-threatening setting in which open sharing of needs, blessings, experiences, and the Word of God takes place in an atmosphere of love and concern. Because of their small size, they are an excellent forum for personal teaching and pastoral care.

Since Bangkok is a city made up of many subcultures, the Hope of Bangkok has organized its pastoral care structure around homogeneous cell groups. We have allowed the members to fellowship at the intimate level with their ethnic and cultural peers, yet the church is a heterogeneous church. In order to maintain a good balance between homogeneity and diversity, we teach and provide fellowship among people of different backgrounds as well. Membership of the Hope of Bangkok Church includes people from virtually all backgrounds, including members of the household of one of the billionaires in Thailand, high-ranking government officers from the immediate family of a past prime minister, as well as slum dwellers and ex-heroin addicts. Some homogeneous groups in the church are business executives, professionals, students, farmers, and laborers.

Effective evangelism, however, should be carried out through the group that is similar to the target audience. We accept the wisdom in the Church Growth Movement principle that "people like to become Christians without crossing racial, linguistic, or class barriers and this should occur with a minimum of social dislocation."[8] We have seen the effectiveness of this principle with the church's Student Fellowship. The student community comprises nearly 20 percent of Bangkok's population. A distinctive evangelistic approach to meet the needs of students has greatly enhanced the growth of this group in the church. By forming the Chinese Fellowship, we have for the first time enfolded ethnic Chinese converts into our church. We have avoided cultural barriers by having a Chinese approach another Chinese.

Applying this principle in our pastoral nurturing ministry, we have found that people are more responsive to small group fellowship when they are being cared for in a homogeneous setting. As they mature spiritually and learn to accept other ethnic groups in Christ, they can be transferred into cell group leadership in their geographical settings and become actively involved in shepherding others. They know that in Christ there is no room for segregation.

A step beyond the care group is the mini-care group, which promotes stronger relationships within the care group. Each mini-care group consists of two or three people from the larger care group, who learn to grow and

---

8. Wagner, Arn, and Towns, eds., *Church Growth: State of the Art*, 71.

serve together especially in evangelism, visiting new believers, and joining together regularly in prayer and Bible study.

Leadership and Discipleship Training

A convert is someone who has genuinely and biblically changed his or her mind Christ-ward. A true disciple is a convert who follows through on his or her conversion commitment by allowing his or her life to be changed to follow Christ all the way. A convert may sometimes slip back and be content in the comfort of knowing that he or she is redeemed and that Christ is there, but a disciple desires to walk closer to God. A disciple is willing to be biblically trained so that life may be transformed into the likeness of Christ. A disciple is involved in serving.

Therefore, having new converts in a church is hardly sufficient for a biblically functioning church. The Hope of Bangkok stresses strong personal and corporate discipleship training, with a vision to see a church full of committed participators, and not merely spectators, in God's kingdom.

Thais are accustomed to the idea that religious devotion means the personal practice of a religious teaching, with or without visiting the temple. Hence, they may only attend Buddhist temples a few times in their lives or perhaps not at all, though they call themselves Buddhists. This attitude often continues after conversion to Christ, which means that getting new converts to attend church can be a real struggle. We have to teach them immediately that Christianity is not simply a religion but a way of life, and that church attendance is not optional but mandatory for spiritual health, growth, and well-being.

Discipleship naturally leads to leadership training. The majority of the leaders at the Hope of Bangkok Church were converted and trained here, so perhaps our model of training new converts to become leaders within a relatively short period would be useful for church development and church planting elsewhere, especially in Christian minority and resistant areas.

Discipleship Training

The Hope of Bangkok Church has strong one-to-one and group follow-up programs with a well-structured discipleship process that follows the initial nurturing. Apart from natural and personal shepherding, there are a variety of programs to enhance spiritual and ministerial development. When nonbelievers accept Christ into their lives, they are pursued through the church's follow-up system, which is care group-oriented. On-the-job training, personal instruction, and exercising of their gifts and talents promote maturity.

When they show sufficient maturity, these believers become cell group leaders. At this point, they join our "David's Mighty Men Groups," which are small discipleship groups led by their immediate pastoral leader. Character training, doctrinal teaching, and ministry development schemes are some of the lessons taught in these groups. Transferable teaching materials are written and taught from the top down to ensure that all levels of leadership are adequately and systematically trained. I, as the senior pastor, meet with area leaders once a week; they in turn meet with those under them. This tier system has enabled the pastoral care of these hundreds of leaders to be more personal and relational.

In a "gospel-virgin" area with a relatively young church consisting mainly of new converts, this system has helped to prevent false doctrines from creeping in. In addition, the unity of the whole leadership has been strengthened.

Leadership Training

A shortage of pastors and of trained leaders is not only a temporary problem to the Thai churches. Historically it has been a thorn in the flesh. The Thai churches and Christians have been brought up without trained pastors. Strong church growth requires competent leaders. Thailand Bible Seminary was established by the Hope of Bangkok Church in June 1985 to offer four levels of training: School of Christian Life, School of Ministry, Bachelor of Theology, and Master of Divinity. All these courses combine high-level academic and biblical teaching with character development and practical training in discipleship. They also provide on-the-job ministerial training through the church's example of effective church growth and church planting. Leaders and potential leaders are trained with the sole aim of pioneering strong, growing churches. More than 1000 have completed this training; most are either serving in daughter churches or have continued with advanced training at our seminary.

A unique aspect of Thailand Bible Seminary is that students are discipled by various pastoral leaders, producing in-depth interaction between students and practicing church-mission leaders. In addition, the various levels of training can accommodate people of different educational backgrounds. The Hope of Bangkok Church is a laboratory in which students test their academic training in real church life situations. Thailand Bible Seminary has grown very rapidly into a strategic and effective training ground for home-grown leaders. Its motto sums up its purpose well: "Godly in Character, Depth in the Word, Effective in Ministry."

Another form of leadership training is more informal. I, as the senior pastor, meet with a group of selected and potential leaders to share Bible teaching, theological insights, concepts, and strategies in church work and missions. This close-knit group meets once a week. Such an opportunity has enabled leaders to share the burden for God's work with developing leaders. Much emphasis is placed on this program.

Member Participation

The Hope of Bangkok Church does not separate believers into "laity" and "clergy." All believers are called to minister with their God-given gifts. In the past, the Christian church has put forth very little effort to tap the potential of the laity.

Clergy and laity distinction must be scrapped, not only in our theological formulation, but also in actuality. I see no room for allowing the people to simply attend church and watch the performance of the "full-time" chosen ones. All gifts must be employed for the advancement of God's kingdom. This is clearly one definite way to demonstrate the priesthood of all believers. There is no place for professional ministries in the church. All clergy must be laity, and all laity must be clergy. God does not and never has called any-one to the "full-time" ministry.

At least 75 percent of those who attend worship are actively involved in ministry. Church growth requires that effective programs equip members to minister more effectively. We emphasize that all should serve God to the full-est possible capacity. To serve God in the way that he has called us is to de-vote our whole being, work, home, time, and possessions to service. Only if time constraints in a secular job prevent one from serving God effectively should "full-time" employed ministry be considered. We have approximately fifty full-time staff in Bangkok and more than 100 in Thailand. Volunteers are a major component of church ministry at the Hope of Bangkok. They serve God with much vigor, strength, and vitality.

Much formal and informal biblical and practical training is given to the laity. Interest clubs meet around many areas of ministry, such as art, evan-gelism, radio, guitar, drums, and drama. People with the same interests are trained to use those abilities to serve God.

Life Example, Sacrificial Spirit

In a survey of church members, the high level of lay participation was at-tributed to the life example and sacrificial spirit of the leader. The leadership lifestyle has challenged the members.

The pastoral team consists of well-educated men and women, successful in their careers, who have chosen to forsake secular "success" to serve God in full-time capacity, with much lower pay. Some serve with no salary at all. This spirit of putting the kingdom of God first has been passed on to the whole church body to the glory of God.

This sacrificial spirit was demonstrated when we were raising money for evangelistic needs. As a young church made up mostly of students, financial backing appeared almost impossible. I prayed about the need and shared it with our pastoral team, inviting each one to seek God personally in this matter. The burden was then passed on to the different levels of leaders and members.

At the end of three months, 10 million Baht (approximately $400,000) was raised in 1986 when membership was around 1000 and the annual average income per person in Thailand was $750.

To fulfill the task of winning this nation to Christ, the leaders sold their cars, houses, and valuable jewelry. Members had the same spirit. Life savings and many valuable items were pooled to participate in this exciting, God-honoring venture. God blessed the church as a whole through this sacrificial act.

Teaching and Preaching

Expository preaching has been vital in the growth of our church. Systematic, structured preaching has enabled members to mature with a firm, biblical worldview. Church members are taught to live holistic and balanced Christian lives. Expository preaching has also taught the church to realize the applicability of the Bible in real-life situations.

Each Sunday there are four worship services in Thai, two in English and two in Chinese. Sixty different two-hour Bible study classes in our Christian education program are offered either before or after regular worship service. At least 60 percent of those who attend worship study in one of these classes.

Worship, the Holy Spirit, and Miracles

At the Hope of Bangkok Church members are encouraged to allow the Holy Spirit to guide them during worship and their daily lives to express their love and gratitude to God. Spontaneous worship and orderly functioning of the gifts of the Holy Spirit have drawn members closer to God. Signs and wonders are performed by the Holy Spirit, especially through members laying hands on one another in prayer. These experiences confirm in people's hearts that God is powerful and still free to work today.

In a country where even nonbelievers believe in miracles by supernatural power, signs and wonders through the God of the Bible have partially contributed to the significant growth of this church. This is reflected in the innumerable verifiable testimonies that members share about God's healing power and answered prayers. The joyful, expressive, lively, contagious, victorious praise and celebration in our worship services are important aspects of the Hope of Bangkok. They remind people that God is alive and in our midst. For fun-loving Thais, this has added to the "fun" of coming to church. God loves his people to rejoice before him, and so do we.

Conclusion

God has used this young movement to effect his work in this nation in a spectacular way. More life and vigor has entered into the Thai church. Tapes of sermons, teachings, and worship choruses from the Hope of Bangkok have influenced a large proportion of Thai churches. Many of the strategies and methods have been used by other churches to bring about visible changes.

We cannot boast or be contented with the growth, as much is yet to be done. We have hardly scratched the surface. We can only say that the strategies applied have been meticulously spelled out for us by the Lord of the church, and to him be the glory in his church both now and forevermore.

Reproducing House Churches
An Autobiographical Pilgrimage

Dick Scoggins

This case study presents our experience planting churches in Rhode Island. Rhode Island has a population of about 1 million; three-fourths of that state population live in metropolitan Providence. Rhode Island is the second most densely populated state in the United States, has the highest percentage of Roman Catholics (67 percent), and one of the lowest percentages of evangelicals (2 percent).

I came to Christ through the ministry of Quidnessett Baptist Church (QBC). As part of its vision for renewal, QBC planned to start a daughter congregation in the suburbs of Providence. From the outset, the goal was to start churches that would vigorously grow and produce disciples, leaders, and new congregations.

From 1975 to 1987, I was involved in this effort. We began the Cranston Christian Fellowship (CCF), a church organized along a traditional, centralized, large group church model. This proved to be a valuable learning time for me. As with QBC, CCF strongly emphasized one-on-one discipleship, a program that focused on Christ as the model for personal character development. I learned—both from my own case and from those with whom I worked—that the process of becoming a useful servant for the King involved deep spiritual healing. The discipleship program hinged on teaching new be-

This chapter first appeared in *Urban Mission* 11, no. 3 (1994): 46–54. Used by permission.

lievers the basics of the faith. Practically, however, they learned how to allow God to mold their character. As God transformed their lives, they became better equipped to serve him.

During this time I also learned a lesson about church leadership: God provides leaders from a congregation's midst. It was a lesson I learned by personal experience. CCF had trained me for pastoral leadership by combining opportunities for service with practical training. My lessons were far-ranging, from theology to preaching, to training other men for leadership.

In 1981, I was sent with a group of believers from CCF to plant a church, the Warwick Christian Fellowship. I was intent on training the next generation of pastoral leaders. During this process, I realized the benefits of plural eldership over one pastor with a supporting board. Since I had begun my service in a pastoral position, however, and since people tend to follow the models they are presented, I doubted that truly plural leadership would ever develop as long as I remained the lead pastor. With this in mind, I asked the church to commission me as part of a team of men to the ministry of church planting. My hope was to create a model of plural leadership that could be duplicated in future church planting efforts.

I joined Jim Frost, who had been commissioned as a church planter from Cranston Christian Fellowship to form the Fellowship of Church Planters. We began a church, Lincoln Christian Fellowship, in a northern suburb of Providence that was similar to the CCF and WCF centralized models. In 1987, after progressing with this church, I began to notice a stagnation in the fellowship. It was not a new phenomenon; I'd witnessed similar patterns before. In every case, though, initial growth had been rapid before the congregational population eventually leveled off. Because numerical growth had essentially stopped, any vision of planting daughter churches remained only that—a vision.

Although QBC successfully planted another congregation in 1981, it returned to its original attendance of about 450 and was antagonistic toward further church planting efforts. CCF remained at slightly more than 300 in attendance and had planted no additional churches since Warwick in 1981. WCF, too, had plateaued at about 130; the congregation had neither planted nor demonstrated a desire to plant additional churches. Lincoln had plateaued at 85 and was unenthusiastic about church planting. All these congregations had been formed with a vision for evangelizing, reproducing disciples, and reproducing churches, yet all had lost sight of this original goal.

We seemed no closer to establishing spontaneously reproducing churches than we had been thirteen years earlier. What could be learned from these efforts? Was there a way to realize the vision? Could the barriers to reproduction be overcome? I wondered if my view was an idealistic pipe dream. Was it lunacy in this setting to dream of vibrant churches calling people into a vibrant life in the kingdom of God—a kingdom so powerful that the kingdoms of this world would be turned upside down?

If these were the types of churches God had called us to plant, we were willing to be faithful to his plan by trusting him to provide the laborers we needed. If necessary, we were ready and willing to reach Rhode Island by planting churches one by one. We estimated, however, that this would take about 300 years. On the other hand, we were also willing to try new approaches with the hope of achieving what we believed to be God's plan: churches reproducing as rapidly as the Spirit would allow. The opportunity to try new models came quickly.

New Directions

We were committed to the notion of an itinerant church planter, one who would move on a short time after forming a church. About this time we had begun a small evangelistic Bible study out in a very rural part of Rhode Island. Because the area was quite resistant to the gospel, we had great difficulty imagining that the group would ever become a church like its larger, centralized sisters. As I moved on to explore the possibility of starting a church in the densely populated suburb of East Providence, Jim Frost remained with the rural work, working slowly and patiently. He began to consider how the group might become a house church, a concept we'd then only just discovered.

In examining the house church approach, we were struck by certain aspects of small group dynamics. The house church, in a sense, is a family made up of individuals who, to varying degrees, are able both to give and to receive love. In this environment, the crippling manifestations of sin are more easily brought into the light. Consequently, hurting souls (either voluntarily or by reproof) receive the healing they need to become capable of loving. We have a motto in the house church: "You can run, but you can't hide. And if you run, we will run after you!" We witnessed people learning practically how to love one another—a miracle made evident by amazing healing in interpersonal relationships. The characteristic warmth of a circle of people sitting or often sharing a meal together encouraged rapid assimilation of new people into the church. The level of intimacy was extraordinary.

We began to assess different models of house churches as presented in literature. Of our initial findings, there is one we have come to call the independent house church model. In this model, each house church is completely independent of any others. It stands autonomous, having little if any interaction with other Christian groups. As a team, we rejected this model. Certainly, it takes into account the versatility and vibrancy of a house church, but it ignores the fact that these groups are also volatile.

Although our first effort at house church planting was an isolated house church, we realized that the church would draw strength by cooperating closely with other churches. Densely populated areas seemed ideally suited to our vision of building a strong, interactive system of house churches. Because the house church concept was both simple and flexible, it seemed the perfect vehicle for reaching characteristically diverse metropolitan groups. Already God had used it, demonstrating its effectiveness in engendering not only personal sanctification, but healing and restoration to broken families as well. Given the state of typical urban family life, metropolitan Providence seemed ripe for a house church harvest.

With Jim's rural Chepachet House Church as our guinea pig, we decided to try the concept with the church in East Providence, which had begun as a six-person investigative Bible study. When we started implementing the house church plan, this group of twenty-five-plus members had recently covenanted as East Providence Christian Fellowship; however, they were meeting regularly for Sunday evening worship and were agitating for a Sunday morning service. Undoubtedly, the group was headed toward becoming a conventional church, similar to the other churches we had planted.

I explained to the church that, although we should desire to grow, we must maintain our present intimacy as a small group. I strongly suggested that, rather than having a large Sunday morning service, we move to meeting in two separate homes on Sunday morning, while continuing to meet together Sunday evening.

The group was not enthusiastic about the proposal; they had become quite tightly knit. Many were reluctant to split up, though they realized that we had already lost the intimacy of the smaller group. But instead of considering the implications of size on intimacy, they wondered how the program could be altered to restore intimacy. I could already see that the way forward would be difficult.

After much prayer and discussion, the congregation reluctantly agreed to a three-month trial period for meeting Sunday mornings in two homes. One group met in East Providence, while the other met in the East Side neighborhood of Providence. After the three-month period, the community assessed its growth in relationships, intimacy, and service to one another. The response was overwhelmingly positive; all agreed that this pattern was the Lord's will for EPCF.

Having rejected the independent house church model, we began to gravitate toward a cell house church model. According to this plan, churches would begin as small house groups. However, as these house groups grew and multiplied, they would centralize many of their activities. Eventually, these distinct cells might purchase a common building for these activities. In this way the cells would coalesce to form one church.

It was several years ago that we began to work with this approach. As we have adapted this idea to our experience, however, we have steered a course between the independent and cell house church models. Our current pattern, which we believe is appropriate to what is happening here in Rhode Island, we call a decentralized house church model or house churches in networks.

The Pilgrimage

By the spring of 1989, EPCF was meeting regularly at two locations on Sunday mornings and jointly for services on Wednesday and Sunday evenings. The church was progressing with a solid mix of small and large group activities. One of the members had a business in an office complex and made space available for large group meetings, while we were looking for a building we could rent. All of this seemed very encouraging; clearly we seemed headed toward the cell house church model. We envisioned new members joining a particular house congregation where they would receive their basic discipling and shepherding. This would be their nuclear family—their church. Simultaneously, however, they would develop allegiance to the larger community, their extended family at that time, the East Providence Christian Fellowship. Accordingly, the purposefully blurred definition of church made for divided loyalties among the congregation. They became allied both to small house congregations as well as to the larger church.

In January of 1990 two elders were appointed; later that spring, deacons were appointed in EPCF. At the same time, a third house group began to form out of an evangelistic Bible study. We were well on our way to a centralized church of three congregations.

Unsettling conflict, however, soon arose. The newer group, Mount Pleasant, by and large did not attend the large group Sunday evening services; they pushed for a separate midweek meeting in order to pursue evangelism in a Bible study format. At the same time, attendance from the other house groups began to wane at the Sunday evening meeting. New attenders remained on the fringes rather than being integrated into the large group. The leaders prayerfully evaluated the situation. Some interesting thoughts resulted from this period:

1. There was general consensus that the larger facility for Sunday evening was sterile when compared to the warmth of a home.
2. More energy was going into the large group meetings—meetings which required a great deal of logistical planning (preaching format, kids' clubs, nursery, etc.). These maintenance activities had become so absorbing that little energy remained for growth activities (discipleship, evangelism, personal shepherding). Essentially, the large group was siphoning energy the small groups needed for growth and reproduction.
3. The large group emphasis was losing flexibility. Almost surreptitiously, meeting format and scheduling had become rigid. Un-

doubtedly, the house church's flexibility was one of its greatest strengths.

4. In the large group, interactions were common among old friends from the different house churches. Newcomers, however, tended to talk to those they already knew from their own house group. The large group meetings were not facilitating bonding among the small groups.

As the leadership prayed and discussed these things among ourselves and the congregations, it was apparent that the cell house church model was not an appropriate vehicle for our vision. We discussed the possibility of adapting the model; ultimately, however, we determined that the Lord was leading in new directions.

The Result: A Fellowship of House Churches

In August of 1990, the leadership adopted a new approach whereby the East Providence Christian Fellowship—a centralized church made up of three house cells—became the East Providence Fellowship of House Churches, a decentralized network of house churches. The fellowship consisted of two house churches: East Providence House Church (which met in two separate congregations on Sunday morning) and Mount Pleasant House Church.

The Sunday evening meeting was dissolved; instead, each house church focused its energies on developing a written covenant and vision statement. A person could join a particular house church by signing its covenant and having hands laid on by the leaders.

In addition, all the house churches in the Fellowship agreed to meet as a large group once monthly, on an evening—although during the summer a Sunday late morning or afternoon picnic became the norm. The hope in having two (rather than the traditional three) meetings per week was to allow members time to deepen their intra- and inter-house church relationships. Likewise, the members were encouraged to develop relationships with unbelievers, relationships which could eventually become bridges for the gospel. In practice, the midweek meeting was largely devoted to planning activities. Sunday morning meetings were given over to worship and Bible study. There was no formal preaching service.

This plan of autonomous yet interconnected house churches attempts to preserve the versatility and vibrancy of each house church, while bringing strength to offset some of the dangers that arise from the house churches' volatility. According to this approach, a fellowship of from two to six house churches will form, based on relationships made in the course of the churches' normal growth and reproduction.

The Structure of House Church Fellowships

Each house church in a fellowship stands autonomous; it is responsible to discern the Lord's purposes concerning itself. Accordingly, each house church drafts two documents: a covenant and a vision statement. The covenant defines expectations regarding intra- and inter-house church relationships, both on a personal and congregational level. Each house church writes its own covenant based on the "one another" verses of the Bible. It is general enough that any true follower of Christ could sign it. The covenant also includes a commitment to care for other churches—a commitment practically demonstrated by generous sharing of resources (time and money) as needs arise.

The vision statement describes, for a six-month period, the nuts-and-bolts of accomplishing the dual responsibilities of evangelism and edification. This includes not only receiving new members and shepherding them (discipleship), but also having a vision for growth and reproduction.

Leadership and Decision Making

Each house church has two male leaders. In normal house church reproduction, leaders for an emerging congregation receive their training from these leaders. New house churches started in virgin territory usually have leaders trained by church planters until they are able to reproduce themselves.

The leaders of the house churches in a fellowship meet monthly for fellowship, training, and decision making. This group is called the Fellowship Overseers Board (FOB). We believe that, although each house church has its own particular calling as its primary focus, this should not be to the exclusion of other churches. The churches in the Bible were interested in one another and cooperated by sharing resources and personnel (cf. 2 Cor. 8:1–5). The FOB is a vehicle by which leaders can help one another and coordinate some of their decisions. Decisions that affect only one house church are made by that house church alone. However, an individual house church might face a decision with fellowship-wide ramifications. In that case the church's leaders would bring the decision before the FOB for consultation and prayer.

Elder Ordination

An example of a fellowship-wide decision is the appointment of elders. An elder works primarily within a single house church, but also interacts with other leaders on the FOB. Thus the decision would have fellowship-wide effects. We hold to the principle that one of the primary responsibilities of leaders is to recognize and train other leaders. With this in mind, each leader is trained by another leader. This "mentor" initiates ordination. The mentor brings the matter to the house church and the FOB for prayer and consideration. The house church takes the FOB's input into consideration when it decides whether to ordain. The congregation is the ultimate agent responsible to confirm the call, but the FOB acts as an advisory board for further confirmation.

Church Planter Confirmation

Church planters, in a similar way, receive two confirmations. Although a particular house church commissions them, they are also confirmed at the fellowship level by the FOB. House churches, as reproductive "organisms," are relatively unstable; their populations are constantly changing. The FOB, on the other hand, while by no means unchanging, is certainly more stable than a house church. Thus, while after several years the sending house church may no longer exist in its initial form, the fellowship as a whole most likely would retain at least a few of its original leaders.

Activities suited to occur on a fellowship-wide basis are overseen by the FOB. Seminars and ministry meetings offered for continued edification are generally organized at a fellowship level. Likewise, the FOB frequently organizes activities for a specific group, like teens', women's, and men's groups. These activities are organized on an as-needed basis rather than an ongoing basis. This tends to mediate against these meetings outliving their need and absorbing energy needed for outreach.

The fellowship as a whole also is better equipped to handle the financial needs of missionaries and other supported personnel. Leaders at the house church level are normally unsupported financially.

The Present Situation

In 1991, the East Providence Fellowship had begun moving toward a decentralized fellowship of two house churches; Chepachet was an independent house church. We've witnessed dramatic growth and changes during this time. The total number of house churches had tripled (from three to nine); instead of one fellowship there were three.

The East Providence Fellowship of House Churches now has four elders and four elders-in-training, or "shepherding deacons" (SDS). All serve on the FOB. In addition, three church planters also serve as resources for the EPFHC Fellowship Overseers Board.

Still in the formative stages, the Northwest Fellowship now has one elder. Five other men (equivalent to East Providence's SD) serve on the FOB. Two church planters serve as resources for NWF's FOB. In the past four years, the Fellowship of Church Planters has grown from two to eleven members, in order to continue to help the Fellowship of House Churches grow and reproduce.

The Future

We hope that the changes we have made in our approach to church planting and reproduction will enable us to accommodate whatever harvest the Lord grants. Certainly we have been excited to see the growing number of people who are actively engaged in the expansion of the kingdom. Elders, shepherding deacons, church planters, singles, couples, men, women, teens, and even pre-teens are all finding significant places in God's plan for his expanding kingdom.

We are especially excited about the house church fellowships' interest in the broader world of missions. Financially, the fellowships have been very involved in missions; 50 percent of the offerings routinely go toward missions endeavors. The EPFHC has appointed a missions coordinator to help continue and deepen the interest in cross-cultural missions. The desire in this effort is two-fold: to support those already in this and other harvest fields and to recognize, train, and send church planters. Already these desires are becoming practical realities. According to the first hope, each house church is investigating the "adoption" of a church planting team working in a restricted country. The fellowship's first church planter was commissioned recently to the team. Additionally, a number of people—including men on home assignment from other agencies—have served as church planting interns. The Fellowship of Church Planters further serves the missionary efforts by sending some of its members to "coach" teams in other parts of the world, as well as having sent one of its members to serve a restricted field.

Truly, we have arrived at one horizon only to look beyond to another. We are awed, excited, and fearful of what may lie ahead. Certainly the growth is encouraging; it is, perhaps, a spark. Hopefully, this spark will start a fire of church growth and reproduction—not only in Rhode Island but in southern Massachusetts and beyond. We cannot control the future; we only strive to be flexible, to look ahead, to plan, and ultimately, to accommodate whatever the Lord would bring.

His Word to His World
First Baptist Church, Flushing, New York

William Travis

The First Baptist Church of Flushing is located in the northeast section of the borough of Queens, New York City. With a current population of close to 250,000, Flushing has gone through several ethnic changes in the past forty years, and its diversity is now quite astounding. It currently is 35 percent white (mostly Italians and Jews), 8–10 percent Hispanic, 5–7 percent black, 22 percent Korean, 20 percent Chinese, 4 percent from India, 1 percent Afghan, and representatives of a smattering of other groups. The Afghan community has come into existence since 1980, and a Japanese community that was present has left since 1980. Flushing has a good deal of ethnic fluidity, with the Asian sectors particularly experiencing fast growth in the 1980s.

First Baptist was founded in 1856 and for about the first 100 years of its ministry served a basically white congregation. Today's building had its cornerstone laid in 1890, so the building is approaching a century in age. With the rift that began to occur in the American Baptist Convention (then, the Northern Baptist Convention), First Baptist took its stand on the more conservative side and eventually, in 1946, severed its connection with the Convention and in two years affiliated with the General Association of Regular Baptists (GARB). In 1960 the congregation withdrew from the GARB and joined the Conservative Baptist Association, a membership it still retains.

This chapter first appeared in *Urban Mission* 6, no. 3 (1989): 37–41. Used by permission.

In the late 1940s the first black attenders arrived, and the congregation began what was to become a strong ethnic ministry. The black attenders were not immediately accepted by all the members but they stayed on and became members themselves in the early 1950s.

The 1960s saw a split in the church over three issues: the pastor, a parsonage purchase, and, most importantly, what the church's mission ought to be. With the split came the determination to stay in Flushing as the home base rather than to move elsewhere. This, combined with the already present black members, proved to be the launching of the church into an ethnic ministry.

By the 1960s a fairly substantial number of Chinese had moved into the area and a Chinese group began meeting separately in the church in the late 1960s. After going through some internal splits of its own in the 1970s, the remaining Chinese attenders joined the main body of the church as the church moved to a heterogeneous membership. In 1978 the present pastor, Russell Rosser, arrived. The heterogeneity has remained, and the church has experienced dynamic growth. So integral is this principle that Pastor Rosser describes it as a "non-negotiable, non-tradeable element." While hundreds meet every week in various congregations, all members belong to a single church—First Baptist of Flushing. The "main" congregation in which all the staff participate meets at the Sunday morning worship hour and is itself multi-ethnic.

A year after Pastor Rosser came, two associates were added to the pastoral staff. Henry Kwan took over the Chinese phase of the ministry and Jorge Prado the Spanish and Portuguese sectors. Rosser sees staff as a key ingredient in the urban context and promotes recruitment of qualified persons to lead the various parts of the ministry. He believes the senior pastor should be a facilitator and administrator who lets the staff carry out the various operations of the multiple ministry.

Besides the Spanish, Portuguese, and Chinese congregations, there is a Jewish work run from the church under the auspices of the Conservative Baptist Home Mission Society. An Indian ministry reaches out to the Indian people by celebrating India Independence Day. The small Afghan community has a special interest in New Year's Day and the church provides various activities for such an occasion. J. Christy Wilson of Gordon-Conwell Seminary, a former missionary to Afghanistan, spoke at one of these events. There are several other ministries as well. Friendship International, a division of International Missions, operates out of First Baptist with a special interest in work with Muslims and Hindus. International Missions runs a summer training program to reach Hindu and Muslim people, which has had positive effects on the work in Flushing.

An Early Childhood Center operates a preschool in the church, and is an outreach to the parents. Several years ago the church began a counseling center for the various ethnic groups in the surrounding area. The English Language Institute began in the mid–1980s to reach new arrivals to the United States through English instruction. First Baptist runs an aggressive intern program, with connections to Campus Crusade for Christ and Inter-Varsity. The church hoped to become a site for Conservative Baptist Seminary of the East and has some ties to the urban program of Alliance Theological Seminary of Nyack, New York. Its desire is to provide valuable urban experience for seminary students.

The intern program provides an excellent outlet of overseas training, and it enhances the work of First Baptist as it influences other ministries and sends some of its principles of operation elsewhere. For example, the first Brazilian appointee to Mozambique under Africa Inland Mission did his internship in 1986 under the tutelage of Prado.

Rosser has clearly found a successful niche for ministry. He began as a pastor in eastern Pennsylvania while still in his teens and held pastorates while attending college in Allentown. Later he attended some seminary classes but did not receive a degree. A believer in seminary education, he has served as chairman of the board of the newly formed Conservative Baptist Seminary of the East which has an innovative approach to urban ministry. He is also on the board of the Conservative Baptist Association of America.

Ministry in the city has many special difficulties. Extra stress is generated by mere day-to-day living; thus the need for the counseling center. The constant flow of persons moving in and out of the city causes a consequent turnover in church membership and leadership. Fortunately, the pastoral staff at First Baptist has been very stable and works well together.

Rosser says that urban churches must take in three persons to grow by one. It is Rosser's conviction that baptism helps new members continue with church life. He sees baptism as a very important event in the new convert's life. The church's membership reached about 600 by 1989. So diverse is the congregation that people from five different continents have been baptized in a single service.

Flushing Baptist identifies nine blocks as its ministry area, a population of 90,000. Flushing Fantastic, a community-wide celebration, presents an unusual opportunity for the church. Literature in fifty different languages is distributed (there are 104 languages in the community) and street preaching is done throughout the neighborhood. At other times, films in various languages have been shown in services at parks. The Christmas nativity scene includes a menorah candle as a reminder of Hanukkah, letting Jewish neighbors know that Christians are concerned. Muslim and Hindu festivals are also celebrated in creative ways.

First Baptist's century-old building has upkeep and space problems. Parking is limited. Solving those problems while serving its target area meant looking at creative alternatives: (1) Selling the property, prime real estate, and building a new facility close by would provide adequate parking and a more practical building, but it would disconnect the church from its ministry to the people in the nine-block area. (2) The church also could sell some of its land to a high-rise developer and in exchange receive a second or third floor in the new building for office, gym, and classroom space. The church would obtain parking in a new parking garage connected with the high-rise. The church could continue to carry out their present ministry to the surrounding nine-block area. This idea is the more feasible.

First Baptist has a strong interest in fostering further church ministry through its own members. Since Pastor Rosser began his ministry, twenty-five to thirty members have gone into Christian work, and more are in seminary. The church views its commitment to these people very seriously and requires of them a strong commitment to the church. Each future seminarian must do an internship at the church before being recommended for seminary training. Also, seminarians are required to do an internship at the church while in seminary.

Calvary Baptist Church in Manhattan has operated the New York School of the Bible, which has students from many minority groups. First Baptist began a relationship with the school in the fall of 1986 and is now the site for the Queens branch. The church networks with many other groups that provide experiences for the church members. The food pantry run by the congregation is now channeled through a nearby organization. This gives the church members an opportunity to help without a full-time commitment. The staff thought of starting a Korean ministry; but a nearby Korean Presbyterian Church was very effective in reaching that ethnic group. First Baptist now advises its Korean attenders to go to that congregation.

Rob Boyd, associate director of the Baptist General Conference Home Missions Board, focusing on cultural and urban ministry, states that a church body should reflect the makeup of its community and not lag behind on any changes that occur. Change is easiest when it occurs naturally. Boyd goes on to stress that in God's church self-determination and access to power must be given to minority groups in the congregation. First Baptist of Flushing has pioneered in operating in a multicultural context, to the enrichment of the body of believers and the extension of the work of Christ. God's Word is going to his world.

Between Resurrection and Reconciliation

The Story of New Song Community Church

Mark R. Gornik

Very early on the Saturday morning before Easter, Bubby Crosby awoke tired and sore but ready to begin the day's work. An assistant construction manager with Sandtown Habitat for Humanity, Bubby had spent the previous few nights sleeping on the floor of 1511 North Stricker Street, rowhouse number 21 of 100 houses Sandtown Habitat was rehabilitating in the neighborhood. As each house neared completion, everyone was extra security-conscious. Bubby's overnight presence ensured that no break-ins would tarnish this dedication day.

The staff and volunteers began to stream into 1511 North Stricker. From the neighborhood and across the Baltimore metropolitan area, black and white, affluent and poor, urban and suburban, came together around a shared commitment—the creation of decent and affordable housing for people in need.

Members of Epiphany Episcopal Church, the house sponsor and one of five Episcopal congregations laboring together on what has come to be known as "Episcopal Row," provided the funding and volunteers. The prospective homeowner contributed over 300 hours of "sweat equity."

This chapter first appeared in *Urban Mission* 12, no. 2 (1994): 52–60. Some minor revisions have been made to bring it up to date. Used by permission.

Precious little time remains before the afternoon dedication, the culmination of seven months of hard work by hundreds of people. Activity is swirling. Every space of the house seems to have someone working on it. The sounds of hammers, saws, laughing, and "dedication panic" fill the house as interior doors are hung, plumbing is finalized, the last pieces of carpet are installed, and window shades are set in place. A house is being transformed into a beautiful home.

Good News on Stricker Street

This house is for William and Mary Elliott, both in their sixties. Community residents for over forty-nine years, today, for the first time in their lives, they will own their home. Both are strong Christians. Mr. Elliott in particular will be bringing leadership skills to the block. As the first of twenty homes to be completely gutted and rebuilt on this block, this home's dedication is a great day for the neighborhood.

At 3:30, the sound of gospel singing replaces the hocking and plocking of hammers. Outside the house on the street, more than 100 neighborhood residents, friends, and Habitat homeowners have gathered to celebrate the dedication. It is time to "have church," time to celebrate the goodness of Jesus and acknowledge God as the builder (Ps. 127:1; Heb. 3:4).

As Millard Fuller, Habitat for Humanity's founder, would say, "every house dedication is a living sermon, a tangible demonstration of God's love and power." Leading the service is LaVerne Cooper, co-executive director of Sandtown Habitat. She is particularly pleased this day; this house, which had been vacant for twenty years, had been her grandmother's home. In fact, this is LaVerne's old block; the vacant house next door was where she grew up. Now LaVerne, also a Habitat homeowner, is leading the way in rebuilding her former block.

At the vibrant dedication service, special music was provided by the New Song Community Learning Center Choir. Keys and a Bible were presented to the new homeowners. Other Habitat families presented flowers. Testimonies were offered by the Elliotts, Epiphany volunteers, and other community leaders. Linking the testimonies was the realization that new relationships have been formed across immense racial, social, and spatial chasms. A closing prayer and house blessing was pronounced.

Finally, the moment has come to cut the ribbon. Bubby, a lifetime resident of Sandtown, joins Mr. Elliott and members of Epiphany for the honors. To cheers and clapping, the Elliotts enter 1511 North Stricker Street, new homeowners. Life is affirmed; a community long put down is rising up.

Few events more vividly capture the heartbeat of ministry at New Song Community Church. Sandtown Habitat, one of more than 1000 Habitat affiliates, was begun in 1990 by our congregation. Committed to being a

Christian community development church, we have embraced the rebuilding of our neighborhood. Yes, a vacant house has been restored. But it is much more than that. The community of faith gathered on Stricker Street is properly celebrating Easter—a message both heavenly and earthly. Reconciliation is being joined with resurrection.

Called to Be Neighbors

With a fury that won't still, the statistics of tragedy and misery in our inner-city neighborhoods keep growing. Life for the poorest of the poor in urban America is a day-to-day struggle against relentless forces of death. Since the early 1970s poverty has become more clearly urban, more concentrated in economically depressed neighborhoods within more segregated Latino and African American communities. Neighborhoods are uniformly sicker, hungrier, more unemployed, less adequately housed, more violent, and increasingly discouraged. Add in the pervasive loss of spiritual purpose and meaning, and thus the growth of lovelessness, hopelessness, and distrust, and you have nihilism. It is easy to see why our poorest neighborhoods are becoming unraveled.

Sandtown-Winchester, known in the community as Sandtown, is part of the "other Baltimore," a microcosm of post-modern urban poverty dynamics. Though less than two miles west of Baltimore's famed Inner Harbor development, Sandtown might as well be a world away. While Baltimore's downtown and surrounding suburban communities are thriving economically, inner-city neighborhoods such as Sandtown continue to decline. In Sandtown, unemployment runs close to 50 percent; infant mortality exceeds that of many Two-Thirds world nations. Sandtown is a community of great historic strength and character. But jarred and jolted by many forces, including the post-industrial bleeding of manufacturing jobs, Sandtown has been crushed by the mechanisms of poverty. Household median income was less than $8,500 in the early 1990s, significantly below the poverty threshold. Isolated from the economic mainstream, it is one of Baltimore's poorest neighborhoods.

In 1986, along with Allan and Susan Tibbels and their daughters, Jennifer and Jessica, I moved to the Sandtown neighborhood of West Baltimore to begin New Song Community Church, an inter-racial congregation of the Presbyterian Church in America. When we began, we owned no buildings. Most of our budget came out of our own pockets. Our closest Christian friends called us crazy; others were not so kind.

What was our motivation? Our call was rooted in knowing how much God loved Sandtown, a desire to follow Christ in a spirit of servanthood, a deep concern for the poor, and a commitment to repentance. Repentance, as the biblical witness defines it, is not about feeling guilty or sorry. Rather, repentance involves "owning" our sin, whether rooted in commission or omission. Concretely, repentance means turning from one way of life to an alternative way. Biblical repentance touches every area of life. It is at once spiritual, social, and economic (Isa. 1:16–17; Luke 19:1–10). As white Christians, we believed that it was vital that we turn from our complicity in a culture that is anti-black, anti-poor, and anti-urban, and turn to the biblical obligations of justice and reconciliation.

For the first two years, we focused entirely on building relationships with our new neighbors. Our ministry style was incarnational and low-profile, not obtrusive. Such activities as volunteering at the local recreation center, visiting people in their homes, playing basketball on the outdoor courts, and attending community meetings proved foundational for all that would take place in our church. We listened to our neighbors to gain understanding into the community's felt needs from the inside out. Given the historic and ongoing role of whites in oppressing our community, how we were treated is a testimony to Sandtown's capacity for graciousness. At about the same time we moved to Sandtown, an African American family moved to an all-white neighborhood in South Baltimore. So mistreated that they were forced to live under police protection, they finally gave up and moved away.

But our move to Sandtown was only a small part of New Song's story; central to that story are the people who loved us, embraced us as friends, and helped to form our church community. Isaac, Fitts, Torrey, Elnora, LaVerne, and Bubby, and many others shared in the heavy work of building a church. God knit together a body of faith out of persons from a variety of backgrounds who share a passion to love God and their community.

One Lord, One People

Ethnic, racial, and other conflicts are tearing cities and nations apart, and many believe that our cities are sliding down the Bosnian road. Where will the world look for examples of inter-racial relationships? We believe that a significant part of the church's public ministry must be to model healthy cross-cultural relationships, to look more like the kingdom and less like our hyper-segregated culture (1 Cor. 5:17).

Humanity, the crowning jewel of God's creation, is like the scattered shards of glass from a broken bottle, its original integrity shattered. We are hurting and hurtful. Reconciliation is not cheap; nor is it the absence of conflict. Rather, it is the presence of right relationships—God putting things back together. "And he made known to us the mystery of his will according to his good pleasure, which he purposed in Christ . . . to bring all things in heaven and on earth together under one head, even Christ" (Eph. 1:9–10). At its core, our task in the city involves the reconciliation of a sinful people to a holy God and to one another.

It is clear that reconciliation is always rooted in God's sovereign initiative. Jesus is the one who calls us to himself and each other (Mark 3:13–18). As the master Urban Artisan, God has not given up on us. He is turning a fractured and broken humanity into something beautiful (Psalm 133). Christ's call is not just to "me and my God," but to a new peoplehood, a deep, supernatural togetherness.

The gathering of this peoplehood into the church is not to be based on similar tastes, interests, or appearances. Neither is unity the same thing as uniformity. Rather, the decisive ingredient of reconciled relationships is the grace of God. Unity is founded in the sharing of the same goal and purposes, a commitment to know and love each other, and the complementary use of gifts and abilities. Reconciliation is about celebrating something bigger than ourselves—the reign of God.

For the Lord's people, reconciliation is a posture toward the world. As Robert J. Schreiter put it, "reconciliation is not a skill to be mastered; rather it is something that is discovered: the power of God's grace welling up in one's life. Reconciliation becomes more of an attitude than an acquired skill; it becomes a stance assumed before a broken world . . . reconciliation is more of a spirituality than a strategy."[1] We can inflict tremendous damage on the status quo just by being who we are in Christ (Eph. 1:18). The body of Christ stands as God's demonstration community—of the new city still to come. Thus, the church is God's counter-sign amidst relational and structural brokenness.

As Paul reminded the Corinthians, "Because there is one loaf, we, who are many, are one body, for we all partake of the one loaf" (1 Cor. 10:17). For Paul, reconciliation is the defining mark of the kingdom. The church has the privilege of anticipating in its body-life the reconciled community which will be found in the coming new city of God (Luke 14:16–24: Rev. 7:9–17).[2] At the same time, the local church has its own unique history, reflecting a given social and cultural context (1 Cor. 9:22; 10:31–33). If there is "one Lord," then we are "one people,"[3] and anything less than reconciliation reinforces the idols of the city scape and denatures the power of the gospel.

In the biblical material, justice is intimately connected to reconciliation. "The fruit of righteousness will be peace; the effect of righteousness will be quietness and confidence forever" (Isa. 32:17). Reconciliation is a biblical goal, but as a missiological agenda item, it works only as a part of the whole gospel (Micah 6:8, Luke 4:16–21).

1. Robert J. Schreiter, "Reconciliation as a Missionary Task," *Missiology* 20, no. 1 (1992): 2–10.
2. Geoffrey Wainwright, "The Church as a Worshiping Community," *Pro Ecclesia* 3, no. 1 (1994): 61.
3. N. T. Wright, "One God, One Lord, One People: Incarnational Christology for a Church in a Pagan Environment," *Ex Auditu* 7 (1991): 45–58.

For New Song, reconciliation is not a program, but the very heart of who we are. It is not a commodity to be organized and managed, but a dynamic to enter into. We are intentionally inter-racial. However, it is vital that we communicate to others that our church has not yet "arrived." We are in the process of becoming reconciled, of growing into our identity as one people. There is much work ahead for us, labor filled with great joy but also pain. Added to this, each one of us brings our own brokenness and need for Christ-centered wholeness.

Rebuilding and Reweaving

In 1988, the group that was to found New Song began meeting in my living room for worship. As a congregation, we wanted to address the life needs and concerns of our community. How could we proclaim the good news to an entire neighborhood? First, we would design our worship service in a manner that was both biblical and contextual. Oriented to the unchurched, our service seeks to draw people into the world-changing presence of God. Second, in order for the gospel to have credibility to reach unchurched young people, we needed a "see and touch" presence in the community. We would have to demonstrate God's love, power, and compassion, not just talk about it (Isa. 58:6–10; James 1:16–17; 1 Peter 2:12).

In 1988, we purchased a long-vacant building for our growing congregation. After two years of renovation, we moved in and greatly expanded our outreach efforts. With the church as the foundation and energizing center, we initiated a holistic approach to community development focused on approximately twelve blocks in the north-central section of Sandtown. Believing that reconciliation encompasses every area of life, our current neighborhood-based efforts include:

Sandtown Habitat for Humanity

Started in 1988, Sandtown Habitat builds houses for home ownership for low and very low income families in Sandtown. We are nearing our goal of eliminating vacant housing in our focus area. We will probably rehabilitate nearly 200 houses and build twenty-seven new ones on Leslie Street. We received a great boost when we hosted the 1992 Jimmy Carter Work Project. Sandtown Habitat, with a full-time staff of ten, operates an extensive volunteer program of more than 4000 volunteers a year. Not only do our volunteers play an important role in helping to rebuild our community, but their connection to the life of our community is a model of the regionalism essential to the future of all metropolitan areas.

New Song Community Learning Center

The Learning Center opened its doors in 1991 in response to the needs of neighbors who desired improved education for their children. Its goal is to see children in our community achieve success in education and life. The Learning Center provides educational enrichment and assistance for Sandtown children and youth. More than 100 children are involved in preschool (ages 3–4) and after-school (kindergarten through high school) programs, as well as a summer education camp and a scholarship program. In 1994, we began New Song Academy, a non-public middle school. The Learning Center choir, The Voices of Hope, has recorded their first CD. We look forward to seeing the impact as many of these students graduate from college and return to the community with their skills, vision, and resources to help rebuild.

New Song Family Health Center

As an expression of God's compassion and concern for the whole person and total community, New Song began a health ministry. The Health Center, staffed by volunteer doctors and nurses, provides primary health care for mainly uninsured community residents, both adults and children. We also are involved in preventative health care, including efforts to reduce high blood pressure.

EDEN Jobs

Our newest initiative is EDEN Jobs (Economic Development Employment Network). A job development and placement program for unemployed Sandtown residents, its goal in 1994 was fifty placements, increasing to 100 annually. The program is heavily oriented toward people development. Seed funding and technical support came from World Vision.

Our philosophy of church-based community development is guided by a number of principles. Holistic ministry is spiritual, social, and economic. Renewal percolates up, not trickles down, and addresses underlying issues, not symptoms. Changes that prove effective are grafted onto existing social and family networks. Thus, the bridges to change aren't programs but relationships. Successful development will build on the strengths of people and the community, not bypass them. Everyone has a vital contribution to make. Therefore, broad-based leadership development is primary, not secondary. Like a mustard seed, community development begins small. It involves gentle, non-cataclysmic, and genuine responses to human needs. Those responses, given space and nourishment, grow in depth and scope. The sustaining motivation for confronting poverty is a concern for justice, not economic self-interest. And finally, true development is mutually transformational, not one-sided. It begins and ends with changed hearts.

Underlying this community development strategy are a number of renewal commitments central to the life of our church. They include the clear communication of God's grace, the necessity of kingdom-centered prayer, a heart for the city and the poor, and servant leadership.

As our church began to grow, the Lord blessed us with two strong additions to the pastoral team, Wy Plummer and Steve Smallman, who joined a rapidly expanding neighborhood-based staff as co-pastors modeling racial reconciliation in shared black–white leadership. Over time, our worshiping community has grown to well over 125 people (which is overflowing our sanctuary), with a wider circle of more than 500 people involved throughout the week.

A partner in the rebuilding of Sandtown is Newborn Apostolic Faith Church of the Trinity, a neighborhood storefront congregation led by Elder Clyde Harris. A lifelong resident of the community, Harris serves as director of family nurture for Sandtown Habitat, and our two congregations share a common gospel witness and ministry.

One way we express our unity is in the Sandtown Voices of Unity Choir. This choir includes not only church members, but draws also from Habitat homeowners and other groups and performs at many different functions, including house dedications.

In everything we do, we seek to have the highest standards of excellence. Too often, people who are poor receive society's hand-me-downs. This communicates many negative images. We believe Christ wants us to share our best and finest, to lavish our gifts, talents, and resources in the service of a more just and joyful community.

In a valuable work on racial reconciliation, Raleigh Washington and Glen Kehrein identify a number of principles essential to healthy inter-racial relationships: commitment, intentionality, sincerity, sensitivity, interdependence, sacrifice, empowerment, and calling.[4] Our experience confirms the wisdom of their observations. Every strong relationship takes time and effort. That is why it is so important for us to daily love and forgive each other within a biblical framework (Eph. 4:4–6).

We have also found at New Song that having a sense of humor is vital. While we take our work seriously, we try not to take ourselves too seriously. Sometimes it seems like we may not get a lot done, but we sure have fun together trying. A sense of connectedness to a larger movement of God in our cities has been important. Our participation in the Christian Community Development Association and Habitat for Humanity has served us very well.

Challenges

God has profoundly blessed us at New Song. He has done more than we could have possibly dreamed. Joy, dignity, and hope are being restitched into the swatch of urban fabric where God has called this group of believers (Isa.

---

4. Raleigh Washington and Glen Kehrein, *Breaking Down Walls: A Model for Reconciliation in an Age of Racial Strife* (Chicago: Moody, 1993), 113–220.

58:12). Lives and an entire neighborhood are being changed. We have seen a new foundation set for the growth of our community. Hearts are responding to God's grace.

Ahead lie many new challenges for New Song. After much prayer and reflection, a second New Song work will soon be started—this time in New York City. The vision of what can happen in our inner cities needs to be ever-expanding and risk-taking if it is to stay truly vital. And so the next mission chapter for New Song has two parts—first, to build and keep dynamic the ministry in Baltimore, and second, to extend outward to other cities and communities. What a great privilege and opportunity from the Lord to seek the shalom of the city in new ways. And in so doing, by God's grace, we will continue to move from resurrection to reconciliation.

Harambee Christian
Family Center

Benjamin P. Pierce

The Harambee Christian Family Center was started by John and Vera Mae Perkins in 1982. The Perkinses had spent twenty-three years in Mississippi, starting and developing a Christian community development project called Voice of Calvary Ministries to improve the physical and spiritual quality of life for blacks in Mississippi. In 1982 they moved to Pasadena, California, to travel, write, and retire. The Lord had other plans.

John and Vera Mae became concerned with the crime rate and drug infestation in northwest Pasadena, and when they saw a house for sale in a neighborhood with one of the highest rates of daytime crime and per capita drug use in California they bought it and moved in.[1] Of the five houses Harambee now occupies, three had been used in the drug trade.

Their first step was to start a neighborhood watch. The Perkinses were not very popular with those involved in this "drug supermarket." They would call the police to report who was selling drugs in the area. As a result, their house was firebombed twice by drug dealers and they had bricks thrown through their windows. They didn't leave. While they eventually were given more police protection, the neighborhood remained dangerous. Three murders occurred within fifty yards of their house.

The Perkins' method of fighting for the neighborhood began with a prayer meeting. Then Mrs. Perkins began what would become the main

This chapter first appeared in *Urban Mission* 7, no. 5 (1990): 45–53. Used by permission.

1. "Let's Get Together and Push," audio tape, produced by Harambee Christian Family Center, 1987.

focus of Harambee's ministry—reaching out to neighborhood kids. She and a woman named Adie James started talking to kids on the street in front of the Perkins' home, asking them, "Do you have a grandmother?" Those who seemed to have no strong family relationships were told, "I'll be your grandmother." They began taking kids to camps and outings and getting them to come to "Good News Clubs," backyard Bible studies for child evangelism.[2]

Place of Ministry

Today Harambee targets a ten-block area in northwest Pasadena to influence for Christ. These ten blocks extend from Fair Oaks in the east to Lincoln Avenue in the west, and from Washington in the south to Tremont Avenue in the north. In addition to the area's crime and drug problem, 60 percent of the households are headed by single parents. The neighborhood is approximately 60 to 65 percent black, around 30 percent Hispanic, and the rest a mixture. There has been some growth in the Hispanic population since the Perkins family moved in. However, neighborhood demographics are fairly stable because there is a relatively high percentage of single-unit, owner-occupied homes, instead of mostly rental dwellings as in many inner city locations.

Largely as a result of the efforts of Harambee and the Perkinses, the drug presence and the neighborhood have changed since 1982. The chief cause of crime had been drugs. As the drug trade has declined, so has the amount of crime. There are still a lot of both drugs and crime, but Perkins believes that "kids have a chance in this neighborhood now without being overrun by drugs."[3] When drug infestation builds up in one part of the neighborhood, Harambee will call in the police to keep drugs from ever getting the foothold it had before.

According to John Perkins, the main problem of the ghetto in general and of northwest Pasadena in particular is not an absolute lack of money, at least not in the traditional sense of poverty. Cash is coming into the neighborhood through work, drugs, and welfare. "Money is not the issue, it is the use of the money and skill development that is the heart of the problem. . . . Poverty of money is not our problem; it is poverty of spirit, poverty of motivation, and poverty of education."[4] In light of this, Harambee seeks to give kids and the rest of the community a vision to see (1) that it is possible and desirable to earn their money rather than be given it; (2) that they can earn this money honestly; and (3) that they can get the skills necessary to do it.

2. John Williams, interview with Ben Pierce, May 3, 1988.
3. John Perkins, interview with Ben Pierce, May 10, 1988.
4. Ibid.

Philosophy of Ministry

The philosophy that the Perkinses have instilled at Harambee is holistic Christian community development. This means ministering to people as body, soul, and spirit. An initial element of this philosophy is relocation, or moving into the neighborhood of ministry. The five houses Harambee now owns make it possible for almost all of the full-time staff to live on the premises. In this way, the needs of the community become the needs of those ministering in it, and the relationships formed provide the means to share the gospel and know and meet people's needs.[5]

Evangelism and discipleship are foundational to what Harambee is all about. Harambee's way of evangelism gives the community a three-dimensional view of the gospel, as *proclamation* is intertwined with *development* and *development* is intertwined with *proclamation* and *social responsibility*. Social responsibility means meeting the felt needs of the people, based on the people's own hopes and aspirations.

Harambee participates in economic development by getting kids job-ready and finding jobs. Work has a high priority. The Harambee philosophy of ministry is that, as people work, their dignity as human beings is affirmed. This philosophy and these purposes, plus a high sense of justice, motivate Harambee to help people break out of the cycle of poverty and stand firm in Jesus Christ.[6]

Strategy and Goals

Harambee's primary strategy has been to reach the community by reaching its young people. The core of their ministry to the kids is: (1) Bible studies, fellowship groups, and special events for evangelism and discipleship; (2) tutoring to give academic support; (3) work and life skills training; (4) helping find jobs for kids and supporting them in their jobs; and (5) spending time with the kids and their families, loving them and caring for them. The goal is to lead young men and women to Christ, and to encourage them to go to college and come back into the community as entrepreneurs, job creators, and godly people. This process will produce indigenous young leaders, both for the ministry and the community.[7]

Evangelism, discipleship, education, and enabling go hand in hand. The staff and volunteers seek to give their best efforts to a balance of evangelism, discipleship, and community development.

Perkins sees "nothing big" in future goals and directions for the Harambee Center. "We have the process in place with this facility and existing pro-

5. "Let's Get Together and Push."
6. Perkins interview.
7. Williams interview.

grams." The community has changed much in the years Harambee has been there. The tools for continued and greater change focus on the children. They are plants, Perkins says. They must be tended before they can bear fruit.[8] This tending process takes time. Harambee staff have the major job now to work diligently and patiently with the kids, mainly through existing programs, giving these efforts time to bear fruit in kids' lives.

People and Structures

As the president of Harambee, Perkins is less involved in the day-to-day running of the center than in giving vision to it. He is also the main fund-raiser for the center. He is, say the staff, the "visionary, whose vision is focused outwards towards others"; the "dynamic source of ideas and enthusiasm"; the "seed planter, initiator, and fire-starter, who sparks off ideas, some of which catch and some of which don't."[9] Harambee remains the product of Perkins' vision and energy.

Vera Mae Perkins is the vice president and oversees accounting and finances. She is the day-to-day, overall authority at the center who makes sure that money is used wisely and that the offices run efficiently. She is also the inspiration for new Bible studies and child evangelism. Staff describe her as "the anchor that keeps things going"; "tenderhearted, yet strong," "wise," "steady"; "humble," and "consistent."[10]

The two other permanent ministry positions are youth program director and director of community youth development/outreach director. Program director John Williams oversees all programs and is heavily involved in many of the programs relating to youth. He recruits kids and the volunteers who work with them. He is Harambee's "contact person" and tells the Harambee story to churches, high school groups, colleges, and Christian organizations.

As director of youth development and outreach, Kent Bailey also wears many hats. Bailey gives job training and helps find work so that young people can make honest money and learn the responsibility of holding down a job. He also has responsibility for ministry to junior high and high school kids through weekly fellowship and discipleship meetings. Staff work together closely since aspects of the ministry overlap. Both directors spend much of their time doing very practical things with the kids to instill life skills, with an eye on seeing them saved and discipled.

Four other full-time staff positions all involve direct ministry to the kids and community, though primary job responsibilities are in office and minis-

8. Perkins interview.
9. Elizabeth Robinson and Kent Bailey, interviews with Ben Pierce, May 6, 1988, and May 13, 1988, respectively.
10. Robinson and Bailey interviews.

try management. The staff handles special writing projects, Bible clubs, the newsletter, and an adult literacy program.

Harambee relies heavily on volunteers to help with tutoring, Bible studies, fellowship groups, summer programs, work crews, and skills training.

Daily Life and Ministry

About sixty young people are consistently involved in the ministry of the Harambee Center. There is some activity every day. About half of the core group is black and half is Hispanic. Programs serve primary age through senior high.

Tutoring and skills training covers such skills as typing, computer, wood shop, sewing, piano, graphic arts, and writing. The variety of the skills taught depends on the abilities of volunteers. Volunteers also help kids with homework assignments. John Williams regards the most successful program as a one-on-one matching of children and volunteers. In addition to academic help, participants are forming relationships with people who are good influences. Many relationships extend outside the classroom. One night each week the Harambee Learning Center tutors children in grades one through four.

Evangelism and discipleship happen in programs specifically designed for them and in the way all ministries are carried out, whether overtly spiritual or not. The overt thrust of youth evangelism and discipleship centers in Bible study-fellowship groups. On Mondays, as part of the Harambee School, there is a Bible study and Scripture memorization. On Fridays, the Young Ladies Christian Club and the Brotherhood Club meet for recreation, fellowship, and support for pre-junior high ages. Kent Bailey and John Williams run Friday Night Live for teens, emphasizing recreation and discipleship. On Sunday morning, free breakfast comes before Sunday school and church. The staff also gives pastoral care. They try to keep tabs on how everyone is doing and give counsel when needed. They also try to help the kids to relate to their parents, especially if they are in trouble. This direct interaction is where staff can most directly see young people come to Christ and grow as disciples.[11]

Employment skills are directly taught at Harambee Business Club on Saturdays, a three-hour meeting emphasizing work skills and experience. Small business projects take place on the Harambee property, a silk screening business for customized T-shirts and a cassette recording business. Bailey solicits business from the community and friends of Harambee and supervises the work. The teen employees receive more than minimum wage and they get experience making honest money and taking job responsibility. In the sum-

---

11. Bailey interview.

mers, Bailey works with the city's Summer Youth Employment program, supporters of the center, and employment agencies to find jobs.

Summer day camp meets for eight weeks during the summer for six hours a day. About sixty kids make crafts, participate in sports and field trips, play music, and go on overnight camp-outs. Staff take the older kids to retreats, at which a number have committed their lives to the Lord.

Though not the main emphasis of their ministry, Harambee does minister to adults in the community. One aspect of this ministry is adult literacy training. Harambee also works with families of Harambee kids. This is not an official program, but John and Kent try to get to know home situations and establish trust with the parents, which they hope will open the way for ministry to these families' needs and to sharing the gospel with them. Harambee also sponsors community entertainment in the amphitheater behind the center.[12]

John Perkins' Dreams

John Perkins doesn't expect Harambee Center to be an ever-expanding institution, but he does dream of facilitating the development of similar organizations in other communities as they catch the vision. He also would like to see the formation of a holistic, Bible-based church in northwest Pasadena. He envisions using neighborhood Bible studies and weekly meetings in a public building at which he would teach, to see if a church can be established. This would give the community as a whole the biblical base and foundation Harambee works to instill in children and teens. It also could give longevity to the ministry on which Harambee is built. Another tack such development might take would be to plant Harambees in several communities, which would meet together on Sunday for a worship jubilee.[13]

Optimizing Ministry with Inner-city Youth

Without ministering to the parents of Harambee kids, the influences can be undercut at home. Important to meeting individual needs is for volunteers to spend time developing trust relationships. As a volunteer myself, the most enjoyable and effective time I have devoted was spent playing racquetball with one of my Harambee tutoring students. His responsiveness to me and to the study hall time increased dramatically after our afternoon together. Volunteers maximize their usefulness and increase their own joy in service through sharing one-on-one time, which is what Jesus gave his disciples and is, in my opinion, the surest way to shape young lives.

The other significant challenge facing Harambee-style ministries is to find enough volunteers who speak Spanish. This would enhance their ability to

12. Ibid.
13. Perkins interview.

minister to and tutor Spanish-speaking kids. Long-term staff might want to consider learning Spanish as well.

God's Options

Harambee and its ministry is incarnational and holistic in that it slights neither the proclamation of the gospel nor the development of the community. The committed, spiritual staff are there out of love for the Lord and sincere Christ-centered compassion for the city and its people. Otherwise, the pay and the neighborhood would not attract them.

Programs and strategy reflect a long-term perspective in concentrating on the next generation of community leaders. They develop these future leaders as whole people, suggesting whole answers to minister to their whole needs. But beyond the programs and quantifiable results, an important aspect of Harambee's ministry is simply its presence in the community. The presence of Harambee and the "Harambee people" say silently but unmistakably to the community that God loves them, and that he provides each of us with a better way. The "presence factor" in Harambee's ministry is like that of an elderly believer who went every day to the high school sports practices to be an influence for Christ. A friend told the man that he was probably wasting his time. Sharing Christ with kids was difficult in that environment. The man responded, "I must go, because when I'm there, God has more options than when I'm not." Harambee obediently gives God more options in northwest Pasadena.

Encounter with God: The Guayaquil Model

Fred Smith

In 1973, a model of evangelistic urban church growth was established in Lima, Peru,[1] that has since spread to Argentina, Brazil, Chile, Colombia, Ecuador, and El Salvador. It has proven successful, to some degree, in each of these countries, though it has not always experienced the same exciting success as in Lima. There it still produces exceptionally large crowds (for Peru) and daughter churches. Since its inception, the program in Lima has grown from one church and 120 members to twenty-five churches and more than 10,000 members.

Four Factors

The *Encounter with God* program (or the *Lima Model*) is an urban model for church growth based principally on four factors:

First, development of an impact or Encounter church in highly visible and accessible areas of strategic cities. The term *impact* applies to a numerically large church that is financially capable of supporting a ministry team and has the goal of hiving off 80 to 100 members plus a full-time pastor to start a daughter church. *Impact* also indicates that it is a church that evangelistically affects an area in which it is located and is known throughout the city.

Second, an evangelistic philosophy of ministry that will be satisfied only when the Lord returns. The goal of such a ministry is to win as many as possible

This chapter first appeared in *Urban Mission* 9, no. 3 (1992): 6–13. Used by permission.

1. Fred Smith, "Growth Through Evangelism," *Urban Mission* 1, no. 1 (1983): 19–28.

within the church's sphere of influence. That goal will be considered partially fulfilled when any unsaved person has been converted and nurtured in the faith to at least a "+3" on the Engel Scale. This goal has normally been accomplished through a rigorous schedule of aggressive evangelism, followed by basic doctrinal courses in a "Bible academy" designed with the new convert's needs in mind.

Third, resources concentrated by the sending agency and the national host church. Resources refers to finances and personnel concentrated within one major city in a country. There is no branching out into other cities until the program is well under way in the target city. This usually translates into a period of five to ten years before the program is started in another area of the country. Once the program is established, the first Encounter churches can help in its reproduction in other cities.

Fourth, a financial commitment to an Encounter Fund that is designated solely for the purchase of land and the erecting of buildings for new Encounter churches. This is a graduated percentage that begins at 5 percent and eventually grows to 20 percent of the church's monthly budget. The deciding factor for this percentage is not the number of members but the amount of building completed.

From personal experience I can attest that the philosophy works. Over two years in the city of Lima, using the Encounter philosophy of working with a team and conducting intensive evangelistic campaigns followed by Bible Academy courses, we saw a church grow from fifteen people to almost 200 in eighteen months. This experience made me a firm believer in the Encounter philosophy. I strongly support it and have advocated it wherever I have been invited to speak: Brazil, Costa Rica, Puerto Rico, the United States, and Colombia. But my experience also led to serious questions:

Could this program exist without the infusion of foreign financial resources? If the program depends on First World money, its extent of influence would be limited to those areas selected by First World participants. In some cases this presents no problem; in others it is an unwanted intrusion into local church autonomy.

In the 1980s such funds became scarce as the evangelical world was rocked by scandals. This should have been an indicator that the "good times" for large foreign investments were diminishing and that other funding methods needed to be developed. The Lima Model as it was structured is unable to continue its fast pace under these conditions.

Could this philosophy be adapted to meet the needs of existing churches? Although there are some exceptions, in the main, the Lima Encounter Model works best when establishing a new church in a new area. What of the many churches in the kingdom of God that want to grow and have a desire to extend their influence into Satan's realm? Is the Encounter philosophy out of bounds for them? Or could it be adapted to meet an established church's needs and thus help it to grow to its full potential?

I felt that the program and its philosophy was transferable to other cities and needed to be proven in other settings, though adjusted to meet the local cultural realities. The philosophies for the Lima Model or the alternative Guayaquil Model are the same, although there may be differences as to the scope of the philosophy. If the philosophy is adhered to, there will be visible, positive results in the growth patterns of the churches implementing the philosophy. Such results are guaranteed because the Encounter philosophy is a biblical approach to church planting amid growth.

Adapting to Established Churches

In 1979 I left Lima to pursue doctoral studies at Fuller Theological Seminary, School of World Mission. These questions continually played at the corners of my mind until we returned to the field in 1986. Our logical choice was to return to Lima and continue working in an environment of dynamic growth and exciting results. This was not the route we took. Among the deciding factors as to where to go were the unanswered questions. My wife and I wanted to be in a place where we could apply Encounter principles in established churches and help answer those questions.

We decided to accept an offer to teach at our denominational seminary in Guayaquil, Ecuador's main port and financial center. Our goal was to teach theory in the classroom while putting it into practice in selected churches. Thus I would be training the future leadership of Ecuador in Encounter principles as well as illustrating how they work. At the same time, we wanted to see the Lima Encounter philosophy adopted as official mission and national church strategy.

When we arrived in Ecuador, there was a ten-year-old Lima Model church already functioning. But, in the process of developing, it had, in my judgment, overlooked some basic Lima Model principles. As a result, its impact on the city where it was located, the nation, and the national church has, to date, been minimal. A new model had to be developed to answer our questions. The model developed since the fall of 1987 is now known as the Guayaquil Model of the Encounter with God program.

From the beginning we faced opposition from vested groups. The national church saw the program as a threat to an existing evangelistic program (which was not producing much results but at least was "national"). The Encounter purists felt that the Lima Model could not be altered.

One of the founders of the Lima Model is known to have said something to this effect: "If you want to make chocolate chip cookies, there's only one way to do it. Likewise, if you want to establish the Encounter program, there is only one way to do it (Lima's way)." If one is planting churches in Lima,

Peru, the statement is valid. In other countries, however, one may have to tamper with the recipe, which can be done without changing the end product. There are chocolate chip cookies the way Nabisco makes them and chocolate chip cookies the way Mom makes them. In some cases, Mom does much better than Nabisco.

The Lima Model, mass-produced, will not always find the right environment and will need to be altered to meet its goals. In that case, Mom's local recipe may fit better. Then, too, maybe in one area you have to add nuts to the batter to make it more palatable to local tastes. That can be done without the cookie ceasing to be chocolate chip. In high altitude areas, the whole batter needs to be altered, but you still get chocolate chip cookies. The moral of the allegory is that the Lima philosophy is within reach of any local church.

Let us take the Lima Model and use it where possible. Let us take the Guayaquil Model and use it where the Lima Model will not effectively function. In this way, we can use the Encounter philosophy in various areas in various ways to reach a greater number of lost souls. To say the very least, the Guayaquil Model does prepare the ground for opening the doors to growth through aggressive evangelism. That has been one result in Ecuador. After several years of struggling, the national church is now beginning to recognize the validity of the Encounter philosophy working within their country. They have even asked the mission to help them establish a strategically located church for a thousand members in an as-yet-unnamed urban area of Ecuador. A few years ago this would have never crossed their minds.

The Guayaquil Model

Since the fall of 1987, we have implemented the Guayaquil Model in seven churches with excellent results. The total growth rate in these churches is a 20 percent average annual growth rate, with an above average retention rate for new believers. This is the result of forty-two local campaigns and 810 decisions. As of this writing, three churches await admission to the program and another five are in the process of making the decision to come on board.

The basic aspects of the Guayaquil Model are principles that need to be adapted to a local situation to be of any value.

Work only with churches who subscribe to the four Encounter principles and establish those principles as their long-range goals. This has to be both a congregation's executive committee decision and the national church's general assembly decision. This model only works within the existing structures of the local and national church organizations.

Work only with pastors who have vision for growth. Pastors must not be discouraged by peer pressure, which they will experience.

Use existing resources with no dependence on outside financing. "Existing resources" include monies donated by the mission from its own operating budget. Funds used should already be designated for evangelism and church growth, funds that would eventually be used within the country in some church growth effort. These funds also include any resources the local church can give. The idea is to get the churches started financially and let them go from there, using their own faith and resources. This principle is functioning in four of the seven Ecuador Encounter churches.

Use mission funds only for evangelistic efforts. In the beginning, some monies may be needed for property and temporary buildings in order to get the church on a solid basis for growth. But once those initial needs are met, all funding for material expansion is left to the local church.

The Lima Model is a valid model, but an "across-the-continent" approach is unrealistic. What worked in Lima can work in other places, but not necessarily always in the same mold. Problems in Buenos Aires, Quito, Cali, Bogotá, and Santiago attest to that. Churches in these cities are involved in the Encounter with God program but each one is experiencing its own problems. We could say that there is also a "Bogota Model," a "São Paulo Model," and a "Buenos Aires Model."

Two main characteristics of the Guayaquil Model are its insistence on working within existing local church structures and its independence from any outside funding. These two factors can greatly hinder the pace of development, but they by no means need to destroy the model. Ecuador is proof of this. It took a three-year battle before the Encounter philosophy was recognized by the national church as a valid method for evangelism and church growth. They felt that anything not "Ecuadorian" was of second-rate quality and that all funds, from the beginning, had to be controlled by the national church. Progress has been made in both areas, but in spite of such difficulties, the existing structure needs to be acknowledged. Otherwise the Encounter philosophy could completely alienate the national church from participation, which is not desirable for long-range planning.

The Guayaquil Model of urban church growth can serve well in reaching the maximum potential a church now has. A church that has room for 100 but only thirty attending can use the Guayaquil Model to reach 100 and then go to two services and eventually hive off a daughter church. The church with room for 300 and 100 attending can do the same. The goal is that once those churches have two full morning services, a ministry team and a strong economic base, they will consider buying land and building for a thousand members.

The result of the Guayaquil Model Encounter program is to win souls for the kingdom of God by using all available resources within the reach of a local church that has no hope of receiving the vast amounts of funds necessary for a Lima Model church.

A Comparison

Table 8 summarizes differences between the two Encounter models. This is not a pro–con presentation, but one that can be matched to see what best

Table 8 Comparison of Lima and Guayaquil Encounter Models

Lima Model	Guayaquil Model
1. Establishes new churches. When working with an established structure, pushes for immediate changes or tends to ignore the existing structure.	1. Starts basically with established churches. Works within existing national structures until time is favorable to change them.
2. Aims for at least 1000 members as soon as possible.	2. Aims for as many members as the church can accommodate in Sunday morning services.
3. Constructs architecturally attractive and large buildings.	3. Uses existing structures until funds are available to construct a large mother church or daughter church that may outpace the mother church.
4. Locates in strategic areas.	4. Uses existing buildings but aims for relocation to a strategic area as soon as resources permit or forms a daughter church in a strategic area.
5. Initiates the program with a large infusion of outside funds.	5. Initiates the program with in-country finances only.
6. Uses "outside" direction and control with direct involvement by the sponsoring mission board.	6. Depends as little as possible on "outside" direction and control. Very little involvement by the mission board.
7. Operates outside of existing structures if progress would be slowed by working within the structure.	7. Works within existing structures until systems are changed.
8. Concentrates resources in money and personnel in one city until the church is at the "super-church" level.	8. Allocates up to two missionaries per church, if available. (If not, only basic supervisory services provided.) Uses only the amount of money necessary to bring the church to the point where it can function on its own. The program is open to any church that subscribes to the four Encounter principles.
9. Emphasizes "buildings," then fills them with people.	9. Emphasizes "people," then builds to house them.

fits a local situation. These are general observations to which there are exceptions.

The "building" vs. "people" comparison (9) does not infer a materialistic preference by the Lima Model. The Lima Model is as interested in winning lost souls as is any other church growth model. The goal for the Lima Model

Table 9 Comparison of the Peru and Ecuador Experiences

Peru (Lima context)	**Ecuador** (Guayaquil context)
1. Church was ready for an aggressive evangelistic program after a good experience with Evangelism in Depth.	1. Church not ready for an aggressive program after a so-so experience with Evangelism in Depth.
2. Close cooperation between the national church and affiliated mission board.	2. Not a close relationship between the national church and affiliated mission board.
3. A recently formed national church (14 years old, relatively open to change).	3. A long-developed national church, relatively closed to change, especially from outside.
4. An international organization ready to infuse necessary funds.	4. Limited funds available from mission.
5. An identity crisis within the Catholic Church (a change in church-state status in the national constitution; impotence after the 1970 earthquake).	5. No identity crisis within the Catholic Church. Still recognized as the state religion.

These additional factors separated Lima from Guayaquil after fifteen years of Encounter in Peru and two years in Ecuador:

6. An urban-oriented national church.	6. Still a rural-oriented church.
7. A fully developed philosophy of team ministries.	7. Resistance to team ministries.
8. High level of planning and evaluation.	8. No planning for the future; even less evaluation.
9. A developed discipleship program.	9. A poor concept of discipleship.

is to start big. Build a large church and then fill it! The Guayaquil Model fills the existing building and then builds big.

It should be borne in mind that programs are as much shaped by internal forces (church history, traditions, culture, God's timing) as by external forces (a change agent's worldview and vision, mission involvement, foreign financing and leadership). Table 9 briefly sketches some factors that account for the differences in the Encounter models between Lima and Guayaquil. In each country and/or city, the factors vary.

The Guayaquil Model of the Encounter strategy is a valid method for church growth. So, for the sake of the kingdom, let's move ahead with as many models as possible to win as many souls as possible in the shortest possible span of time.

Resources for Sampling

Eastman, Michael, ed. *Ten Inner-City Churches*. 1988. East Sussex: MARC/Kingsway Publications (Lottbridge Drove, Eastbourne, E. Sussex, England, BN23 6NT). A chapter-by-chapter look at ten urban "non-super" congregations in the U.K. An opening chapter outlines the agenda of concerns Eastman sees reflected in the case studies. Rich insights written popularly.

Freedman, Samuel G. *Upon This Rock: The Miracles of a Black Church*. 1993. New York: HarperCollins Publishers (10 East 53rd St., New York, NY 10022). A year in the life of East New York's St. Paul's Community Baptist Church and its revitalized ministry under the leadership of Pastor Johnny Ray Youngblood. It is filled with detailed looks at its members and the community central to the life of the congregation.

Neighbour, Ralph, Jr. *Where Do We Go From Here? A Guidebook for the Cell Group Church*. 1990. Houston, TX: Torch Publications (P.O. Box 19888, Houston, TX 77224). A classic apology for the cell group church, providing both a theological basis for the model and in-depth discussions of key questions relating to its methodology. Extensive case studies draw primarily from Australia, Korea, and Singapore.

Romo, Oscar. *American Mosaic Church Planting in Ethnic America*. 1993. Nashville, TN: Broadman Press (127 Ninth Ave., North, Nashville, TN 37234). A comprehensive picture of theological, philosophical, and methodological wisdom on ethnic church planting. Romo's leadership in this area in the Southern Baptist Convention has resulted in the development of 7,000 congregations among 101 ethnic groups. This is a catalog of strategies used in that process.

Sample, Tex. *Hard Living People and Mainstream Christians*. 1993. Nashville, TN: Abingdon Press (201 Eighth Avenue South, Nashville, TN 37203). Analysis of the lifestyles of those battered by such problems as abuse, addictions, unemployment, and poverty, persons who live on the edge of American life. The second part of the book offers concrete suggestions for structuring the church's worship and ministry to meet these needs. Includes eleven pages of suggestions for further reading in the area.

Scoggins, Dick, and George Patterson. *Church Multiplication Guide: Helping Churches to Reproduce Locally and Abroad*. 1994. Pasadena, CA: William Carey Library (P.O. Box 40129, Pasadena, CA 91114). Focus on practical areas of church multiplication. Ten models of reproduction are introduced, with ample illustrations from around the world.

Sider, Ronald J. *Cup of Water, Bread of Life: Inspiring Stories about Overcoming Lopsided Christianity.* 1994. Grand Rapids: Zondervan Publishing House (5300 Patterson S.E., Grand Rapids, MI 49530). Ten exciting chapter-length samples of evangelical ministries from around the world that combine evangelism, concern for the poor, and social ministry in an integrated way. The final chapter looks at eight central features found in the samples.

Vaughan, John N. *Megachurches and America's Cities: How Churches Grow.* 1993. Grand Rapids, Baker Book House (P.O. Box 6287, Grand Rapids, MI 49516). Demographic and historical overview of the contemporary megachurch model. A list of twenty strengths of the model are sketched in the concluding chapter. Little attention to the model's problems. Valuable statistical appendixes.

Index of Subjects

Index of Names

Index of Biblical References

Genesis

1:27–28 70
4:17 71, 197
11:1–9 197
11:2 71
11:4 71
11:31–12:4 197
12:2 71
12:3 53
19:1–29 197

Exodus

1:8–10 166
1:8–2:7 166
2:10 166
2:11–15 166
2:16–22 166
3:1–4:17 165
3:11 165
18:1–12 166
18:13–27 166
23:27–28 78
25–40 70
32 70
35:30–34 70
36:3–7 70

Leviticus

25:39–42 72

Numbers

1:54 77
13:28 76
13:31–33 71
14:9 78
26 77
27:21 75

Deuteronomy

6:11 78
33:8 75

Joshua

6:16 78
7 71

1 Samuel

8:5 71
8:11, 13 71
8:14–17 71

2 Samuel

24 77

1 Kings

3:7–15 73
4:6 71
4:7–19 71
5:7 73
5:13 71
9:15 71
9:15–22 71
9:20–21 71
12:26–30 72
13:32 72
22:39 72

2 Kings

17:9 72
18:13 72
19:25 72
23:8 72

2 Chronicles

2:12 73
11:5 73
11:5–12 72
14:6–7 73
16:6 73
17:12 73
26:2, 6, 9, 10 73
27:4 73
32:3–5, 29–30 73

33:14 73
34:10–13 73

Psalms

22:29 73
48:2 73
68:31 73
69:35 73
86:9 73
127 175
127:1 70, 236
133 239
137:1, 2, 5, 6 73

Proverbs

1:4 75
3:21 76
5:2 76
8:12 75
11:22 76
22:3 76

Isaiah

1:10–17 70
1:16–17 238
2:2–3 74
8:12–13 78
10:1–4 72
32:17 239
40:9–10 73
58:6–10 240
58:12 242
60:1 72
60:3 73
60:19–20 72
61:1–4 175
62:11–12 72
65:17 72
65:17–25 80
65:18 72
65:20–25 72
66 175

Jeremiah

11:13 72
22:13–17 72
29:4ff 80n
29:7 202

Ezekiel

5:5 73
16 80n
16:49–50 97

Daniel

2:14 75

Amos

2:6–7 72
4:1–2 72
5:12 72

Micah

6:6 97
6:8 97, 239

Matthew

5:5 201
5:16 110
9:35–36 96–97
10:16 70
12:6 74
12:42 74
13:47–48 165
16:18 74
24:14 53
25:2 69
25:31–46 96
28:19 53

Mark

1:21 74
3:13–18 239
12:30–31 101